2 v 1 Attacking Drills and Exercises
and How They Apply to the Larger Game

First published August, 2007 by
WORLD CLASS COACHING 15004 Buena Vista Drive, Leawood, KS 66224 (913) 402-0030

ISBN 0-9788936-4-4

Author – David Goldstein
Edited by Tom Mura

Front Cover by Mark Palmer of p2 creative

Diagrams created using the session planner on www.soccerspecific.com.

To contact David Goldstein, email him at dgoldstein01@sprynet.com.

Published by

WORLD CLASS COACHING

Chapter 1

A Chip in the Kaleidoscope

Short Introduction As To How This Is Just The Alphabet or Chip in Soccer Needed

A Chip in the Soccer Kaleidoscope

Knowing the concrete details of soccer to teach players how to play does not mean making the players play in concrete.

The patterns of 2 versus 1 are a staple that all players must understand and be able to execute. In attacking soccer there are many chips in the kaleidoscope. 2 versus 1 is a tactical staple, a staple that provides creativity between teammates to pry open the organized and compact defenses in the modern game. Players must know and be able to use all the 2 versus 1 patterns. Players must be imbued with the technical ability to execute the patterns. Great players use tactical understanding with technical versatility to be creative and surprising. Add mental, technical, and physical speed to the mix and the soccer public has something to watch that is special. Some other chips in the kaleidoscope of attacking soccer are:

1) 1 versus 1 tactics
2) 2 versus 1 tactics (As noted)
3) combination play tactics (Defined as the use of three or more players to achieve a movement)
4) small group tactics: 3 versus 3 through 6 versus 6
5) mentality for purposeful possession soccer: taught in left/right/split support
6) transition periods of the game
7) free kick and dead ball situations
8) counter-attacking
9) technical command
10) style of play: created through the culture of the sport, the mentality of the players, expectations of the fans and most importantly the attitude of the coach and other leadership figures
11) physical attributes of players
12) mental attributes of players
13) tactical attributes of the players
14) team shape or system of play: 11 versus 11
15) width, length and depth to the overall attacking game
16) team group tactics: 8 versus 8 and Up
17) place, conditions, opponent, and stakes when playing
18) direct play (separate from counter-attacking)
19) the culture around the players, team, club and/or country
20) the courage of the coach
21) patience (This is noted separately from mentality because the human condition is almost always one of impatience, particularly for tangible goals as defined by wins and losses.)

This book examines 2 versus 1 almost exclusively. It is those patterns of play that take two people to execute that are examined and parsed. These 2 versus 1 patterns will be discussed almost exclusively in terms of their use for penetration. There is some examination of 2 versus 1 for possession. However, the beauty of 2 versus 1 is the penetration and creativity that it allows players in the game of soccer. These patterns are used all over the field to move forward and/or to keep the ball. 2 versus 1 patterns are critical to the penetration of attacking third space and the creation of scoring opportunities. The ability for two players to see the opportunity, read all the visual cues accurately, have the technical command and then exploit the situation at speed is one of the great moments in soccer and in all of sport. The eventual use of combination play, defined as three or more people working the balls' offensive movement together, can not be done without a base understanding of all the 2 versus 1 patterns. There is a cursory look at combination play in the book.

There are two issues that need to be discussed before delving into the patterns of 2 versus 1. The first topic comes from understanding the dynamics of 1 versus 1. It is **180 degrees versus 360 degrees.** The topic refers to and illuminates the issue of a defender needing to defend on a 180 degree line to prevent penetration while an attacker has the privilege of receiving the ball and playing in a 360 degree circle. This allows an attacker to hold the ball at will against a single defender. This is of course provided that the players' technical ability is proficient. The defender must gamble if they try to win the ball by invading the attackers 360 degrees of space. Defending into the attackers 360 degrees of space makes it possible for the attacker to beat the defender towards goal and through the 180 degree space defenders must protect. This penetration is exactly what the defender is trying to avoid. The defender, to prevent scoring opportunities, defends on a line of 180 degrees to prevent the attacker from crossing that line and moving forward at goal. The attacker operates with 360 degrees. Advantage attacker! All players and coaches should keep this concept clearly in the forefront of their tactical understanding.

The second critical concept that all coaches need to keep in focus is that a defender has to try and prevent two possibilities from occurring. **Defenders must prevent both passing options and dribbling options.** It is the great dilemma inside each confrontation for a defender. Players who understand this defensive problem have a great advantage. Attackers can approach tactical confrontations with a two pronged solution. The attacker that can see which of these two options, passing or dribbling, that the defender is trying to take away can exploit this knowledge by choosing the other option. A defender can take away one option completely but can rarely take away both. Visual cues learned through experience and some teaching from an instructor will help players to read the defender's intentions to take advantage of their decisions.

The dilemma becomes even more complicated for the defender if the attacker will use all 360 degrees to play in and not force the issue of penetrating through the defenders 180 degrees. The effort to penetrate the 180 degrees should be when it is advantageous for the attacker to do so. This 180 versus 360 degree dilemma is why modern defenses are built in zonal layers and two defenders are often required to pressure and/or cover in the area of the ball. One defender alone is often in deep trouble in the modern game.

Diagonal dribbles, often from the flank, by an attacker exploit this issue of 180 degrees for the defender verses 360 degrees for the attacker. This is done by "nibbling" at the edge of the 180 degree line of the defender with the diagonal dribble. The attacker can gain ground with a penetrating dribble without entirely leaving the protection of the 360 degree bubble. This concept of "nibbling" is important for all players. This movement is highly useful in the midfield and attacking thirds of the field. It is also extremely important for slower players to be successful with their dribbling options.

Because the diagonal dribble does not directly confront the defenders 180 degree line of defense the defender must decide whether to control the dribble or attempt to win the ball outright. To simply control the dribble the defender may eventually have a situation where the attacker can shoot at goal since the diagonal dribble not only moves across the field but penetrates toward the end line as well.

The other option, to tackle, is made more difficult because defenders must stretch into the 360 degree bubble to win the ball. This often causes them to foul by over committing. This creates free kicks in dangerous positions. Additionally, the defender that misses the tackle when they over extend into the 360 degrees often leaves teammates scrambling to cover the attacker and reorganize the defense. Finally, the defender that times their extension into the 360 degrees incorrectly may find that the attacker has read their intent and is changing directions through the 180 degrees that should be protected but are not because of the attempted tackle. This leaves the attacker with a more direct route to goal. This is the situation that the defense was trying to avoid by protecting the 180 degrees to goal but is lost by the defender over reaching into the 360 degrees of the attacker.

Once these two concepts are clearly understood by the attackers then using or threatening to use a teammate in a 2 versus 1 situation puts the defender in a near hopeless situation of trying to stop the pass and the dribble options simultaneously. It really can't be done by a single defender. The attackers that recognize which option is being chosen by the defender, to prevent the dribble or the pass, will be able to penetrate with the other choice. Attackers simply have to choose the option that the defender leaves open and they will be successful. When the game gets more realistic with 2 versus 2 and layers of zonal defenses both attackers must recognize what each of the defenders are trying to take away and must exploit this more complex set of visual cues. The attackers should also look ahead to the tactical situation that will occur should their move be successful. This mental preparation for how to deal with defenders that will readjust to the new situation is essential to the complete success of scoring and the speed at which the game is played.

The consequence of a defender having to stop two options is that it forces modern defenses to provide a covering defender(s) to stop attacking movements. Without the extra defensive help attackers would be too free to disrupt defenders working alone. It causes modern defenses to compact the area they are defending trying to gain a man advantage. This in turn means attackers must anticipate the covering defender(s) appearance mentioned in the paragraph above. It means that 2 versus 1situations often have to be created more than once to break down organized, compact defenses. This in turn leads to combination play and the kaleidoscopic effect that soccer creates at higher levels of play.

These two concepts help attacking players to read the game and exploit what the defense gives them. The 360 degree circle allows attackers to hold the ball and slow the game up to gain time, create the situation that they want to occur or get teammates around them. With a player in support of the attacker the option to dribble or pass gives the attacker two options while a defender can really only stop one option at a time. The supporting attacker is what creates the opportunity for 2 versus 1. The support provides the passing option. Without these passing options the game would become just single player confrontations. With the options comes a body of knowledge that players must have command of to reach the highest levels of the game. 2 versus 1patterns are a critical building block in the tactical repertoire of soccer. The support must come at speed and at the right time to be realistic.

2 versus 1 is a set of patterns that can, should and do occur on a regular basis with competent players and teams. It is a chip inside the kaleidoscope of soccer. This chip mixes with other chips, is refracted off the mirrors in the tube, and becomes a magical set of ever changing patterns that make up the larger game of soccer itself. Every player must know the patterns, how to recognize their possibilities and how to exploit them in the flow of the game. 2 versus 1 is a corner stone of tactics in soccer.

Teaching 2 versus 1 in its' rudimentary forms needs to be learned by an isolation of the pattern. Having said that, it is also important to teach 2 versus 1 in environments of multiple players, most often taught through small group games. This training of players, often with a man advantage to the attackers, (referred to as a Plus situation through-out the book) is done so that players can learn to identify and create the 2 versus 1 confrontation within the larger picture. Inside of every 3 versus 2 is a 2 versus 1 solution. Inside of any 4 versus 3 is a 2 versus 1solution and so it goes. Eventually, when players are sophisticated enough the can attack numbers down and still create 2 versus 1situations and combination play.

Eventually, 2 versus 1 must be taught as 2 versus 2 so that the player supporting the attacker and receiving the ball learns to take part of their visual cue for the correct response from a second defender as well as the defender marking their teammate. The complexity of making the correct decision grows astronomically as other defenders are introduced into the environment.

Additionally, the issue of 2 players working in concert to keep possession of the ball from a defender is important to address. 2 versus 1 for possession of the ball can be difficult to execute, but is simple enough in its guidelines.

The object of the man off the ball is to "sharpen" their angle of support making them self available to receive a pass. The sharpening should be before pressure on the ball is so great that the attacker with the ball can not make a pass. The goal of the passer is to release the ball to their teammate when the defender is closer to the ball carrier or the defenders' momentum is towards the ball making the defender committed away from the supporting attacker. The pass should be timed to be made before the pressure by the defender makes a pass impossible. It is also important to try to pass the ball to a teammates feet but this is not always possible. Passes paced properly into space that the supporting attacker can reach before the defender can react to them are appropriate.

The issue of 2 versus 1 for possession is of some importance. Just as in 2 versus 1 for penetration, the players working to release the pressure on the ball while maintaining possession must be have the option to pass or dribble to solve their dilemmas. The defenders' job is to isolate one of the attackers and turn the tactical situation into 1versus 1. The attacking player off the ball must be willing to work hard, up to and including making a run around the player with the ball, who may be temporarily isolated and shielding the ball, to avoid any 1versus 1 isolation. This releasing of a defender's pressure on the ball carrier is essential. Running into usable space to support a shielding attacker is critical. The attacker who has taken up a shielding position over the ball will receive defensive pressure until support arrives. Because of the support run by the ball holders' teammate passing options, faked passes, take over, false take over, or dribbling out of the pressure are all options. The defender must decide to jump the passing lane or to defend the dribble which frees the ball carriers decision making because their teammate has become available. Other patterns also become available and make it hard to defend because of the proximity of the supporting attacker which allows a passing option to coincide with the dribble option.

The central issue of 2 versus 1 for possession is to release pressure on the ball. This helps a team to gain or maintain possession of the ball. 2 versus 1's for possession are frequently used to relieve pressure in the defensive third of the field to begin building out of the back. The tactical patterns of possession are used all over the field but are rarely a long lasting part of the game. 2 versus 1exercises for possession may last for 60-120 seconds. 2 versus 1 for possession is an anaerobic experience that in the real game will not last that length of time. Once pressure is off the ball in the match the attackers should then look for penetration as the next order of business. Or the attackers should look for a series of passes that allow possession by the team and will eventually allow penetration. Game tactics, score, opponent, result, entertainment of the fans can all be taken into consideration by the team as a collective to decide what to do with the ball. Bear in mind, 2 versus 1 for possession is not a long lasting affair. It is to relieve pressure on the ball to gain time and space for other tactical decisions to be become possible. Possession produced by 2 versus 1 to relieve pressure is usually a quick pass or two in a game. It can also be a dribble created by the perception of the defender that a pass is imminent.

The last point in possession situations to bear in mind reaches back to the 360 degree concept. If there is high pressure on the ball, the attacker carrying the ball needs to shield and keep possession. While shielding is most often conceived as a stationary movement the player with the ball is not required to be stationary but can be slowly moving away from pressure with a shielded dribble. The supporting attacker may have to run all the way around the defender to the far side of the attacker in possession to reach a good supporting position. If a defender invades the 360 degrees or moves into the passing lane of the supporting attacker dribbling out of the situation will most likely be the solution. Even in exercises that emphasize possession attackers will end up using the take over, false take over, flick and spin, wall passes and almost all of the 2 versus 1patterns that are used for penetration.

There is an important teaching point that needs illumination at this point that effects the information for the entire book. In both possession and in penetration if a defender is playing passively to gain time then the ball carrier must commit that defender by dribbling at them; passing the ball into a dangerous position that forces the defender to respond or the supporting player must threaten the defense with a run into a dangerous space. Passive defending to gain time can be an intelligent decision in matches. It is most often counter productive to teaching and learning in 2 versus 1exercises. The coach should instruct the attackers to commit the defenders, usually as quickly as possible, something they will need to do in matches, or the coach must demand that the defender be aggressive which will set up the 2 versus 1patterns. Forcing a confrontation by committing the defender or the coach requiring the defender to commit creates 2 versus 1patterns. The attacker must read if the defenders' commitment is defending against the dribble or the pass. After the attacker reads the defender they should choose the opposite option. If the defender is attempting to prevent the dribble the attacker should pass. Conversely, if the defender tries to take away the pass to the supporting attacker then the ball carrier should dribble past the defender.

There are visual cues that attackers can use, among them are closing angles, speed of approach, positioning of supporting defenders, attackers' position and control of the ball relative to the defender, body language, risk for defender if beaten with a dribble, area of the field, and physical attributes of the defender are just some of the cues that a sophisticated attacker can use. Many of the visual cues are reading the body movement, body stance, and eyes of the defender.

It would also be helpful at this juncture to define a couple of concepts so that the reader can know how a word reference connects to a clear concept. The concepts are **"Open"** body shape, **"Sharpening"** the angle of support, good **"First Touch,"** and the shape of possession soccer, **Left/Right/Split Support.**

"Open" Body Shape

The players need to keep their body shape "open" so they have vision of the field. This means that their shoulder is most often pointed at the ball or ball carrier that they are supporting. Their chest supported directly at the ball causes the player to close up and lose vision of the field; this in turn slows the pace of the game because the player does not know where they will want to send the ball to next. This will create the situation where a player will need to take two touches at least, one to move the ball into a position where they have vision to make an informed decision and a second touch to use the decision.

"Sharpening"

The players need to "sharpen" their angle of support; even if it just two feet, to be available to receive a pass from their teammates. This means that the player without the ball needs to make it possible for the attacker with the ball to send them a pass that the defender can not cut out or obstruct. Some coaches call this "showing" and others call it creating a good angle of support.

Good "First Touch"

The players need to have a "good first touch." A good "first touch" is one that gives your team an advantage in either possession of the ball or penetration of the defense. Many coaches think that a good "first touch," often referred to as a "positive" touch, to be only a touch that takes the ball forward towards the goal the team is attacking. A good "first touch" is not so limited. It is any touch that gains an advantage for the team whether the touch is forward, backwards or sideways. A good first touch is a concrete indication that players are thinking ahead to what they will do next after receiving the ball.

The Shape of the Possession Game: Left/Right/Split Support

Left/right/split support is the basic tactical structure for the game. This means that any player that has possession of the ball should have teammates who are in "sharpened" angles to receive the ball. The player in possession should have support on their left, a support player on their right and a support player in a split position. This shape is only mentioned because in later exercises it is important to know this concept to help the players understand how to create it, how to use it to attack from and then create it again. The speed of movement by supporting players to the tactical situation that is about to occur from a pass or dribble is an indication of how quickly and how well the teams' players understand soccer. The quicker the understanding, the quicker the play can become as the speed of the players movement picks up.

It is hoped that this initial discussion leaves the reader with a foundation to refer to for the rest of the manual. The rest of the book will deal with 2 versus 1patterns and exercises that will instruct there use. Please review a little educational methodology.

People learn in three basic modalities; **seeing, hearing and doing.** Players need to see what is required and for some hearing is helpful. But **doing is the most important aspect of learning.** Don't over burden the players with long lectures or over elaborate or spend too much time repeating visual demonstrations. Get the players doing and get them active to learn most effectively.

The more a player does and is required to be involved in the thinking process about what they are doing the deeper the learning sets in and the more often it will be used in real matches. Involve the players with "Socratic" questioning and not simply with supplying answers. The Socratic Method is asking questions of the players to illicit thought and answers through personal engagement. The personal involvement of the player in the process gives empowerment and responsibility which are critical to the educational process. This demanding the players to think out the solutions has been shown in studies to dramatically increase information retention.

Chapter 2

Patterns

The following names are 2 versus 1 patterns. This section of the book will explain these patterns. Chapter 3 deals with exercises that will teach the patterns. Chapter 4 will examine where on the field the patterns are often used and why these may be safer patterns to use in certain areas of the field.

1) **Wall Pass**
2) **False Wall**
3) **High Wall Pass**
4) **Low Wall Pass**
5) **Flick and Spin Walls Pass**
6) **The X Pattern A) Off the Dribble: B) From the Pass**
7) **False X**
8) **Curved Runs and Overlaps**
9) **False Curved Runs and Using the Runner Late**
10) **Double Pass (straight return pass)**
11) **Double Pass (diagonal return pass)**
12) **False Double Passes**
13) **Take Over**
14) **False Take Over**
15) **Diagonal Run/Straight Pass**
16) **Straight Run/Diagonal Pass**
17) **Straight Run/Straight Run**
18) **Diagonal Run/Diagonal Pass**
19) **Dummy Patterns**
20) **Wall Passes (vertically, diagonally, horizontally)**

General Teaching Points for 2 versus 1 Patterns:

1) The first pass is almost always to the supporting players' feet. (The X Pattern, Diagonal Run, Straight Run and the Curved Run can be exceptions) The first pass should be to the top foot of the supporting attacker to prevent easy interception by the defense. If the supporting attacker is not marked tightly then the pass can be any where that gives a technical or tactical advantage to the attacker receiving the ball.
2) The second pass is almost always into the space in front of the attacker who played the ball first.
3) If a player is running slowly or is standing still this is a visual cue to pass to feet.
4) If a player is running at high speed this is a visual cue that a pass should be into the space in front of the runner.
5) Body feints and dribbling moves intended to "freeze" the opponent are crucial to creating good passing opportunities for the second attacker.
6) The rule of physics: "For every action there is an equal and opposite reaction;" is a truth about all 2 versus 1 patterns. For every wall pass pattern there is a False Wall possible, for every Take Over there is a False Take Over, for every X Pattern there is a False X Pattern and so on.
7) A good "first touch" is necessary to prepare the ball for the next move the attack wants to make. This is a universal technical issue that should always be addressed.
8) "Sharpening" to make clear passing lanes from one attacker to the other and is critical for 2 versus 1 patterns and necessary in all aspects of the game. Some coaches refer to this as "showing" or creating a better "angle" of support.
9) "Open" body shape is not always possible in 2 versus 1 patterns but should be strived for when ever it is possible to achieve.
10) Attackers should read the angle of approach by defenders to see if the defender is intending to deny the pass or the dribble.
11) Attackers should read the speed of approach by the defender to see if they should commit the defender and force the timing of the attack. Too slow an approach by a defender can

demand the attacker to commit the defense by either dribbling at the defender or passing the ball into a dangerous area that their teammate can exploit which in turn will cause the defender to commit because of the danger.

12) Attackers should read the speed of approach by the defender to see if it is at a high rate that would allow a quick pass to be effective or if the speed of approach by the defender is to fast then dribbling is an option. An attacker who is facing a defender that's speed is out of control leaves two solution their problem. The first choice is to use the momentum or speed of the defender to use a quick dribbling move and defeat the defender. The second is to use a quick pass to the supporting player and again use the momentum of the defender to get past them.

13) The attacker should look beyond the first defender they come in contact with to see where other defenders are and where vulnerable space to exploit might be had. The ability to have enough technical command and control so that the attacker's head is up to see the space beyond the first defender is a crucial skill.

14) The attacker should look at the spacing of their teammate and them self to determine time and motion to execute the move in relationship to the defenders.

15) Passes to supporting teammates should leave the ball in positions that multiple options are available to the player receiving it. Passes that leave only one option are gambles to absolute success or absolute failure. That is why the first pass is to the top foot of the supporting attacker is so important. This kind of pass is not always appropriate but passes that allow options are more difficult for defenses to deal with effectively. (See Diagram 1 A, page)

16) Disguise is a critical piece to successful patterns. That is why for every 2 versus 1 pattern there should be an equal and opposite action.

17) There should be the choice for a supporting attacker to simply keep possession of the ball if the 2 versus 1 pattern fails to materialize properly.

18) Area of the field may determine a preferred choice of a pattern. An example of this would be in the defending third a curved run back behind the ball carrier and out around them is safer to execute than a diagonal run out in front to receive a straight pass up field. The reason is simple. The curved runner is always available to receive the pass should pressure get to great to handle. In a diagonal run there is a moment where an astute defender can see that the pass is intended and the supporting attacker is for just a split moment behind the defender and unavailable. A defender willing to gamble a little will jump the passing lane at this exact moment and close to deny the dribble thus turning a 2 versus 1 into a 1 versus 1. The curved run keeps the supporting attacker available at all times and the 2 versus 1 intact.

19) A defenders physical approach is often an indicator of their psychological status. Attackers should take advantage of players who are; unsure, confused, are slow to decide, over committed, angry, lack focus, look tired or show other signs of physical or psychological weakness. The attackers should react accordingly with the 2 versus 1 pattern that their teammate and they can create and will allow them an advantage in the situation.

20) Attackers should often gamble in the attacking third with a choice that will create the most havoc for the defending team.

21) Attackers need to commit the defender by attacking them with their movement. This should be done as soon as the numerical superiority is recognized or created. Almost all 2 versus 1 patterns require committing the defender to first make the pattern occur and then to make it successful.

22) A lot of players show a great deal of reluctance to give a marked player the ball. Many times giving an attacker the ball when they are marked or will be marked quickly is part of creating a pattern of play. Giving the ball to a player who is marked or will be is another way of forcing the defense to commit to the attacker. From a warfare perspective it is sometimes better to know where the enemy is or force them to be where one knows the how and when of their movements. Curved runs, X Patterns, Overlaps, Double Pass Patterns, all benefit or require that an attacker who is marked receive the ball to start the pattern. This concept has not been illuminated before this but is essential to teaching 2

versus 1patterns and to encouraging players to pass to teammates that are marked.

23) Passing a ball can be destructive to a defense but most often leaves the organization of the defense intact. Dribbling forces defenses to reorganize the entire defense to meet the disruption of a dribble.

24) Physical match-ups of the defenders attributes with the attackers attributes should not be overlooked in reading a 2 versus 1 pattern and the likelihood of its success.

25) Experience has no substitute in using teammates and 2 versus 1patterns to disguise intent, be deceitful, creative and unpredictable about attacking movements.

This author is sure that there are other cues not listed and that others have learned how to read a defender. Believe it or not I used shadows on the ground, the sense of air pressure, and of course the sense of touch to read an opponents' where about and intent.

Wall Pass:

This pattern is one of the foundations of all team sports that resemble soccer. It is called a give and go or a pick and role in basketball. It is usually the first pattern that children pick up by themselves or have taught to them by youth coaches. In concept it is simple; a player gives the ball to their teammate and the teammate gives it back to them as the first player runs by their opponent. Here are some keys:

Keys to the Wall Pass

1) The first pass is to the foot of the supporting teammate.

2) The first pass should be to the top foot of the teammate. This is the foot away from the defender marking them. (This allows the player to decide to return the pass as desired, to hold the ball in a shielded position or to turn away and dribble while keeping the ball away from the defender.) The quality and placement of the pass is what allows the player to decide what option is appropriate.

3) The pass should be made to the supporting player's foot when the initial player making the pass is 1 to 1.5 yards away or closer to the defender that is marking them. The timing of the pass depends on the skill level, physical attributes of the attacker; the physical attributes of the defender and the timing of the attacker. A pass sent too soon will be read by the defender who will be able to turn and run with the attacker making the return pass either impossible or highly susceptible to interception. If the attacker holds the ball to long the defender will be close enough to cut the initial pass and thereby ruin the wall pass pattern. Timing the release is critical.

4) The first pass is most deceptive and hard to read for the defender when an attacker uses the outside of their foot with a flicking motion created with the ankle. This method of passing also keeps the attacker in a running stride and therefore more explosive in sprinting by the defender.

5) The supporting player or wall player should try and show up on the shoulder of the defender that is pressuring the attacker dribbling the ball. This allows a good angle of support for a passing lane that is not easily shut down. (See Diagram 1, page 14.)

6) The return pass should be in one touch whenever possible and in no more than two touches. Taking two touches is usually to slow to get the pattern done and successful.

7) Whenever possible the first pass to the player performing the wall function and the return pass should be on the ground. (I am of the firm conviction that the passes should be on the ground if possible. But if they need to be in the air to exploit the tactical situation it should be in the technical command of the players to get the ball in the air and return it in the air. Many coaches insist that all passes always be on the ground which dooms many tactical opportunities to failure. "On the ground if you can, in the air if you must;" is how I ask my players to play.)

8) The attacker passing to the supporting player should make an explosive run into the space behind their defender. (This will change to some degree if there are covering defenders or defensively crowded space.) (See Diagram 1, page 14)

9) The receiving player should receive it with the top foot away from their defender. This automatically shields the ball and lets the player choose how to respond to the situation they find them self in at that moment.
10) The pass back to the running attacker is into the space in front of the runner and behind the back of the defender so that the attacking player may penetrate while keeping a good tempo to their run.
11) The run by the attacker initiating the wall pass should be on the far side of the defender away from the where the ball was passed. This forces the defenders' vision to be split between seeing where the ball is located and seeing the penetrating runner. This not allowing the defender to see both the runner and the ball at the same time is a crucial part of the wall pass pattern.
12) A good "first touch" is necessary to prepare the ball for the next move the attack wants to make.
13) The wall player or second player to touch the ball must read two visual cues:
   a) Has the defender tracking the first player made a good recovery run into the space where the return pass should go? If they have then the return lane for the pass will be blocked. In this case the ball should not be returned. If lifting the ball into the passing lane or even over the opponent is not possible then other options must be exercised.
   b) Has the wall passer's defender marking them moved to a position to intercept the return pass? If the defender has then the return passing lane will again be blocked. A lifted flick pass in the air can get the ball past the defenders shin? If this type of flick pass is not a possibility then the wall pass is off and other options must occur.
14) If the wall pass is no longer possible the attacker with the ball has three options: shield the ball; choose the false wall option, or they can play the ball off to another attacker.

All these decisions for a simple wall pass. (See Diagram 1, page 14.) The concept of a wall pass is simple, the execution is hard. The wall pass keys are guidelines to help the players read and execute those specific tactics successfully. There are three basic kinds of speed for a soccer player. It is extremely helpful if all the players have all three kinds of speed but a combination of any two will usually make a player successful and will define their particular attributes to add to the game. These kinds of speed are critical to the success of any 2 versus 1 pattern.

Three Kinds of Speed

1) The speed of the decision to execute the pattern must be as quick as possible. Tactical recognition must be immediate and use of that knowledge at the same pace. This is most often referred to as **"mental"** speed.
2) **Physical** speed should be as high as possible without loss of control.
3) Command of the ball is crucial if players are to create any speed of play that demands ball movement. All 2 versus 1 patterns of course demand the use of the ball. This kind of speed is referred to as **"technical"** speed. How fast can a player receive the ball and get the task they want accomplished done? Can a player create the desired situation and result with a minimum number of touches required to execute the desired goal. In this book the desired goal is the execution of 2 versus 1 patterns.

Diagram 1: Wall Pass

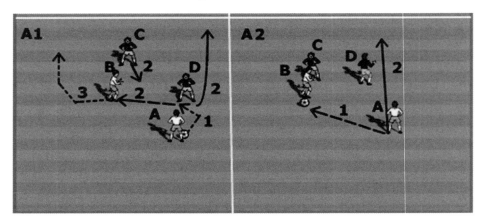

Diagram 1, page 14, shows the basic components of a Wall Pass. In Square A1 the attacker with the ball commits the defender as closely as possible. The attacker, labeled A, lays the ball off to the supporting attacker, labeled B. Using an outside of the foot pass is the most deceptive form of passing and keeps the attacker in running stride. The supporting attacker should be approximately even with the shoulder of the defender. When working with players I instruct them that the supporting attacker, player B, should have their chest even with the defender who is confronting the attacker with the ball. In Square A1 that would be the defender labeled D. Attacker A makes an explosive run on the opposite side of the defender D so that the ball and the run split the vision of the defender.

In Square A2 the attacker receives the return pass behind the defender. This pass is made by the supporting attacker, labeled B. Again, notice that the run and the position of the ball splits' the vision of the defender, labeled D, between the ball and attacker A who is making the penetrating run forward. Remember that a good pass to the supporting attacker, player B, is to their top foot. The ball and the defender are on opposite sides of the attacker which allows the attacker to automatically shield the ball.

How does a Wall Pass evolve into a False Wall? If everything went according to plan the wall pass was executed and play has flowed on. However, if either of the two situations in point 13 occurred then option 3 must now become one of the possible decision for the attacker now in possession of the ball. The points are reviewed here as well as being discussed on page 11.

Review of Points 13 and 14 of Wall Passing

13) The supporting attacker who returns the ball must read two clear cues.
   a) Has the defender tracking the first attacker made a good recovery run into the space where the return pass should go? If they have then the return pass is blocked and the ball should not be returned. Returning it will cause it to be intercepted by the defenders' positioning as they recover.
   b) Has supporting attackers' defender moved to a position to intercept the return pass? (This is referred to for my players as having the defender jump the passing lane.) Will a flick pass in the air get the ball past the defenders shin? If no then the return passing lane is again blocked.

14) If either of these two defensive actions has occurred the wall pass is off and different solutions need to be applied to the situation. Possible solutions include holding the ball by shielding; use the false wall option by dribbling away from the intended wall pass or knocking the ball off to a third attacking player. Option to solve a broken pattern should then occur:

Option to Solve a Broken Pattern

1) The wall passer can shield the ball and hold it. That is one of the primary reasons attackers should pass the ball to the supporting teammates top foot. The ball is out of reach of the defender and in a shielded position because of the quality and positioning of the pass.
2) The wall passer can roll away from the defended area and dribble out of the situation. This allows the player to keep the ball and attack in another direction. This movement is referred to in this manual as a False Wall Pattern.
3) The player after dribbling away from the wall pass and using the False Wall Pattern has two options directly related to the 2 versus 1 pattern. First, they can simply dribble out of pressure away from the intended pattern. Second, they can, after one or two dribbles pass the ball back behind their defender across the grain of flow to the original target of the wall pass. This is a surprising move. (See Diagram 2A, page 17.)
4) The attacking player now in possession of the ball can use a third attacking player to combine with the player who made the first pass and is making the penetrating run. This creates the concept of combination play.
5) The attacker can use a third player to move the ball away from the 2 versus 1 pattern and have the flow of the game go into other choices or areas of the field. This option is not discussed at length in this book.

False Wall

The False Wall Pattern is crucial to all players. What it does is allow the supporting player options to use should the initial Wall Pass be disrupted by the defenders. A good recovery run by the defender marking the attacker who is trying to run into the space behind the defender marking them will disrupt the pattern. The defender that is marking the supporting player involved in the wall pass can also "jump" the passing lane and make a return pass impossible. Without the following options the player would be stranded. (See Diagram 2, page 16)

Keys to the False Wall

1) The first pass needs to be made to the "top" foot away from the defender.
2) A good "first touch" is necessary to prepare the ball for the next move the attack wants to make. There are four possible decisions of what to do with the "first touch."
    a) Send the ball back to the penetrating attacker either on the ground or in the air.
    b) Shield the ball away from the defender.
    c) Pass the ball to a third player to create combination play or move the play away from the intended 2 versus 1 pattern.
    d) Use the False Wall Pattern which is to turn away from the intended pattern of play and dribble in the opposite direction.
3) The attacker that initiated the wall pass needs to make a hard run behind their defender. This run helps commit the defender marking the supporting player who is receiving the ball. The quality of the run will help entice the defender marking the supporting player to jump the passing lane which allows the other False Wall options to be more easily executed.
4) As stated the supporting player who receives the ball in the wall pass pattern can shield the ball and holds it if desired.
5) The supporting player receiving the ball in the wall passing pattern turns away from the intended wall pass pattern with a dribbling movement. Their first touch taking the ball away from the originally intended wall pass pattern allows deception to disrupt the defense. The first touch is often with the outside surface of the top foot and the ankle just flicks the ball to the intended space.
    • Any surface that allows the player to turn is acceptable. (See Diagram 2, page 16.)

6) The top foot continues as the first stride of the attacker and shields the ball from the defender that is marking the attacker.
7) The attacker using the False Wall Pattern should remember that they can carry the ball and then play it back against the grain with a deceptive pass behind both defenders that were marking the attackers.
8) Although the option is not discussed at length in this book the use of a third attacker to accomplish the wall pass, the creation of combination play, is another possibility for the sophisticated attacker.

Diagram 2: Using the Top Foot: False Wall and Shielding Options

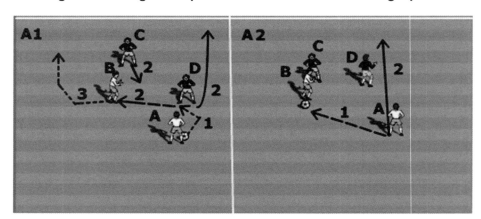

In Diagram 2, page 16, Square A1 the defender, player C, jumps the passing lane for the return pass in the wall pass pattern. Player C's run is numbered with a 2. Because the ball was played to attacker B's top foot it is not easy to dispossess the attacker and when the defender over-commits into the passing lane, the attacker labeled B, simply uses the False Wall Pattern to avoid the defender and turn away from the intended Wall Pass. The ball is shielded from the defense the entire time because it was served to the top foot of attacker B.

In Square A2 both defenders play the Wall Pass Pattern well. Defender D recovers back through the passing lane and tracks attacker A thus clogging up the return pass. Defender C plays attacker B honestly by not over-committing. This makes the Wall Pass almost impossible to execute and the False Wall a difficult but viable option. By having the ball played to the top foot of the supporting attacker, player B, the attacker is able to simply hold the ball in a shielding position while assessing other options.

Diagram 2A: False Wall Option: Playing the Ball Late

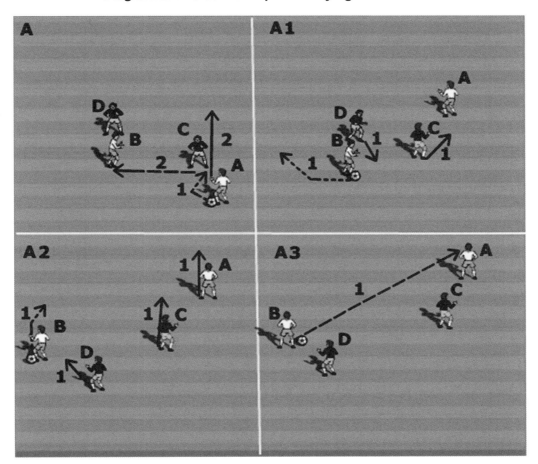

In Diagram 2 A, page 17, Square A, the attacker, labeled A, commits the first defender by dribbling at them, then passes the ball to the supporting attacker, labeled B and makes a penetrating run behind the defender labeled C.

In Square A1 the defender labeled D jumps into the return passing lane, indicated by the player run numbered 1, while defender C starts to make a recovery run, also numbered with a 1, chasing after attacker A. Because the passing lane is closed the supporting attacker, labeled B, dribbles away from the intended Wall Pass and into a False Wall Pattern.

In Square A2 the supporting attacker, labeled B, dribbles up field into a position where they can now pass to attacker A, the intended target in the Wall Pass. Both defenders are now making recovery runs numbered by 1's while attacker A continues to penetrate forward which is also numbered with a 1.

In Square A3 attacker B returns the ball behind the defenders to attacker A who originally passed the ball and has continued their normal run for a wall pass. The supporting attacker, labeled B, who has used a False Wall to turn away from the original Wall Pass now passes the ball in behind the two recovering defenders with the pass numbered 1. Remember, there are also two other options not shown in this diagram.

Options:

1) Shielding or holding the ball
2) Third person Combination Patterns

Lower Wall Pass

The Lower Wall pass is executed with the supporting attacker for the first pass positioned well below the defender pressuring the attacking player initiating the pattern with the first pass. The positioning of the supporting attacker forces the pass to be sent a little earlier then the conventional wall pass pattern. The defender that is static or has their momentum towards the attacker first carrying the ball is easier to beat with this pattern.

The Lower Wall Pass Pattern will require the attacker who initiates it to be highly explosive with their penetrating run. This need for explosiveness is necessary because there is more space required between the attacker committing the defender and the defender for the initial pass. The pass to be open to the supporting attacker down field must be released earlier, 1.5 to 2.5 yards before the attacker reaches the defender.

The main of the advantage of the Lower Wall Pass is that the return pass can be square into the space behind the defender that was just committed. This variation is effective against defenses built with depth. Players can still attack with the wall pass but the square pass avoids a deeper lying defender. A normal wall pass sends back a diagonal ball that can be cut out by defenders positioned with depth. (See Diagram 3, page 20.) The Lower Wall Pass returns the ball square instead of diagonally which avoids covering defenders more effectively.

Keys to the Lower Wall Pass

1) The first pass is to the top foot of the supporting teammate.
2) The first pass should be to the top foot of the teammate. This is the foot away from the defender marking them. (This allows the player to decide to return the pass as desired, to hold the ball in a shielded position or to turn away and dribble while keeping the ball away from the defender.) The quality and placement of the pass is what allows the player to decide which option is appropriate.
3) The pass should be made to the supporting player's foot when the initial player making the pass is 1.5 to 2.5 yards away or closer to the defender that is marking the dribbling attacker. The timing of the pass depends on the skill level, physical attributes of the attacker; the physical attributes of the defender and the timing of the attacker. A pass sent too soon will be read by the defender who will be able to turn and run with the attacker making the return pass either impossible or highly susceptible to interception. If the attacker holds the ball to long the defender will be close enough to cut the initial pass and thereby ruin the wall pass pattern. Timing the release is critical to success.
4) The first pass is most deceptive and hard to read for the defender when an attacker uses the outside of their foot with a flicking motion created with the ankle. This method of passing also keeps the attacker in a running stride and therefore more explosive in sprinting by the defender.
5) The supporting player or wall player must show up below the shoulder and down field of the defender that is pressuring the attacker dribbling the ball. The supporting player must use the concept of "sharpening" to effectively provide support. The initial timing of the first pass is difficult because it is done earlier and without a good angle of support the timing of the initial pass is difficult because the passing lane is more easily shut down. (See Diagram 1, page 14.)
6) The return pass should be in one touch whenever possible and in no more than two touches.
7) Whenever possible the first pass to the player performing the wall function and the return pass should be on the ground. (To reiterate my conviction; the passes should be on the ground if possible. But if they need to be in the air to exploit the tactical situation it should be in the technical command of the players to get the ball into the air and return it in the air if necessary. Many coaches insist that all passes always be on the ground which dooms

many tactical opportunities to failure. "On the ground if you can, in the air if you must.")

8) The attacker passing to the supporting player should make an explosive run into the space behind their defender. (See Diagram 1, page 14.)

9) The receiving player should receive it with the top foot away from their defender. This automatically shields the ball and lets the player choose how to respond to the situation they find them self in at that moment.

10) The pass back to the running attacker is into the space in front of the runner and behind the back of the defender so that the attacking player may penetrate while keeping a good tempo to their run. However, the return pass is square not diagonal which helps elude defense that are well structured in depth. .

11) The run by the attacker initiating the wall pass should be on the far side of the defender away from the where the ball was passed. This forces the defenders' vision to be split between seeing where the ball is passed and seeing the penetrating runner. This not allowing the defender to see both the runner and the ball at same time is a crucial part of the wall pass pattern.

12) Sometimes it is necessary for an attacker in possession of the ball to make the pass to a supporting defender down field from them because the rate of the defenders pressure is coming faster than the supporting attacker can "sharpen" their angle of support.

13) A good "first touch" is necessary to prepare the ball for the next move the attack wants to make

Remember the unique issues involved in the Lower Wall Pass Pattern:

14) The supporting attacker stays deep behind the defender of the dribbling attacker. In a regular Wall Pass the supporting attacker attempts to be approximately square with the defender that their teammate is committing for a wall passing option.

15) The supporting wall player must work hard to create and keep a passing lane open to them. The supporting attacker may need to "sharpen" their angle to create or provide a good passing lane to them. The supporting attacker can move wider of the defender that the attacker is committing if the pass is getting held to long. The supporting attacker does not want to come back very much if at all towards the attacker committing the defender because that will force the return pass to start into diagonal angles.

16) Depth behind the defender forces the return pass to be square and not diagonal.

17) The attacker committing the defender and starting the Lower Wall Pass Pattern must release the pass a little earlier in the sequence and make a very explosive run to get into the space behind their defender.

Diagram 3: Lower Wall Pass

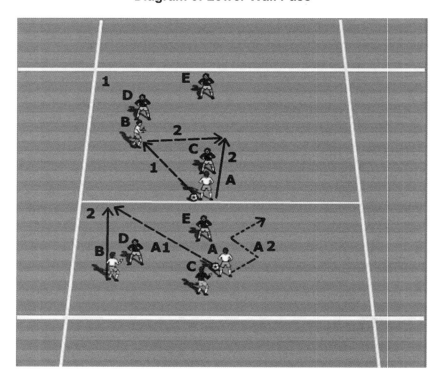

Diagram 3, page 20, illustrates that the position of the third and most deeply positioned defender. (See Square 1, player E is providing depth to the defense) This makes a return wall pass that is diagonal impossible. A deep running diagonal pass would be cut out by the covering defender, player E. The attacking players must deal with this by creating a supporting position that allows the return pass to be square behind the first defender and away from the covering defender.

This is done by the supporting attacker taking a slightly different position, one that is deeper down field from the first defender and not on the defender C's shoulder as is the case in the first wall pass that was illustrated. In Square 1 (See Diagram 3, page 20.) the supporting attacker, labeled B, has not moved up high on the shoulder of the defender but has taken a position further down field below defender C.

This forces the dribbling attacker that commits the first defender to pass the a little earlier to avoid having it cut out by defender C. This takes an excellent sense of timing for the attacker. The attacker must use one of two possible visual cues to help them be successful.

1)   A defenders' forward momentum running at the attacker helps the attacker to explode into the space behind the defender to receive the square pass back.
2)   Or ironically the exact opposite should occur. The defender is standing statically and their lack of momentum allows the attacker to accelerate into the space behind the defender to receive the square return pass.

In Square 1 (See Diagram 3, page 20.) the reader can see the attacker's pass being slipped by the defender. In Square 1 (See Diagram 3, page 20.) the reader can see that because of the supporting position of the other attacker, attacker B, they are able to return a square pass back and avoid the covering defender. In Square 2 the attacker can now decide whether or not to send back a standard wall pass in return, option A1 or to dribble in option A2. With more attackers there are of course other options which include combination play.

Diagram 3A Low Wall Pass Patterns

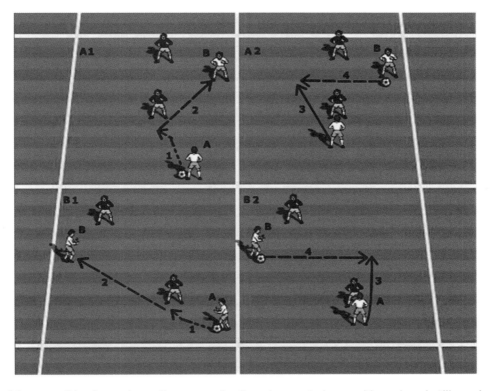

Diagram 3A, page 21, shows two other ways for the players to be positioned and still produce a Low Wall Pass Pattern. In section A1 and A2 the two attacking players are "stacked" up or in a line together when they start. Attacker A dribbles the ball, numbered with a 1, to commit the defender and then passes to attacker B with a pass numbered 2. In Square A2 shows attacker A making a run in behind the defender and receiving the square pass back from attacker B. The run by attacker A is numbered with a 3 and the pass from attacker B to attacker A is numbered with a 4.

In Diagram 3A, page 21, squares B1 and B2 show how a diagonal run from attacker A can set up the Low Wall Pass. In Square B1 attacker A dribbles the ball diagonally, numbered with a 1, at the closest defender and then lays the ball off the ball with a pass numbered 2. In Square B2 attacker A makes a run in behind the defender they committed with a run numbered 3. Attacker B returns a square pass which is numbered with a 4.

It is important that players learn that relative starting points can lead to patterns and how to use the relationship of the space between them and the positioning of the defenders to choose and execute 2 versus 1patterns. It is the speed of the thought and the speed of the following actions of two players understanding the possibilities that makes the patterns effective. Add the critical element of technical command and the players can now force the game on the defense.

High Wall Pass

Sometimes a players support for the wall pass is neither even or below the defender but in a position that is higher or up field from the attacker with the ball. This requires a slightly different solution to the situation for the attacking players. Diagram 4 will illustrate that a wall pass can still be created but requires a diagonal run by the attacker who first passes the ball up field to the supporting player. The return pass is straight downfield and works like a split pass in the concept of left/right/support shape. (See Diagram 4, page 22.)

Keys to the High Wall Pass

1) The keys applying to Wall Passes are still effective in this pattern. Here are the exceptions:
2) The initial carrier of the ball must commit the defender before passing off the ball and because of the supporting attackers position up field the dribble is diagonal at the defender. (See Diagram 4, page 22.)
3) The supporting attacker should be a little higher up field than the defender to be in a good position to return a pass to the attacker committing the defender. The return pass will be straight down field because the attacker committing the defender has not only made a diagonal dribble to commit them but must continue with a diagonal run behind the defender to receive the pass back. (See Diagram 4 section A 1, page 22.)
4) The run by the attacker penetrating behind the defense is diagonal. This pattern is very similar to another pattern later described as Diagonal Run/Straight Pass. (See Diagram 12 A, page 48.)
5) A good "first touch" is necessary to prepare the ball for the next move the attack wants to make.

Diagram 4: High Wall Pass

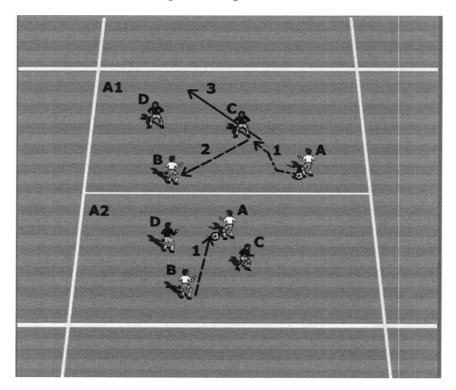

In Diagram 4, page 22, the supporting attacker, labeled B, is up field from the attacker, labeled A. Attacker A is committing defender C with the dribble numbered 1. Attacker A then passes the ball to attacker B with the pass numbered 2. This pass is back up field from the direction that the attacker wants to go. Usually this means that the supporting attacker, labeled B, is closer to their own goal than the teammate who is committing the defender with the dribble. The solution is a High Wall Pass which will have its' first pass back up field and then splits the defenders with a straight pass down field

In Square A1 the attacker, labeled A, dribbles to commit the defender. The dribble is numbered 1. In Square A1 the pass is hit backwards, numbered 2, to the supporting attacker. The pass should be to the foot furthest away from the defender nearest the supporting attacker. Attacker A then makes a hard diagonal run in behind the defender labeled C with a run numbered 3.

In Square A2 the supporting attacker splits the defenders with the straight return pass. This leaves attacker A with the ball behind the defense with the hoped for results.

Diagram 4 A: High Wall Pass Lateral Movement

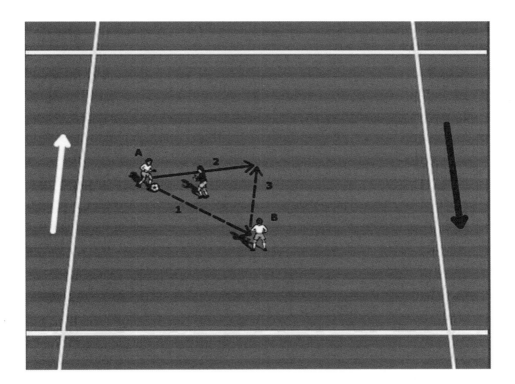

Diagram 4 A, page 23, shows the use of the High Wall moving laterally across the field rather than forward at the goal that the team is attacking. Player A makes a pass back up field numbered 1 to player B who returns the pass to player A. Player A is making a run, numbered 2, approximately parallel with the goal they are attacking and the pass from player B is numbered with a 3. This allows mobility in the attack and is another way to use the High Wall Pass other than to attack the goal with the movement.

Flick and Spin Wall

Most often the first attacker who delivers the ball in a wall pass is already in motion. In the Flick and Spin variation the first attacker can be moving or standing statically while marked. Being able to be static to start the Flick and Spin Wall makes it a little unique from other wall pass patterns. The diagrams will show the Flick and Spin wall from a moving position and from a shielding position. (See Diagram 5 and 5 A, pages 25 and 26.)

Keys to the Flick and Spin Wall:

1) It is best if the attacker with the ball who starts the Flick and Spin is "shoulder on" to the defender marking them. This means the attackers' shoulder is placed into the chest area of the defender which maximizes the distance between the defender and the ball held by the attacker. This position creates a full body width to shield the ball.

2) The wall pass can be made to either side of the attacker but the most deceptive is to use a supporting player to their back. To do this the player must be able to "flick" the pass to the supporting player with the outside of the foot, although there are other technical choices for serving the ball. If the player is directly facing the supporting player then the pass is most often with the inside of the foot. Other technical applications are perfectly acceptable.

3) After the attacker makes their first pass the attacker making that initial pass will "spin away" in the opposite direction from the pass to receive the ball back. This spinning run will split the defenders' vision between where the ball was just passed and where the player is making their run. This is an attempt to force the defender to choose how to respond, follow the ball or follow the man.

4) The attackers' teammate who is receiving the ball must decide whether to give the return pass based on both the reaction of the defender who is marking the attacker making the spin move and the defender of the man receiving the pass. If the passing lane is open then the return pass is given. If the passing lanes are closed then other options must be chosen.
   a) Shielding the ball.
   b) A False Flick and Spin Move that dribbles away from the intended pattern.
   c) A third player is used to create combination play or to move the ball into better situations for the team.

5) All the other guidelines for wall passing apply to this situation including making the first pass to the wall player to the top foot away from their defender.

6) The return pass will be into space and is usually a diagonal pass if the first attacker penetrates straight down the field. Any initial pass that is made to a supporting teammate in a square position will force the return pass to be diagonal.

7) If the attacker spins into a diagonal run behind the defender the pass will become a straight one into the space the attacker is penetrating. This straight pass is caused because the supporting attacker is either in a position up field or down field from the attacker giving the initial pass. (See Diagrams 5 B, 5 C and 5 D on pages 26, 27 and 28.)

8) One other unusual aspect to the Flick and Spin wall is that the attacker who initiates the first pass will often temporarily loses sight of the ball as they spin away. This action must occur and is therefore a little unique in the execution of the tactic. The attacker should relocate the ball visually as quickly as possible.

9) A good "first touch" is necessary to prepare the ball for the next move the attack wants to make

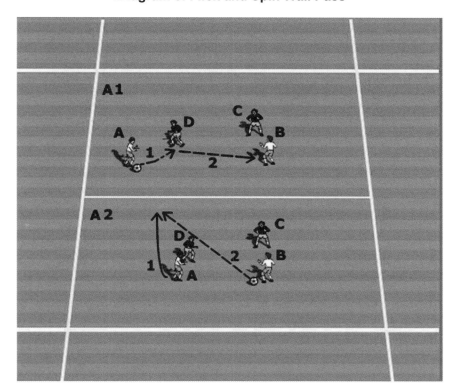

Diagram 5, page 25, illustrates the Flick and Spin move initiated from dribbling. The Flick and Spin Wall Pass is one that takes getting comfortable with to use. In Square A1 the attacker, labeled A, is dribbling towards their support, labeled B, while committing the defender, labeled D, at the same time. The dribble is numbered with a 1.

In Square A1, attacker A, after committing defender D, passes the ball to the supporting attacker. This pass, numbered 2, should be to the top foot, the foot away from the defender marking the supporting attacker. The defender in this case is labeled C.

In Square A2 the attacker that just passed the ball spins in the opposite direction from the pass. This run is numbered with a 1 and the run takes attacker A into the space behind the defender, labeled D. The supporting attacker, player B, returns the ball with a pass numbered 2 to their teammate. This pass is often a split pass between two defenders.

Diagram 5 A: Flick and Spin from a Static Position

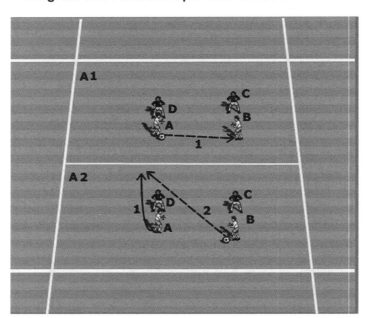

In Diagram 5 A, page 26, the movement starts with the attacker, labeled A, who is in a static shielding position. The rest of the pattern is the same as in Diagram 5, page 25. In Square A1 attacker A passes the ball to attacker B with a pass numbered 1.

In Square A2 the Spin Run is made in behind defender D by the attacker labeled A. This run is numbered 1. The return pass by attacker B is numbered 2 and splits both defenders C and D.

Diagram 5 B: Flick and Spin-Up Field

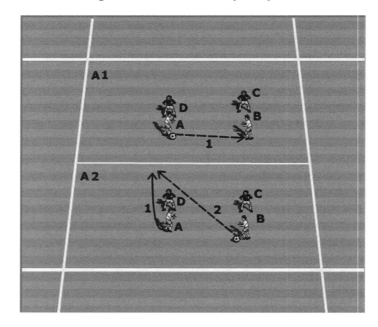

In Diagram 5 B, page 26, the position of the attackers makes a slight adjustment necessary. The supporting attacker, labeled B, is up field from the direction of the attack. This does not mean that a Flick and Spin solution is not available. The Flick pass in Square A1, numbered 1 is back up field.

What must change is that the Spin by the attacker labeled A must change from straight down field to a spin that becomes a diagonal run behind the defender. The pattern of the run is shown in Square A2 and is numbered with a 1. The return pass is made by attacker B and is numbered with a 2. In this diagram the support player is shown in a position that is not only up field from the attacker with the ball but is also behind the attacker with the ball. This makes the pass a little more surprising but is possible with good peripheral vision, verbal communication and players that look ahead of the situation that they are currently in to see what will occur as they receive the ball.

Diagram 5 C: Flick and Spin Down Field

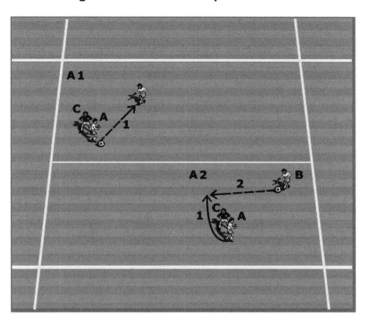

In Diagram 5 C, page 27, the Flick and Spin move is done with the supporting player, labeled B, in a position down field from the attacker, labeled A, who is in possession of the ball. In Square A1 the pass from player A to player B is numbered with a 1. In Square A2 attacker A spins away from the pass to split the vision of the defender, labeled C, from the ball and themselves. The Spin run is numbered 1 while the return pass from player B to player A is numbered with a 2.

Diagram 5 D: Flick and Spin Backwards

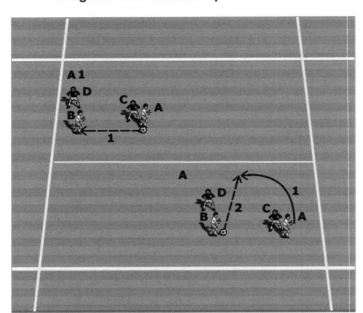

The purpose of Diagram 5 D, page 28, is to show that the Flick pass can be done in what some would consider a blind position. The pass in Square A1, numbered 1, is made by attacker A with their back to the supporting attacker B. This is a surprising move and can catch even well trained defenders off guard.

The return pass in Square A2 is numbered with a 2 and the Spin run by attacker A can be either straight down field or as shown in this case slightly diagonal in direction. Whether the Spin run should be straight or diagonal in this case depends on the positioning of defenders down field and if the attack has penetrated the last line of defense with an eye to get to a shooting position that is most advantageous.

Diagram 5 E: False Flick and Spin

Diagram 5 E, page 29, is shown to make sure players and coaches understand that in any pattern of play there is the exact opposite opportunity. In this case attacker A uses a body feint or dribbling motion to indicate that the pass is going to be made to attacker B. Once defender C has bitten on the feint and tried to stop the pass, attacker A can simply dribble out of the pattern.

The X Pattern

The X pattern is very much like the wall pass except that the "wall" is making a diagonal run that is in motion and often uses a deceptive outside of the foot pass to return the ball into the area that the player has just vacated. (Other technical surfaces are acceptable.) The reason that it is called an X Pattern is because the first attackers' diagonal run is crossed over by the second attackers' run through the same space that their teammate just ran through. The shape of the letter X is formed on the ground by their runs after they have both run over the same space. The passes themselves form a V shape in their pattern.

The pattern is very similar to a wall pass but the supporting player is in motion rather than in the more traditional static support of a wall pass supporter. In addition the X Pattern can be created with just two passes or it can be created with a dribble and a pass. These two points make the X Pattern unique. The pattern can be used anywhere on the field but is most safely used in the midfield and in the attacking third. The X Pattern can be devastating to defenders in the opponent's penalty box and is a thing of beauty to watch when teammates combine on the same page to execute it and score.

Keys to the X Pattern:

1) The movement can be produced with a dribble and a drop pass to the player "Xing" behind the dribbler. (See Diagram 6 A, page 30.) The movement can also be created with a pass sent to the diagonal runner with the return pass sent into the space that the attacker receiving the ball just ran through. (See Diagram 6 B, page 31.)
2) The pass is made so that it arrives on the hip of the runner and on the foot farthest away from the defender.
3) The return pass is made back into the path that the diagonal run or dribble just vacated.

4) After the first pass the attacker who just passed the ball runs explosively into the space just vacated by the runner who just made the diagonal run.

5) The attacker making the first run is the passing target running diagonally behind the defender of the man with the ball. (See Diagram 6 B, page 31.)

6) The X Pattern can also be created by a diagonal dribbling move done by the attacker with the ball. The supporting attacker simply waits for the space to be cleared and then times the run back into the space created by the diagonal dribble. (See Diagram 6 A, page 30.)

7) The switching of the space or areas occupied by the two attackers is what makes the X Pattern so hard for defenders to track their marks. This provides a momentary advantage of time and space for the attack.

8) A good "first touch" is necessary to prepare the ball for the next move the attack wants to make.

9) This pattern is useful in creating scoring opportunities and deceiving defenders any where in the midfield. The pattern can be used in the defensive third but tends to have a higher inherent risk if the teammates fail to be on the same page.

Diagram 6A: X Patterns Dribbling

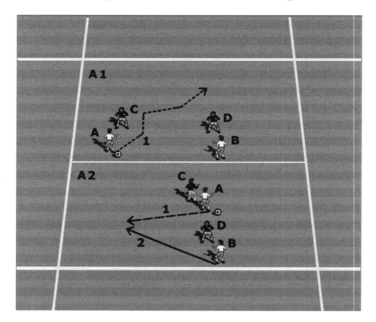

Diagram 6 A, page 30, shows the X Pattern created from the dribble. In Square A1 player A is dribbling from left to right which is numbered with a 1. The dribble goes between the defenders labeled C and D. This will cause the defensive structure to be disrupted as the defender labeled C tracks the attacker labeled A.

In Square A2 you can see that space has been opened up behind the attacker labeled A because of their dribbling. Attacker B now runs explosively into the space created by the dribble of attacker A, which creates an X Pattern on the ground. (This X Pattern on the ground is clearly shown in Diagram 6 C on page 32.) This run by player B is numbered 2 in Square A2. The pass to attacker B is made by attacker A and is numbered with a 1 in the diagram.

Diagram 6B:X Pattern from Passing

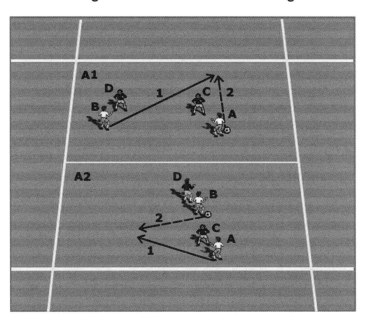

In Diagram 6 B, page 31, the X Pattern is achieved a different way. In Square A1 the attacker, labeled B, runs in front of the defender labeled D and behind the defender labeled C. The run is numbered with a 1 in the diagram. Attacker A passes the ball straight down field into the path of attacker B's run. This pass is numbered 2.

In Square A2 the attacker, labeled B, who just received the ball simply lays it off back into the space that they just ran through. The attacker, labeled A, who made the original pass cuts into the space just created by their teammate's run. Attacker A's run is numbered with a 1. The pass from attacker B to attacker A is numbered with a 2. The two runs together create an X on the ground. (See Diagram 6C, page 32, to see the X Pattern on the ground.) It is very helpful if the players have the technical ability to use the outside of the foot with an ankle twist to send the ball back from attacker B to attacker A because the pass is back into the space behind the run that player B just made. Any technical skill is acceptable to make the pass but the outside of the foot used in a twisting motion is an overall useful skill and particularly useful in executing this pattern.

Diagram 6 C: X Patterns Shown on the Ground

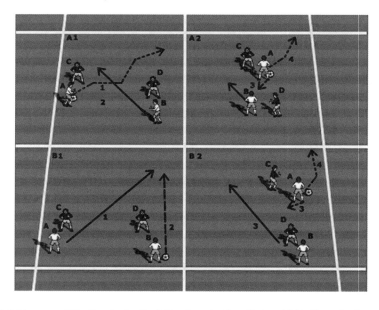

Diagram 6 C, page 32, is shown so that the reader can see the X Pattern left on the ground. In Square A1 the dribble pattern is shown with the second attacker making an X over the dribbling move. In Square A2 the passing pattern is shown and it can be seen that the two runs together create an X Pattern on the ground. This is source of the name for this 2 versus 1 pattern.

Diagram D and E: False X Patterns:

Diagrams 6 D and 6 E, page 32, illustrate that the key to the False X Pattern is the ability of the attacker with the ball to create the illusion of a pass. This is done with body feints or step over type dribbling moves that look like an attempt to pass the ball. All these can be achieved in the following ways. It could be a momentary hesitation of the body. It could be a partial swivel of the hips and then just flowing on into the space that the attacker was moving into in the first place. It could actually be a step over move and then reacceleration forward after freezing the defender with the move.

In Square A1 and A2 the False X Pattern is shown using the dribbling pattern. In Squares B1 and B2 the False X Pattern is created from the passing option. It should be remembered that for every action there is an equal and opposite action possible. In each example attacker A uses a feint to confuse the marking defender C. That feint is numbered with a 3 and the dribble by attacker A after the feint is numbered with a 4. In both the examples above the attacker using the feint has dribbled the ball or received it from a pass. In Diagram 6 F, page 33, the attacker that would send the initial pass in an X Pattern uses a feint to indicate a pass and then dribbles as the defender over commits and jumps the passing lane.

Diagram 6 F: False X Pattern

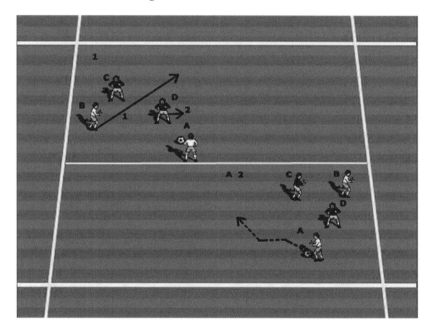

Diagram 6 F, page 33, shows that the False X Pattern is created by the run, numbered 1, by attacker B in Square A1. Defender D in Square A1 "jumps" the passing lane with a run numbered 2. This leaves space created by the run of attacker B, who is being tracked by defender C, open. Because defender D jumped into the passing lane defender D is no longer in a good position to prevent the dribble by attacker A.

In Square A2 the choice left open because of the defending choices of players C and D is for the attacker A to dribble into the space created by attacker B. This dribble is numbered 1 in Square A2.

Curved Run Pattern and/or Overlapping Runs

The Curved Run from behind is an excellent way to get a 2 versus 1 advantage momentarily on the field. Most often used on the flanks this is not the only way to use this movement. There is an interesting way for two strikers to use the curved run at the top of the box to create a shooting opportunity. (See Diagram 7 C and D, pages 36 and 37.) The Curved Run is also used in the midfield and to move out of the back third of the field.

The difference between a Curved Run and an Overlapping Run is the starting position of the supporting attacker in relationship to the attacker with the ball.. If the attacker is in a wider position than the ball the run will simply be straight and usually forward up field. This does not require the supporting attacker making the penetrating run to curve around their teammate with the ball. If the ball is outside on the flank and an attacker wants to make the run out and around the attacker with the ball then the run will by nature turn into a curved one. The supporting attacker starts in a position that allows backwards supporting passes and then turns into a penetrating run as they move forward past the attacker with the ball. The Curved Run is a little unique in that it supplies good support of the ball during the whole run and then turns into a penetrating run as it moves forward of the ball carrier.

Keys to the Curved Run

1) The space outside of the holder of the ball should be clear of opponents.
2) If the space is not already clear of opponents then the ball carrier can dribble diagonally into the interior of the field to open the space for their teammate to exploit with the curved or overlapping run. This dribble is most often from outside to the inside of the field.
3) When a curved run is created in the interior of the field then there may not be a clear inside or outside to use for reference.
4) Keeping some space between the ball holder and the supporting runner is helpful but exact amount of space between the two attacking teammates is not always predictable. Having large amounts of space between attackers executing the pattern is not a requirement for the pattern to be successful.
5) A player can run straight forward from behind to accomplish the same thing as a curved run. This is referred to in this manual as an overlapping run. The curved run that starts inside of the man with the ball and runs out and around is the traditional concept of the curved run.
6) It is helpful, maybe necessary, for the dribbling attacker to move diagonally. This is for two reasons:
   a) The diagonal run creates space by drawing defenders out of the area being dribbled out of by the attacker. This space can then be used by the second attacker.
   b) A diagonal dribble makes it easier for teammates coming from behind the ball carrier to catch up, pass the position of the ball and penetrate space forward of the ball. Catching a teammate that is sprinting straight forward with the ball as the supporting attacker tries to run, catch up and pass the ball carrier is a difficult if not nearly impossible movement to execute.
7) The holder of the ball must recognize whether their defender is trying to take away the dribbling option or the passing option to the runner outside of them. When they recognize the choice they are given they should exploit that choice given to them by the defender's position and not force one choice over the other because it was "expected."
8) A body feint or lunge may be useful in getting the defender tracking the dribbler of the ball to over commit into the interior of the field. The feint will usually create a little more space for the attacker with the ball to send a pass out to the curved runner that will make it hard to cut out the pass. The move may also freeze the opponent which will also allow an easier pass to be made to the overlapping attacker. This temporary freezing of the opponent will also make it harder for the defender to turn and catch the supporting attacker making the penetrating run if the ball is sent to them. The defender's static position verses the supporting attacker's running stride is an advantage to the attacker.
9) A good "first touch" is necessary to prepare the ball for the next move the attack wants to make.

Diagram 7 A: Curved Run

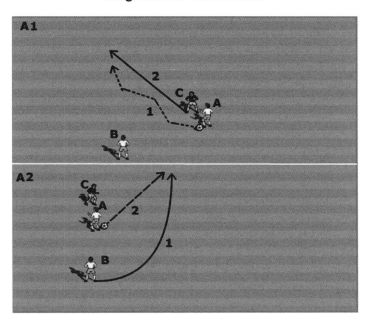

In Diagram 7A, page 35; Square A1, space is created for the overlap by attacker A dribbling into the interior of the field. This dribble is numbered with a 1. This dribble draws defender C out of the way and creates space for attacker B to exploit. The defender's run is numbered 2

In Square A2 attacker B curves out and around attacker A which gives the movement its' name, Curved Run. The run by attacker B is numbered 1. The pass made by attacker A to player B as the Curved Run is made is numbered with a 2.

Diagram 7 B: Straight Run Overlap

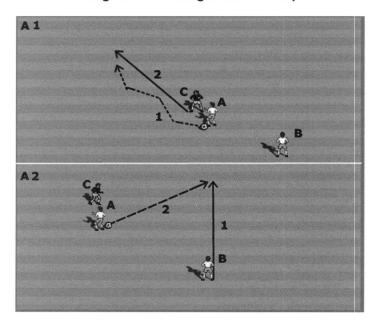

In Diagram 7B, page 36, the space for the overlapping run is already created by the wide position of attacker B. In Square A1 the attacker with the ball, labeled A, dribbles to widen the space for their teammate to overlap into before giving the pass to the player. The dribble by attacker A is numbered with a 1 and the tracking run by defender C is numbered with a 2.

In Square A2 attacker B makes a run forward, numbered 1. Attacker A sends a pass numbered 2 to attacker B. The supporting and then penetrating effect by the supporting runner is the same in the Curved Run pattern or the straight Overlapping Run. Space created in a wide position on the field is created by one attacker in possession of the ball and an attacker from behind exploits the space by making a run forward. The run can either by Curved or Straight and accomplish the same thing.

Diagram 7 C: Curved Run Used by Strikers

In Diagram 7C, page 36, striker A passes the ball shown by the broken line numbered 1 to striker B. Striker A then makes a curved run, shown by the solid line numbered 2 around the far side of striker B. Striker B passes the ball, shown by a broken line numbered 3, into the run of striker A which allows a shot on goal. The shot on goal is shown with the broken line numbered 4.

The difficulty for the defenders is that they must switch assignments or let the shot go uncontested. This means that defenders C and D must change assignments from marking attackers A and B. If striker A's defender, labeled C, tries to follow in a man to man manner then there will be space for striker B to exploit with a dribble. If defender C who is marking striker A tries to shadow their mark behind the line of restraint the shot will most likely be gone by the time the defender can run around their fellow defender. The run by the defender is longer to reach the point where the ball will be struck from to score than the attackers run to shoot it.

It also means that if defender C runs around to the far side of the other defender to block the shot potential space is opened up for striker B to exploit with a dribble. This only leaves the defenders with the decision to switch player assignments. If the switch required by the defenders is recognized to slowly the shot will already be taken at goal unimpeded by the defense. A slight movement by the dribbling or shielding attacker which creates momentum in the opposite direction from the pass or freezes defender D will help the curving attacker to have the space and time needed to shoot.

There was an excellent example of this movement in a Scottish Premier game. The ball was sent from the flank, attacker B dummies the ball and was received by the attacker C at the top of the box. The first striker then curved around their fellow striker and upon receiving the pass struck a shot that bounded off the post. This pattern use is shown in Diagram 7 D on page 37.

Diagram 7 D: Curved Run Pattern from Scottish Game

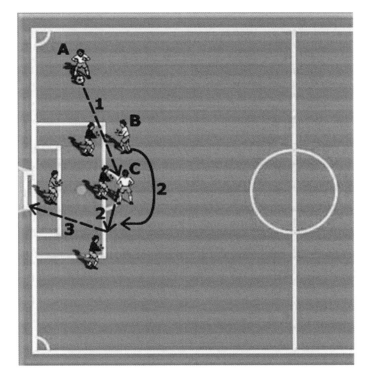

Diagram, 7 D, page 37, show the initial pass made by attacker A, numbered 1, was dummied by attacker B who then ran around attacker C. The run by attacker B is numbered 2. Player C held the ball long enough for the run to develop and to freeze the defender before passing the ball to player B. The pass by player C is numbered with a 2. Attacker B then shot the ball at goal which is numbered with a 3 and in the game struck the post.

Playing the Curved Runner Late
This pattern is both deceptive and disruptive to defenses. What is required is that the attacker creating the space with the dribble for their teammate beats their defender into the interior of the field. Then instead of continuing the dribble the player passes the ball behind the defender they just beat with the dribble to the teammate that is making the Curved Run. (See Diagram 8 A, page 38.)

Diagram 8A: Using the Curved Runner Late

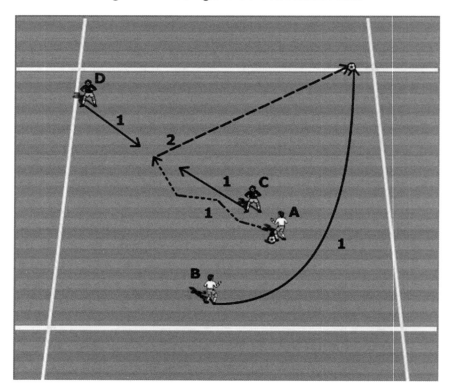

In Diagram 8 A, page 38, the same pattern of dribbling is used by attacker A to create space for attacker B to play wide in. The dribble by attacker A, the run to defend it by defender C and the Curved Run by attacker B are all numbered 1. However, instead of the defender C catching up and getting between the goal and the attacker the dribbler has beaten their defender and now elects to pass the ball out wide to attacker B after they have beaten their marking defender. This pass is shown in behind defender C and is numbered with a 2. The reason for making this pass is because other defenders, in this diagram labeled D, will slide over from the interior of the field and arrive to apply pressure on attacker A. This will mean that the pass by attacker A will split two defenders C and D as defender D arrives to contain the dribble and the other defender, C, tries to catch up to the dribble. This late pass commits two defenders to trying to stop the ball and creates more space for the attacking teammate to use when receiving the pass.

Diagram 8 B: Using the Straight Overlap Late

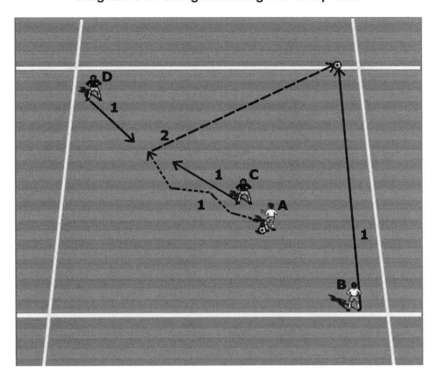

In Diagram 8 B, page 39, attacker A is dribbling to create free space outside for teammate B. Player A beats their defender in Diagram 8 B while player B makes the straight run outside. Attacker A sends the pass back outside to player B who is continuing their run up field. All the same reasons for the late pass still apply. A defender, labeled D, will be sliding out from the interior of the field to contain attacker A. This commitment of two defenders to stopping the ball creates more space for attacker B to exploit.

False Curved Run:

The False Curved Run is named separately in this manual but is just a logical extension of using the opposite action from the one that is implied by the attacker's movements. As coaches we can not overlook this concept. All a False Curved Run really is, is the defender jumping into the passing lane which allows the dribbling attacker to continue dribbling and accelerate away from the defender who positioned them self to stop the pass by jumping into the passing lane thereby leaving the dribbling option open for the attacker with the ball. This goes back to the basic assumption that a defender can stop the dribble or stop the pass but can not stop both options at the same time.

The False Curved Run or Overlap is a simple concept. All that happens is a defender jumps the passing lane leaving space to dribble. An attacker can also use a stop and go move or a movement that indicates a pass will be made to the supporting attacker which creates the situation for the dribbling attacker to exploit. In any case a False Curved Run and/or Overlap is just an attacker making use of a defender's inclination to prevent the pass from being completed rather than stopping the dribble. The term used regularly in the book is when a defender "jumps" the passing lane then the attacker should use the dribble to beat the defender's decision to prevent the pass.

Diagram 8 C: False Curved Run

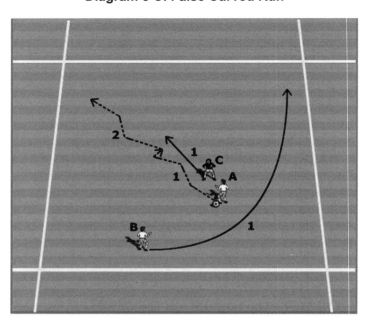

In Diagram 8 C, page 40, attacker A dribbles to the inside of the field to create space for attacker B to exploit with a Curved Run. Defender C reacts by defending the dribble. All of these actions are numbered with a 1. There is a point in attacker A's dribble where a pass is threatened to the outside of the field to the run being made by attacker B. This feint often creates hesitation or an attempt to jump the passing lane by defender C to prevent the pass to attacker B. This in turn allows attacker A to reaccelerate into the interior of the field and continue with the initial dribble. The feint creates the illusion of a normal curved run use and is used to create the option of continuing to dribble instead of making the pass to attacker B. The continued dribble is numbered 2 and extends on from the dribble numbered 1 by attacker A.

Double Pass (straight return pass)

This pass is most often used at or near the top of the box to exploit 2 versus 1 that usually consists of a midfielder coming forward towards a striker who is in their direct path. The pattern, however can be used anywhere on the field. (See Diagram 9, page 41.)

Keys to the Double Pass (straight return pass)

1) The first pass from the midfielder is straight into the strikers' feet. If the defender is not already marking the striker closely this should draw the defender to the striker in a close marking position. This tight marking is a desirable situation for this pattern.
2) The return pass is straight back to the feet of the midfielder. The midfielder should have started moving forward towards the striker and the pass that is being returned.
3) While the pass is returning the striker backs away square from the defender. The attackers' chest should be turned towards the defender so they can see the defender. The attacker should create just enough space for a pass by "sharpening" wide of the defender so the pass can not be cut out.
4) It is also possible for the attacker who has just returned the pass to turn forward with their back to their teammate. This body language is a clear demand for the ball to be played through into the space in front of the attacker. This is highly acceptable but leaves fewer options for the attackers and therefore is easier to read defensively than sliding sideways with the attacker's chest to the defender.
5) The attacker attempts to open a passing lane just wide enough to receive the pass back

again. To wide a passing lane and the defender is given more recovery time. To narrow a lane and the defender will intercept the return pass.

6) The midfielder carries the ball just long enough to commit the defender then slips the ball to the striker so that the ball runs right across their teammates' chest.

7) The attackers need to be careful of the offside rule if they are penetrating the last line of defense.

8) A good first touch in behind the defender leaves the striker with a good shooting opportunity. (This pattern can also easily evolve into a wall pass.) (See Diagram 9 section A3 option 2, page 41.)

9) The striker needs to be aware of the defender's movement forward that might put them in an offside position and should adjust to stay on the defenders shoulder. (In the match they can also watch adjacent defenders to make sure they stay onside.)

10) The return pass to the attacker should be to their lower foot, the one closest to the goal. This will increase the speed of attack with the first touch to goal. However, as with other situations other technical solutions are possible, acceptable and may be required.

11) If the attacker opening up the passing lane does not do so correctly other ways for the pass to penetrate to the back of the defense is with a sharp incline chip pass served with backspin so that it will not roll to the keeper or to bend the ball around the defender.

12) A good "first touch" is necessary to prepare the ball for the next move the attack wants to make.

Diagram 9: Double Pass Straight Return Pass

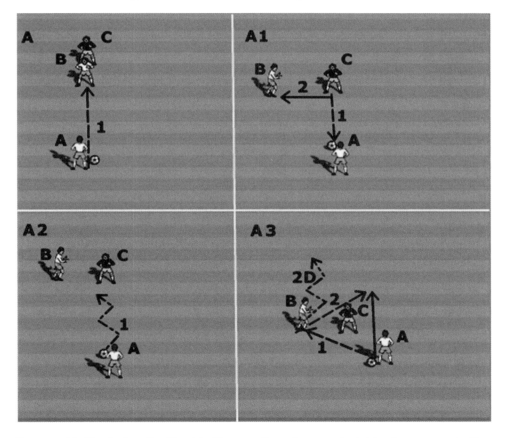

Diagram 9, page 41, illustrates the Double Pass pattern from a straight return pass. In Square A attacker A initiates the move with a pass to the striker, attacker B. The pass is numbered with a 1. In Square A1 attacker B has sent the ball back to attacker A and has moved wide of the defender labeled C. The pass back is numbered with a 1 and the run by attacker B is numbered with a 2. Attacker B keeps their chest and face to the defender labeled C. This can be done if the attacker backs away from the defender as they open up the passing lane. This movement keeps attacker B's body shape open allowing them to see what the defender is doing.

In Square A2 player A makes a short dribble to commit the defender. This dribble is numbered with a 1. In Square A3 there are two possible outcomes to a well timed pass from attacker A to player B. One is for player B to take a touch forward to dribble, this option is numbered 2D. The other option is for attacker A to keep their run going and receive a return Wall Pass from attacker B. This option is numbered with a 2. This pattern is seen most dramatically at the top of the box and is used to penetrate a flat defense while creating shooting opportunities.

Double Pass (diagonal return pass)

This pass has almost all the same attributes as the Double Pass Straight Pass. There are two differences that make this 2 versus 1 pattern unique.
   a) The first is the angle of the return pass from the striker to the midfielder.
   b) The second is a spin movement by the attacker around the defender and into a diagonal run that allows a straight penetrating pass to be sent in and gets the attacker behind the defense.

Keys to the Double Pass (diagonal return pass)

1) The first pass from the attacker is straight into their teammates' feet to draw the defender into a close marking position against the attacker receiving the pass.
2) The attacker initiating the first pass will need to drift wide of the striker while still staying up field from them to receive the diagonal pass back. The decision to drift left or right and therefore demand the diagonal pass back in a certain area is determined by which side the defender is marking the striker on. If they are slightly to the left of center so that the spin move around the defender will be to the right then the area that the supporting attacker should choose will be to the their right. This forces the defender to choose between sight of the ball and sight of the attacker they are marking. The supporting attacker will drift in the opposite area if the defender is marking more to the right. If the defender is marking the striker dead center then the supporting player should choose the side that will allow their fellow attacker to shoot with their stronger foot.
3) The return pass goes back diagonally to the original attacker so that a split or penetrating pass can be sent in behind the defenders. This return pass is not possible with the straight return pass that was just examined in the last section. The diagonal pass moves the position of the ball into a spot where a split pass can be sent forward and in behind the defense.
4) While the pass is going back the striker must spin away from the direction of the diagonal pass. This will split the defenders vision of the attacker and the position of the ball. The attacker will then ultimately make a diagonal run behind the defender to receive a split pass behind the defense. (This is similar to the Flick and Spin Wall Pass Pattern when the supporting attacker is up field.)
5) The attacker will usually pass the ball through the split pass in one touch to help keep their teammate onside. (If the defender reads the split pass and steps into it then it frees the midfielder to dribble the ball in the direction just vacated by the defender and shoot or pass the ball themselves. This is the False Double Pass Pattern from the Diagonal Pass) (See Diagram 10 B, page 44.)
6) A good touch in behind the defender gives the attacker a shooting opportunity.

Diagram 9 A: Double Pass Diagonal Return Pass

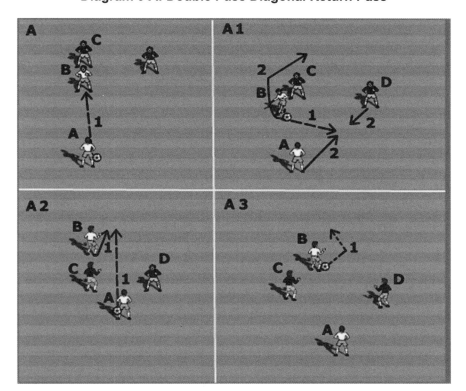

In Diagram 9 A, page 43, Square A, the attacker labeled A passes the ball to attacker B just as they did in the first Double Pass Pattern. The difference is the return pass from player B to player A, which is not straight back but is now laid back diagonally. The return pass is shown in Square A1 and is numbered with a 1. Attacker A steps forward to the diagonal pass, this run is numbered 2, as attacker B spins away from the direction of the ball and then around the defender into the space directly in front of the ball. This run is also numbered with a 2 and moves around defender C. It is very similar to the Flick and Spin move up field.

In Square A2 this allows attacker A to send a straight split pass behind the defenders C and D. The pass from attacker A is numbered with a 1 and the continuation of attacker B's run is also shown with a 1. Square A3 simply shows how the final picture would look with the defenders chasing attacker B who is dribbling forward. The dribble is numbered with a 1. (See Diagram 9A, page 43.)

False Double Pass Patterns:

Once again all the False Double Pass Pattern is for the attackers to respond to defenders who try to jump the passing lane instead of protecting the potential dribble. In the case of the straight return pass the visual cue is that the defender tracks the attacker moving wide and leaves a lane of space open for the other attacker to dribble through. (See Diagram 10 A, page 44.) In the case of the diagonal return it is caused once again by the defender turning and tracking the penetrating attacker while running through the potential passing lane. Again all that is needed is that the supporting attacker sees the space opening up and attacks it with the dribble. (See Diagram 10 B, page 44.)

Diagram 10 A: False Double Pass Dribbling Option from Straight Pass

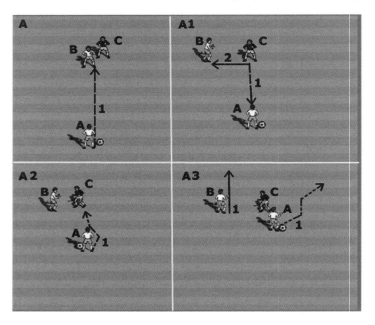

Diagram 10 A, page 44, shows exactly the same patterns of movement as 9 until Square A2. In Square A attacker A passes the ball to attacker B. In Square A1 attacker B returns the pass and opens up a passing lane while keeping their body shape open to defender C. In Square A2 attacker A dribbles to commit defender C with a dribble numbered 1, defender C starts trying to jump the passing lane to attacker B. This reaction by defender C to the run by attacker B creates the difference in Square A3. In Square A3 attacker A recognizes that defender C has moved to prevent the pass and chooses to dribble rather than pass the ball. This dribble is numbered with a 1. This dribble is allowed because the illusion of the Double Pass Pattern and the attempt by defender C to stop it from occurring.

Diagram 10 B: False Double Pass Dribbling Option from Diagonal Pass

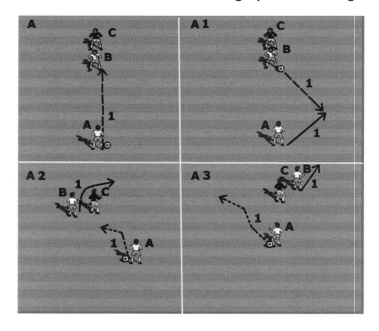

In Diagram 10 B, page 44, what is illustrated is a possible solution for an attacker when the defender, labeled C, makes a recovery run by tracking attacker B which in turn blocks the passing lane. The attacker B receives the ball in Square A from attacker A. The pass is numbered 1. In Square A1 attacker B passes off the ball diagonally, numbered 1and attacker A steps forward to receive the pass with a run numbered 1.

In Square A2 attacker B spins around the defender C in an attempt to get the ball back behind the defense. This run is numbered with a 1. Defender C however, starts making an effective recovery run which disrupts the ability of attacker A to return the pass to attacker B. In Square A3 where the pass should be sent forward defender C's good recovery run and closing of the passing lane prevents the pass from occurring. The attacker A, now in possession of the ball, does not have a workable Double Pass Pattern anymore.

One of the best options for the attacker with the ball is to dribble into and across the area where attacker B's run pulled defender C out of the space with the run. This solution is shown in Square A3 and attacker A's dribble is numbered 1. There are a myriad of possible solutions but this is an effective one because it exploits the space that the defender had to surrender to achieve the blocking of the passing lane.

Take Over

All the rage in coaching circles for awhile there are not a lot of opportunities for this to occur on the field and with the present emphasis on players keeping their spacing it lessens the chance of it occurring. However, adding this maneuver to your players' repertoire is a good idea. Take Over patterns can occur anywhere on the field but in the tighter spaces of the attacking third or in the middle third of the field is where the pattern is most likely to occur. Areas of the field that players tend use the Take Over are near the penalty box and in the middle third of the field. (See Diagram 11 A and 11 B, pages 46 and 47.)

Keys to the Take Over

1) Communication is paramount. There is nothing quite as embarrassing as when two players both think they are taking the ball and a smashing good tackle occurs between teammates or they both thought the other was taking the ball and it is left laying there for the defender to take as both attacking players run away neither one in possession of the ball..
2) The Take Over is essentially like a hand off in football but done with the feet.
3) The player in possession of the ball will usually be closer to a defender and the opponent's goal than their teammate, who is coming in close to take the ball over or leave it if the dribbler decides to keep it.
4) The Take Over is done left foot to left foot or right foot to right foot. Anything else causes a collision to occur.
5) The Take Over should occur at less than full speed so that acceleration can take place after the exchange. This acceleration will help lose the defenders.
6) If the attacker carrying the ball has a defender that is slightly ahead of their hips then the supporting teammate should take the ball. The opposite is true if the defender is trailing or scrambling to catch up with the dribbler. If this is the situation then the dribbler should keep the ball in the Take-Over pattern. (This relates to a 1 versus 1 principle about when to stop the dribble abruptly or when to feint the stopping and still dribble forward. The visual cue for stopping the dribble is if the defenders hips have passed the attackers hips, if the defenders hips have passed the attackers hips then jam on the brakes, the defender will continue on by the stopped dribble. If the defender's hips have not gone past the attacker's hips and are still behind them then a feint to stop that slows the defender's run will be effective when the attacker reaccelerates forward with the defender behind them. Players executing the Take Over should read where the defenders hips are that is marking the dribbling player. If they are behind then a feint to exchange the ball and keeping it is most

effective. If the defenders hips are in front of the dribbling attacker then exchanging the ball and the direction of movement is most effective.)

7) It is best for the carrier of the ball to just leave the ball for the take over rather than attempt a tiny little pass to their teammate. (Although sending a heel pass to the attackers' teammate after a False Take Over has occurred can be quite surprising to the opposition.)

8) If the carrier of the ball wants to keep possession, a little cut dribble making the ball closer to them will allow them to keep the ball.

9) A good "first touch" is necessary to prepare the ball for the next move.

Diagram 11 A: Take Over

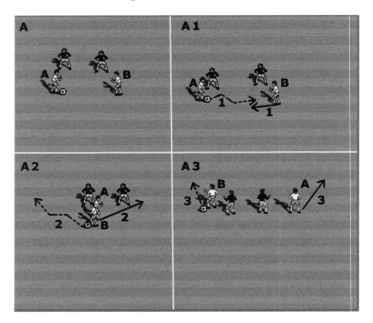

The Diagram 11 A, page 46, shows how two attackers in close proximity can use this to their advantage by changing who has possession of the ball from a dribbling move. In Square A both attackers, A and B, are shown facing each other. In Square A1 attacker A dribbles the ball straight at attacker B who makes a run right next to attacker A. What matters is that in Square A2 the exchange of the ball is done with the same foot, right to right or left to left. If opposite feet are used by the two attackers then a collision will occur. Square A3 shows that the ball has exchanged possession from attacker A to attacker B and that they are now moving away in opposite directions.

Diagram 11 B: False Take Over

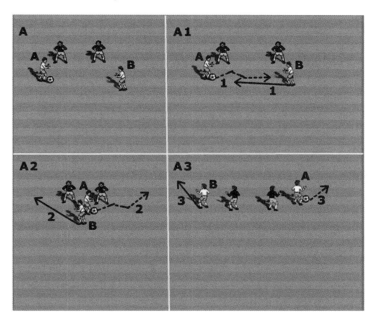

In Diagram 11 B, page 47, all the same rules apply but the ball is kept by the dribbler of the ball. The illusion of the Take Over can create a little space for the attackers to work with and a quick acceleration can leave defenders in poor defending positions. Square A shows the attackers A and B facing each other. In Square A1 the ball is dribbled forward by attacker A and attacker B makes a run right past their teammate. Square A2 shows the ball being carried forward by attacker A and no switch of possession has occurred. Square A3 simply shows the desired results and who would end up with the ball.

In making a decision to choose to keep the ball or exchange it in the Take-Over Pattern it is best to keep the ball if the defender who is marking the ball carrier is trailing the attacker in possession of the ball is behind the hip of the attacker with the ball. This means that the defender is trailing behind the attacker slightly and any feint or move that can slow the defender up a little can leave that defender in the attacker's wake when the attacker reaccelerates. It is therefore helpful if the attacker is below top dribbling speed. This trailing position of the defender allows the attacker to use the feint of a Take Over to explode forward with the ball and lose the defender.

The opposite decision is true if the defender who is tracking the attacker with the ball is slightly ahead of the attacker or in front of the attacker's hips. This position by the defender allows for a better opportunity for the attackers to use a Take Over to lose the defender who is in a good position to stop the attacker from moving forward with the ball off the dribble.

To explain these ideas to the players it is clear if they are told that they should continue to carry the ball (False Take Over) if the defender marking them is behind the hip of the ball carrier. And if the defender is in front of the attacker's hip then the attacker should let their teammate have the ball. (Take Over) "Defender behind your hips, carry it, defender in front of your hips give it."

Diagonal and Straight Runs

These are straight forward enough concepts. A diagonal run with a straight pass occurs when a teammate runs behind a defender from a slightly wider position than the attacker with the ball creating a diagonal slash across the field. The diagonal run can be from inside to out or outside to inside in relationship to the interior or flank areas of the field. The passing teammate can exploit this run with a straight penetrating ball.

The second pattern is a diagonal pass to a player who is making a straight run in behind the defenders' space. Either pattern can be done without the idea of penetrating towards goal. The runs however, are used constantly to penetrate behind defenses and create scoring opportunities. These concepts can best be simplified by a soccer saying: "Diagonal runs to straight passes and straight runs to diagonal passes." (Author unknown) (See Diagrams 12 A, 12 B, 12C, and 12 D pages 48 and 49.)

Diagram 12 A: Straight Pass with Diagonal Run

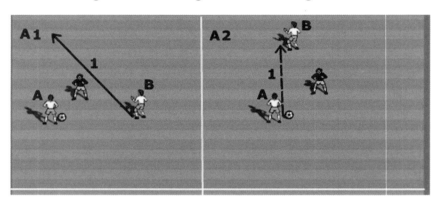

Diagram 12 A, page 48, shows the starting positions in Square A1 of attackers A and B. Attacker B makes a diagonal run in behind the defender in Square A1 that is numbered with a 1. The straight pass by attacker A to exploit attacker B's diagonal run is shown in Square A2 and is numbered 1.

12 B Straight Run with Diagonal Pass

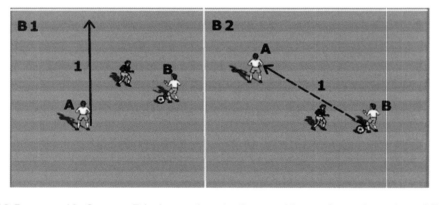

In Diagram 12 B, page 48, Square B1 shows the starting positions of attackers A and B. Attacker A makes a straight run into the space behind the defender in Square B1. This run is numbered 1. In Square B2 attacker B then sends a straight diagonal pass out in front of the run by attacker A. this pass is numbered 1.

Straight Run/Straight Pass

In this pattern the supporting attacker must run to a position on the field where their run places them to a position on the field that is "square" of the attacker with the ball. (See Diagram 12 C and D page 49.)

Diagram 12 C: Straight Run and Straight Pass

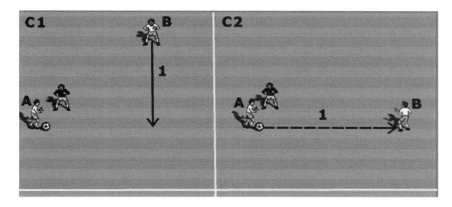

Diagram 12 C, page 49, shows attacker B making a run back past the pressuring defender of attacker A thus making them self available for a pass. The run is labeled 1. In Square C2 the pass is shown from attacker A to attacker B and is numbered with a 1. This run is most often used in possession situations.

Diagram 12 D: Straight Run and Straight Pass

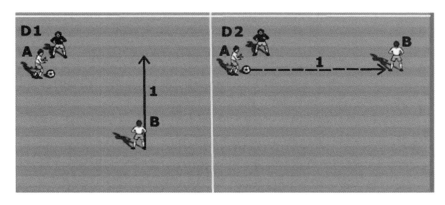

Diagram 12 D, page 49, shows the exact same concept except the run by attacker B in Square D1 is made from behind the attacker, A, who is in possession of the ball. Square D2 shows attacker A passing the ball to attacker B. The pass is numbered with a 1. This run is to also secure possession of the ball for the team as a whole.

Diagonal Run/Diagonal Pass

The supporting attacker must cut diagonally into space towards the teammate in possession of the ball. This run creates some great passes to the back of the defense or past a single defender when the attacker with the ball is quite far away from the attacker making the run. The pass and the run make a V shape or arrowhead shape on the ground. This run and pass can be a close quarter move or can be done from flank to flank where the ball and penetrating attacker meet in the middle of the field. (See Diagrams 12 E, F and G pages 50 and 51.)

Diagram 12 E: Diagonal Run and Diagonal Pass

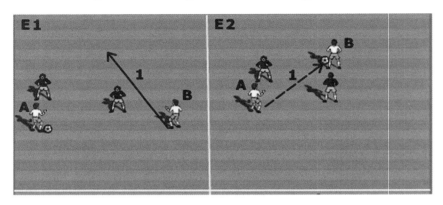

In Diagram 12 E, page 50, one of the advantages to the Diagonal Run and Diagonal Pass shown is that the attacker numbered B is now directly behind the defender when they receive the ball. This makes it difficult for the defender to make any recovery run that will not force them to foul attacker B. Attacker B makes a diagonal run in Square E1 which is numbered 1. And attacker A sends a pass numbered 1 to attacker B in Square E2. The run and pass are simultaneous.

Diagram 12 F: Diagonal Run and Diagonal Pass

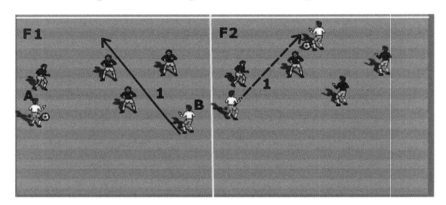

In Diagram 12 F, page 50, shows that it is possible to penetrate defenses in depth with the Diagonal Run and Diagonal Pass. Attacker B makes a diagonal run in Square F1 that cuts right through the defense. The run is numbered with a 1. In Square F2 the ball is passed by attacker A to attacker B behind the defenders. This pass is numbered 1. In Diagram 12 F, page 50, the pattern used is a Diagonal Run with a Diagonal Pass and if the run and the pass are shown at the same time there is a V shape or arrowhead shape drawn on the ground. This shape can be used to explain the run and pass to the players.

Diagram 12 G: Diagonal Run to Diagonal Pass over Distance

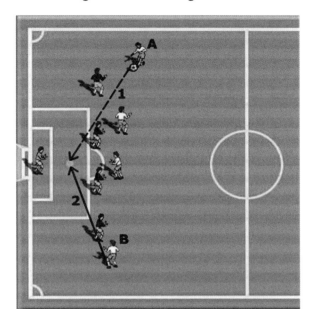

Diagram 12 G, page 51, illustrates the ability of teammates A and B to use the Diagonal Pass and Diagonal Run to converge at a spot that would be impossible to reach with any other pattern. It is a good way to get into a dangerous scoring position that could not be achieved by attackers A and B in any other way. A well timed run and pass are needed to avoid the offside rule.

Dummy Patterns

These patterns are often used by strikers using each other in tight situations near the edge of the penalty box. The movement catches defenders by surprise just enough to leave creases for the strikers to pass the ball through. It is not a move that is exclusive to strikers or the penalty box area. But a Dummy Move is often most surprising and effective in this area of the field because of the close proximity of the strikers to each other and when successful the scoring opportunities that they provide. Diagram 13, page 52, shows how a Dummy Move could be used by attackers in the final third of the field. Diagram 13 A shows another way to use a Dummy Movement on the field. (See diagrams 13 and 13 A page 52.)

Diagram 13: Dummy Movement

In Diagram 13, page 52, attacker A passes the ball to attacker B. This pass is numbered with a 1. Attacker B lets the ball slide by them, this can be done just outside of the body or more often between the legs, and the pass numbered 1 continues on to attacker C. After attacker B lets the ball past them with the Dummy Move they make a run numbered 2 into the space behind the defender marking them. Attacker C then send a pass numbered 2 into the path of attacker B's run who then shoots the ball at goal. The shot on goal is numbered with a 3. Once the Dummy Move has been made the pattern is similar in this case to a Wall Pass or Flick and Spin Pattern discussed earlier in the book.

Diagram 13 A: Dummy Move Made in Other Parts of the Field

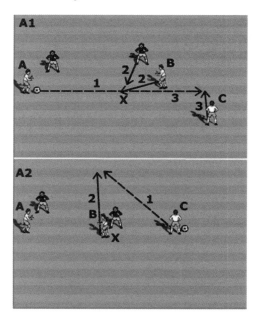

Diagram 13 A, page 52, shows a Dummy Pattern used in another part of the field. It could also be used in the final third to penetrate a defense but it is not likely to be used in the defending third of the field because failure would most likely lead to a catastrophic result. However, one should never say never in soccer and the best players are always doing surprising things.

In Square A1 of Diagram 13 A, page 52, attacker A sends a pass, numbered 1 to attacker B who is making a run towards attacker A. The run by attacker B is numbered 2. The pass and the run attract the attention of the defender who also makes a run to what is likely an interception point. However, in this example attacker B arrives at the point labeled X first and lets the ball slide past them or through their legs. The continuation of the first pass is labeled 3 even though no new contact has been made. Attacker C steps up to receive the ball after attacker B Dummies it.

In Square A2 attacker B makes a Straight Run in behind the defenders, numbered 2 and attacker C sends a Diagonal Pass in behind the defense, numbered 1, that meets the run of attacker B. The Dummy move by attacker B committed the defender into an attempt to win the ball and commit their momentum forward. This in turn allowed the attackers B and C to use a Straight Run/Diagonal Pass Pattern to penetrate the back of the defense one the Dummy Move had committed the defense.

Wall Passing Used Diagonally and Horizontally

One of the interesting points to wall passing and wall passing patterns is that they are almost always taught in straight or vertical movement down field towards an opponents' goal. This is a limited use of the patterns and a coach may need to instruct their players that there are other uses and directions to use with wall passing patterns. Wall passes are not always used in just vertical movements at higher levels of play. They are of course used to attack straight at goal in the traditional concept of the wall pass. But they are also used to move horizontally across the field and in their most varied form are often used diagonally. The diagonal movement of wall passes is often from flank positions to penetrate the penalty area. But the movement and concept should not be limited to just this area of the field.

None of the principles of the wall pass change but for some people it is hard to visualize the diagonal wall passes from the flank or the use of horizontal wall passing across the field. This is because the supporting wall passer no longer has to be in any one position. They can be either above or below the defender being exploited with the wall pass. The pattern is the same but because the direction of the runs is different the concept initially confuses players and some coaches. The use of the wall pass to move across the field both horizontally and diagonally is important for players to know and be comfortable executing.

Diagram 14 A and 14 B: Diagonal Wall Passing

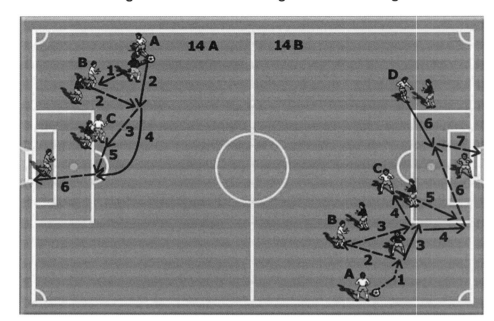

This use of wall passing is not often pointed out, taught or practiced with players. The left half of the above soccer field is Diagram 14 A and the right half is Diagram 14 B. I hope that I made this clear enough that if you just walk through it slowly all the lines should come clear.

The reader can see in Diagram 14 A, page 54, the attacker, labeled A, use attackers B and C to create wall passes diagonally across the field. Attacker A uses a Low Wall Pass Pattern with attacker B and a Curved Run with attacker C to get into a scoring position behind the defense.

Attacker A sends a pass numbered 1 to attacker B. Attacker A then makes a run past the defender. The run is numbered with a 2 which allows the pass back from attacker B. The return pass is also numbered 2 because the pass and the run are essentially simultaneous. Attacker A then passes the ball to attacker C with a pass numbered 3. While attacker C holds the ball in a shielded position attacker A makes a Curved Run around attacker C. The run by attacker A is numbered with a 4. Attacker C then plays off the ball with a pass numbered 5 for attacker A to shoot at goal which is numbered 6. This attack is done across the field in an East to West motion and not in the more traditional North to South manner of penetrating a defense and attacking the goal.

In the right half of field the reader can see Diagram 14 B, page 54. Another East to West attack is demonstrated using 2 versus 1patterns to penetrate the defense. Attacker A uses attackers B and C to cut diagonally across the field. The first pattern that A and B use is a High Wall Pass followed by a more traditional Wall Pass that combines attacker A and C which leaves attacker A with the ball in a position to pass the ball behind the defense to attacker D who shoots the ball at goal.

Attacker A starts the sequence by dribbling at the first defender; the dribble is numbered with a 1, and then passes the ball to player B to combine for a High Wall Pass. The pass to attacker B is numbered with a 2. The return pass by attacker B is numbered 3 as is the run by attacker A past the defender. Attacker A then passes the ball to attacker C to start a wall pass. This pass is numbered with a 4 and the run by attacker A to get behind the next defender is also numbered with a 4. Attacker C sends a penetrating pass back to attacker A, who receives it behind the defense. This pass is numbered with a 5. The attacker A is now in a position to cross the ball to attacker D who is making a run towards attacker A in front of the goal mouth. Both the cross by attacker A and the run by attacker D are numbered 6. The shot on goal is numbered with a 7.

To reiterate, these 2 versus 1patterns are used in an East to West manner that allows penetration of the goal area. They are used frequently in the modern game and as coaches it is quite useful to instruct the players about these uses of the patterns to diversify the ability of players and teams. Becoming unpredictable as an attacking team is crucial to disrupting well organized and trained defenses.

Diagram 15: Horizontal Wall Passing Across the Field

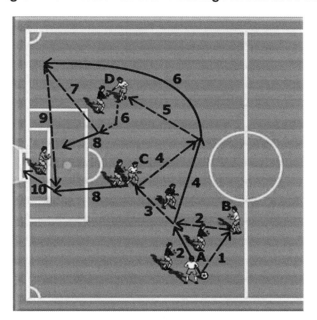

Diagram 15, page 55, shows an example of horizontal wall passing. Horizontal wall passing is often used in moving the point of attack from one side of the field to the other. In Diagram 15, page 55, attacking player A (on the bottom of the diagram near the center of the field) begins their run horizontally across the field by wall passing with supporting attacker B. This 2 versus 1 pattern is a High Wall Pass. Attacker A sends a pass to attacker B which is numbered with a 1. Attacker A then makes a run past the defender and receives the ball from attacker B. Both the pass by attacker B and the run by attacker A are numbered with a 2.

Attacker A then combines with attacker C by using a Low Wall Pass Pattern. The pass from attacker A to attacker C is numbered with a 3. The return pass from attacker C to attacker A and the run past the defender by attacker A are both numbered with a 4.

Attacker A now combines with attacker D who is wide on the opposite side of the field from where attacker A started the movement. The pass from attacker A to attacker D is numbered with a 5. Attacker A then makes a Curved Run around attacker D which is numbered with 6. Attacker D uses the Curved Run to use a dribble to the interior past the defender. The dribble is numbered with a 6. Attacker D then chooses to make a late pass to attacker A who is now in the flank position. This pass is numbered 7.

To finish the move both attackers D and C make runs into the box which are numbered 8. Attacker A sends a crossing pass into the box numbered 9. The movement is completed with a shot by attacker C numbered 10.

In moving the ball from flank to flank a team usually does it using the traditionally understood method of using the ball to switch the point of attack from side to side. But the players themselves can use logical moves to flow from side to side on the field. This kind of mobility requires that all the players on a team understands how to create both the small group support shape and the entire shape that the team needs to be successful.

Summary:

These are the 2 versus 1 patterns used most regularly. It is hoped that the above section has illuminated the 2 versus 1patterns in the game of soccer. They can be used singly or strung together in a series of choices. A curved run around a defender can develop into a diagonal run behind that same defender, time permitting. The patterns are used in little bursts all over the field and then the game goes on to left/right/split support or into a 1 versus 1 dual or then again the ball may be switched across the field to another point of attack. The game is a kaleidoscope of a few pieces ever changing and being spun into something that make each game unique because of the quality of the players, the teams involved and/or the players' tactical and technical evolution.

Players and teams should, must, know the different 2 versus 1chips of the soccer kaleidoscope or the eventual artistry of creativity and combination play can not occur. Think of the patterns as letters of the alphabet. Without knowledge of letters one can not form words, without words sentences, without sentences beautifully put thoughts can not be formed. Eventually, if we are lucky, we get great writers who have the knowledge of letters which brought them to writing literary masterpieces.

Teachers and coaches must keep this evolution clearly in mind when developing players and team play. This is true from the youth level to the professional level of play. Just knowing the letters or chips is not enough. Players and teams must be free to use the letters or spin the chips in the kaleidoscope if they are to evolve into masters of the game that can take the breath away. While it is clear that there is and must be structure in soccer it must be tempered with artistic creativity. If as coaches we restrict our players to just learning the letters and structure the environment to harshly all that can be accomplished is a dyslectic jumble of letters that are misunderstood, robotically performed or are simply chosen at unintelligible moments. Great art is not only the complete comprehension of the component elements but the ability to create something beyond them.

Evolution to Combination Play

This is a short note to discuss the issue of combination play. This book is about 2 versus 1. But with a little thought the concept of combining with a third player to deceive or exploit the defense can be readily extrapolated and understood. Many coaches consider 2 versus 1 combination play. At a rudimentary level this would be true because two people combine to be more effective through working together. This would seem to categorize 2 versus 1 as combination play. However, for my money, the concept of combination play starts when three or more people see a pattern emerging on the field and work in concert to take advantage of this situation.

Frequently, the need for combination play is the result of defenders doing an excellent job of denying passing lanes and marking the attackers in the 2 versus 1 pattern. The attackers trying to execute a 2 versus 1pattern can still often accomplish their objective and the pattern by passing the ball to a third teammate that because of their support position is able to send the ball to the penetrating attacker from the original 2 versus 1 pattern.

Third player combinations can be taught to players and practiced in exercises. I can still remember when just starting a community college program watching an opposing team, coached by Teddy Mitalis up in the Seattle, Washington area, using combination play patterns to warm-up the team with before the game. The team I coached had inexperienced non-club players and from watching the warm-up and the level of sophistication of the players it was clear that we were in for a long evening. We were.

Combination play takes the obvious 2 versus 1 pattern away from the direct and obvious use of that pattern to a third player who now sends the ball into the runner from the original 2 versus 1 tactic. Using a third or even fourth person can make 2 versus 1 into a ballet of motion and effective inter-passing. (A simple example is given in Diagram 16, page 57.) More examples are not given for the simple reason that the possibilities are endless. What players and coaches need to do is, with a little thought and experience, see that this concept can be expanded almost endlessly making a team more cohesive, creative and deceptive in attack. Please bear in mind that the same approach of having a pattern and its' exact opposite can create chaos in a defense. This is also true when three or more players start playing on the same page. The permutations of dribbling and passing with just three players in any direction, in any pattern, using just combining three passes or dribbles made can reach into the billions. When three or more players start combining on the same page then the game gets exciting. Add exceptional technique and soccer becomes a recipe for endless diversity, entertainment, beauty and joy.

Diagram 16: Combination Play

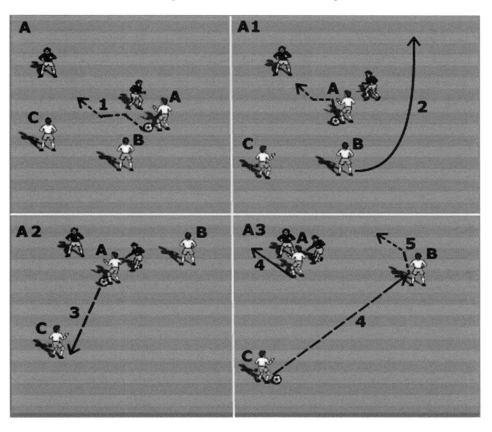

Diagram 16, page 57, is an example of combination play that is created out of the Curved Run 2 versus 1 pattern. Curved Run pattern created by attackers A and B in Square A has been prevented from succeeding by the positioning of the marking defender who is defending the attacker with the ball and the defender who is providing cover for the marking defender. Attacker A starts the Curved Run Pattern by dribbling into the center of the field with a dribble numbered 1.

In Square A1 the defender is cutting the passing lane to attacker B who is making the Curved Run. The run by attacker B is numbered 2. The marking defender is steering the attacker A into the second covering defender which will allow the defense to double the ball.

In Square A2 attacker A solves the problem by dropping the ball back to attacker C. Attacker C has a passing lane open to attacker B who is making the Curved Run. The pass by attacker A to attacker C is numbered with a 3.

In Square A3 the combination of the three attackers working together to successfully complete a 2 versus 1 pattern is shown. Attacker C passes the ball to attacker B who has continued their curved run despite the fact that a direct pass from attacker A has been shut down. The pass numbered 4 by attacker C finishes the original 2 versus 1 pattern by using a third attacker. The play continues with a dribble by attacker B numbered 5.

This is what combination play is all about. Bear in mind that the threat of using a third attacker and not involving them with direct possession of the ball is a subtle form of combination play. Just the threat of what the third attacker can do can force defenses and defenders to adjust their positioning and decision making. To create this play attacking teammates must work hard to support each other and provide options to the ball carrier or none of this is possible.

Visual Cues:

There are several visual cues that attackers can use to decide what to do. Truthfully, the list is endless and can be quite subtle. Among the visual cues are a defenders' closing angles, speed of approach, positioning of supporting defenders, attackers' position and control of the ball relative to the defender, body language of teammates, the attack's gain if the defender if beaten with a dribble, area of the field, physical attributes of the defender, physical attributes of attackers, hearing verbal communications between defenders, receiving verbal information from teammates, position of the ball upon reception, depth in the defense, are just some of the cues that a sophisticated attacker can use.

On the other side the supporting attacker must use visual and verbal cues like angle of support, speed of movement, positioning of teammates, risk involved, body language, amount of pressure on the ball positioning of the defender(s) and other information supplied by their fellow attackers to assess choices or relative chances of success. The use of 2 versus 1 is predicated on all this and more. An attacker's technical command alone will severely cripple or increase the possibilities available. The higher the technical skills the more choices for the attack and the harder it gets for the defense to stop an attack. These nuances should be taught to players as they get more sophisticated. Teaching is from the Simple to the Complex so make sure that the players understand the basic movement or pattern and then in the flow of small sided teaching games show and explain the nuance that would lead to a better decision.

The issue of technical command increasing or decreasing a player's and team's choices is why highly experienced coaches chant the paraphrased mantra, "technique, technique, technique" and what players must learn and develop from an early age. What appears to hamper many coaches of younger players from creating an environment that truly supports this mantra is that when learning anything mistakes will happen. In competitive sports like soccer mistakes means losses. The irony of learning to be great is that one must slip, fall and fail to reach the heights of commanding the view from the mountain top. Most coaches in America will not let failure occur and create safe highly organized environments to produce wins, which parents correlate with competency which in turn means the Directors of Club Soccer continue to get paid. Win and get paid is crushing our ability to create highly technical, creative players. There are other reasons why America continues to struggle to create world class players but this is one of the culprits.

There are highly useful and flexible shapes and patterns to the game. The system of play is selected to high light the strengths of the players and minimize their weaknesses'. The ultimate goal of a coach is to give the players the tools to think, react and perform both independently and within the group dynamic to succeed in the dual goals of both playing well and getting results.

Chapter 3

Exercises to Teach 2 versus 1

Exercises to Train 2 versus 1

Exercise 1: 1 versus 1 with Side Support
(Grid 10-12 x 12-15 yards) (See Diagrams 17, 17 A, 17 B, 17 C, 17 D, pages 63, 64, 65 and 66.)

Keys to Exercise One

1) A player scores by stepping on top of the ball to stop it on the end line of the grid.
2) The player and team retain possession of the ball and can now attack the other end.
3) The coach can also give points for successful 2 versus 1patterns that are either executed or the threatened execution causes the defender to misread the tactical situation and the attacker succeeds because of the ruse.

4) There are two neutral players, one on each side of the grid, that support who ever has the ball.

5) The "game" lasts from 30-120 seconds depending on the fitness level of the players. This is an anaerobic exercise and as such can not be stretched much in time length without forcing the players to slow play or slow the work rate down so that they can use an aerobic energy supply.

6) The neutral players switch in and swap roles with the players who were just active. (This is a work to rest ratio of 1 to 1 which in anaerobic work and is just about as high as it can get)

7) The two players in the middle keep competing until time has expired.

8) When the defending player takes the ball away they become the offensive player and attack from end to end. Which ever player has the ball is attacking and the other player in the middle of the grid is defending.

9) When possession first changes the player that is newly in possession can attack either end first. After reaching one end line successfully they must then attack the other end to score again.

10) When one of the players reaches one end of the grid they "turn" and attack the other end of the grid. The defender does not need to give room for this "turn" to occur. (Younger players may need a "free turn" to play.) Besides dribbling moves or body feints that throw off the defender and create space to turn the 2 versus 1pattern Flick and Spin is a solution to eluding a tight marking by a defender. An attacker who has their body turned to the field of play will have a lack of easy vision into the space that they want to attack next.

11) Neutral players need to sharpen their angle of support along the sideline to be available for the wall pass. They do not just stand in one spot on the side waiting idly. They are active supporters of the players in the middle of the grid.

12) Neutral players should be playing the ball back in one touch and no more than two touches. If the return pass from the side support player is intercepted then it is a lesson about the timing of the 2 versus 1. A second touch by the side support player can be allowed so that a player in the middle of the grid who immediately recognizes that they have not timed the run correctly can readjust their run to correct the error and maintain possession. Do not let the side players hold the ball for long periods of time which disrupts the purpose and flow of the exercise.

13) The attacking player in the middle should be sure to knock the first pass into the "top" foot of the neutral player. Remind them of where the support players' top foot would be in a game. It is the foot that is furthest away from the direction of the grid the players are attacking. In the real game there would be a defender close to the support player between the supporting attacker and the goal. The ball should be served to the foot away from where that defender would be in a game.

14) Have three or four extra balls by the grid so the game does not have to stop every time it is knocked far away from the grid. This helps any fitness element of the exercise that the coach might be expecting to occur for the players and team. It also keeps a better flow and rhythm to the exercise.

15) If a defender does nothing but back up to defend the coach can not allow this decision. (Delaying is a good idea in a game when a player is facing 2 versus 1. Almost all situations where a defender is outnumbered delay is the right decision unless passing lanes can be closed and a player is isolated, or the ball is passed into a dangerous position that requires the defenders immediate response.) But no wall passing can occur with the defender using delaying tactics. The defender must try and attack the ball in the exercise. (When the coach is teaching defense do not let a defender rush forward at an attacker when they are outnumbered 2 to 1. A defender needs to delay for help or angle their approach so that they cut out passing lanes to the second attacker and isolate just one of the attackers.)

16) It is alright for the attacker to dribble by the defender. This is because a defender can take away the dribble or they can take away the pass but they can not take away both options. If the passing lane for the wall pass is taken away by the defenders' positioning what the coach wants the attacker to learn is to dribble in that situation in the game. This is a fundamental concept for attacking players and the exercise must reflect this idea.

17) Attackers should commit the defender as quickly as possible. This is usually done by the attacker dribbling at the defender. The timing of the pass is critical to the success of the movement. There are two possible errors.
   a) If the pass is sent to soon then the attacker will not be able to run explosively past the defender into the space behind them to receive the pass. The defender will have time to recover and intercept the return pass.
   b) If the pass is sent to late the defender will be in position to intercept the pass as it leaves the attackers' foot.
18) Encourage the use of the outside of the foot to make the wall pass as late as possible. This helps disguise the pass as long as possible and keeps the attacker in running stride to make an explosive run past the defender. The coach can also encourage a toe poke to keep the pass disguised. (The toe is not a forbidden surface. It is just another piece of the technical puzzle.) Other technical surfaces are always acceptable.
19) A good "first touch" is necessary to prepare the ball for the next move the attack wants to make. Do not let the players take a touch first and then think about the situation. Mental speed is an attribute that needs constant use. The use of a good first touch shows concretely that an abstract thought about what should happen next is going on in a players' mind.
20) A coach should select a grid size that allows enough success to encourage the players to work hard but enough failure to force improvement.

While there are twenty guidelines for the exercise and this would appear to make it complex it is in fact a fairly simple exercise once the coach and the players learn the structure. Additionally, many of the keys are teaching points and not just rules that structure the exercise itself. Lastly, many of the guidelines in this exercise are ones that are used for every exercise that a coach selects for instructing the players and are repetitive in nature.

Methodology Note:

The following diagrams are in place to allow a visual support for the lengthy list of explanations for the exercise. Remember that people learn in three modalities. The first is to hear, usually in lecture form. Strangely this is often our most common way of conveying information to others but it is often the least effective. The second method is to instruct players with information by seeing usually associated with a demonstration. For a slightly larger portion of the teams' players this method is more effective. The third "instructional" method is doing. Instructional is in quotations because the learning that is going on is a self application supported by information from the coach and fellow players. Most people in the world learn best by doing. Make the lecture short and sweet. Let the players see what is required once maybe twice. Then let the players do, and do and do. Information from the coach that is sent through hearing or seeing now can be used briefly through-out the exercise to reinforce positives, help players improve or correct what they are doing.
In addition the "Socratic Method" of instruction has been shown to help players retain information at a much higher level. The Socratic Method is to ask players questions and illicit answers or solutions from them rather than lecture of explain the answer. One study showed a 60% increase in retention of information if the student had to work out the answer for themselves after being questioned rather than being given the answer by the instructor.

Diagram 17: 1 versus 1 with Side Support: Wall Pass Example

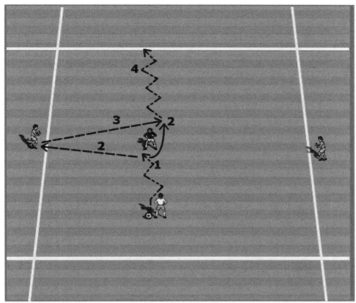

In Diagram 17, page 63, a standard Wall Pass Pattern is used. The attacker, the white player, is executing a regular wall pass with the side support player on the left side of the grid. The white attacker commits the defender with a dribble, numbered 1, and then knocks off the pass to a supporting side player. The pass to the side support player is numbered with a 2 and the return pass by the support player is numbered with a 3. The white attacker in the middle of the grid has made a run to penetrate the space behind the defender. That run is numbered with a 2 and intersects with the return pass numbered 3. The attacker then dribbles to the end line which scores a point for them. The dribble is numbered with a 4. The attacker then turns and attacks the other end of the grid. If the defender wins the ball they then attack to the end line of the grid. The player that wins is the one who has reached the end line most often in the allotted time period.

Diagram 17 A: 1 versus 1 with Side Support: Flick and Spin Example

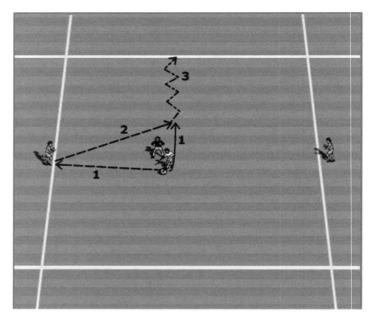

In Diagram 17 A, page 64. a Flick and Spin Pattern is used. The attacker, in white, in the center of the grid is marked closely by the defender. A Flick and Spin Pass option is used with the side support player to penetrate behind the defender and reach the grids' end line. The pass is sent wide to a support player and is numbered with a 1. The white attacker spins away from the defender, splitting the defenders' vision of the ball and them self. This run by the white attacker is numbered with a 1. The penetrating attacker then receives the ball back from the side support player with a pass numbered 2 and the white attacker dribbles to the end line. The dribble to the end line is numbered with a 3. The attacker would now need to turn and attack the other end of the grid. Remember that the side support players should be moving up and down the sides of the grid to make them self available for passes by the attacker in the middle of the grid.

Diagram 17 B: 1 versus 1 with Side Support: High Wall Pass Example

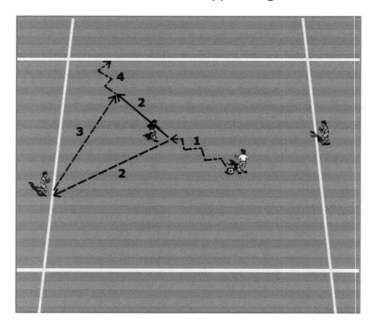

In Diagram 17 B, page 64, the High Wall Pass Pattern is used. The dribble by the central attacker, in white, commits the defender. The dribble is numbered with a 1. Because the supporting attacker has not sharpened their angle of support to be even with the defender the attacker must use a High Wall Pass to penetrate. The attacker must send a pass back up field from the direction they are attacking to the support player. The pass is numbered 2. The run by the white attacker to penetrate space behind the defender is also numbered with a 2. The supporting attacker sends a pass, numbered 3, back to the central attacker and the attacker reaches the line with a dribble numbered 4. The pattern requires a diagonal penetrating run behind the defender to a pass that is essentially straight down field. The white player would then turn and attack the other end line.

Diagram 17 C: 1 versus 1 with Side Support: Low Wall Pass Example

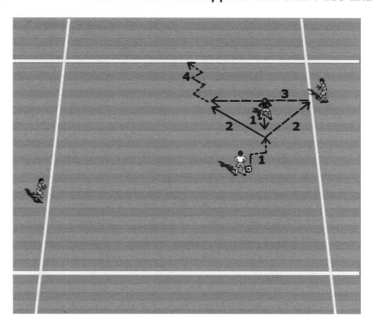

In Diagram 17 C, page 65, the example shows the Low Wall Pass Pattern. The attacker in white starts by committing the defender with a dribble numbered with a 1. The pass to the supporting attacker must be sent a little earlier than in other wall passing patterns because of the supporting players' down field position. In this case the forward momentum of the defender helps the attacker execute the Low Wall Pass. The forward momentum of the defender is shown as a run numbered with a 1. In Diagram 17 C, page 65, the explosive run by the white attacker is numbered 2. This allows the attacker to get in behind the defender for the return pass, numbered 3. The white attacker then finishes the move to the end of the grid with a dribble numbered 4.

Remember to create the Low Wall Pass Pattern the attacker must take advantage of one of two possible situations created by the defenders' actions. The first is that the defender is standing statically which will allow the attacker an advantage in momentum and explosion. The other advantage that can occur is shown in Diagram 17 C, page 65, by having a defender that is moving forward and therefore is exploited by their forward momentum. Timing the pass to the support player is the critical element to this pattern.

Don't forget the side support players should be "sharpening" their angle of support to improve the chances of success for any pattern. In this case the pressure is moving forward faster than the support player can react to it and get in the conventional Wall Pass support position. This problem is one of the two reasons for Low Wall Passes to exist. It is important to remember that one of the reasons that the Low Wall Pass will work is the forward momentum of the defender that makes the run into the space behind them much more likely to occur. It is also important to show the players how this return pass is square and can avoid defenders that are in good position of depth. In this exercise there are not defenders in depth so the coach would have to stop and show how this pattern would be used to avoid or eliminate covering defenders.

All through this exercise there will be lots of opportunities to refine the decision making of the attacking players. The refinements will be for both the player in the middle of the grid and the support players that are on the side.

Diagram 17 D: 1 versus 1 with Side Support: False Wall Pass Example

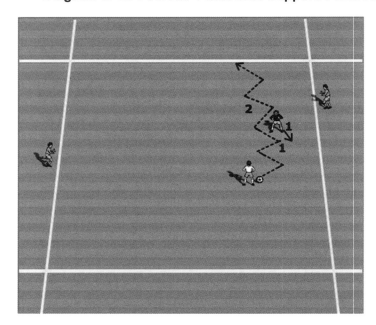

Diagram 17 D, page 66, is diagramed to remind the reader that the option to dribble past a defender is always acceptable. The defenders' position in reaction to the white attackers' initial dribble is to jump into the passing lane for the supporting attacker. The run by the defender to cut the passing lane is numbered with a 1. The initial stage of the white attacker's dribble is numbered with a 1. The decision for the attacker to continue dribbling past the defender and not pass the ball predicated on the positioning of the defender is numbered with a 2. A False Wall Pass Pattern is in response to the concept that a defender can stop the dribble or the pass but not both. If the dribble is blocked use the pass and combine to penetrate behind the defense. If the pass is blocked then the attacker should dribble, thus the name False Wall Pass.

Exercise 2: 1 versus 1 Inside a Square with Supporters on All Sides of the Square
(Grid 10-15 x 10-15 yards)
(See Diagrams 18 A, 18 B, 18 C, 18 D, pages 68, 69 and 70.)

1) A point is awarded for each completed wall pass.
2) A faked wall pass that sells a defender into jumping a passing lane and allows the attacker to retain possession is also awarded a point.
3) The game lasts 30-120 seconds, depending on age and fitness level. Remember that longer work periods will force the players to change energy sources from anaerobic to aerobic.
4) A pair of the neutral players switches in to take their turn. (There are two sets of neutral players to rotate in so the work to rest ratio is 2 to 1. This is a demanding work rate but not brutal.)
5) The attacker with the ball in the middle of the square is trying to learn to see wall passes and the support for it in all directions. Dribbling to commit the defender for a wall pass, shielding for flick and spin walls, dribbling when the defender tries to jump the pass are

some of the many of possibilities.

6) The neutral players should return the pass in one touch. Allow two touches if there is no good return pass and the runner has to rework their run to receive the pass back. Neutral players who hold the ball too long cause the loss of possession for the attacking player.

7) Neutral players should be trying to sharpen along the sideline to create good support angles with their "sharpening." This makes the support players available to the players inside the grid and avoids mental shut down for the players on the side.

8) If the defender wins the ball they then attack. Scoring and possession goes back and forth based solely on who has the ball.

9) Have four to six balls near the grid to keep the exercise flowing.

10) It is alright for the attacker to dribble by the defender. This is because a defender can take away the dribble or they can take away the pass but they can not take away both options. If the passing lane for the wall pass is taken away by the defenders' positioning what is required of the attacker to learn is to dribble in that situation in the game. The exercise must reflect this concept. In fact most exercises past the fundamental stage of instruction should reflect these passing and/or dribbling options.

11) Encourage the use of the outside of the foot to make the wall pass as late as possible. This technical selection helps disguise the pass as long as possible and keeps the attacker in running stride to make an explosive run past the defender. The coach can also encourage a toe poke to keep the pass disguised. All technical options that will allow success are acceptable.

12) A good "first touch" is necessary to prepare the ball for the next move the attack wants to make.

13) If a defender does nothing but back up to defend the coach can not allow this decision. (Delaying is a good idea in a game when you are facing 2 versus 1) But no wall passing can occur with the defender using delaying tactics. The defender must try and attack the ball in the exercise. When teaching defense do not let a defender rush forward at an attacker when they are outnumbered 2 to 1. A defender needs to delay for help or angle their approach so that they cut out passing lanes to the second attacker.)

14) Players playing in the middle compete until the time has expired.

15) Attackers should commit the defender as quickly as possible. This is usually done by the attacker dribbling at the defender. The timing of the pass is critical to the success of the movement. There are two possible errors.
   a. If the pass is sent to soon then the attacker will not be able to run explosively past the defender into the space behind them to receive the pass. The defender will have time to recover and intercept the return pass.
   b. If the pass is sent to late the defender will be in position to intercept the pass as it leaves the attackers' foot.

16) In this exercise support players on the edge of the grid can have two touches if needed to help the attacker rearrange their run because the initial pattern failed to form correctly. Attackers often fail to time the initial pass properly so this is not an uncommon occurrence. The coach should make sure that the tempo of the exercise still stays as high as possible. The support players will tend to take for ever when trying to decide where to send the ball with their second touch. Make it a turn over in possession if the supporter does not play quickly.

17) A coach should select a grid size that allows enough success to encourage the players to work hard but enough failure to force improvement. Having a success rate of 70 to 80 percent is appropriate. Succeeding at a lower rate tends to frustrate players, which diminishes personal confidence, belief in the topic being taught and a lower work rate. Succeeding at a higher rate tends to breed over confidence and also lowers work rate out of boredom. In any exercise there should be enough challenge that leads to some failure but enough success to keep the attention and motivation of the students high.

Diagram 18 A: 1 versus 1 with Side Support on all Sides: Flick and Spin Example

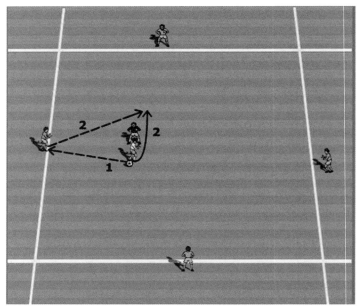

Most of the 2 versus 1 patterns can be used in this exercise. Diagram 18 A, page 68, shows the use of the Flick and Spin Wall Pass from a static position. A Flick and Spin pattern when the attacker is marked tightly is done quite easily with a teammate that is square to them. A static Flick and Spin can also be done with the support player up field from the attacker who is in possession of the ball. It is possible but not as likely to occur with a teammate that is down field from the attacker with the ball.

The diagram shows the attacker in white and in possession of the ball facing away from the supporting player on the left side of the grid. The white attacker sends a pass behind them with a pass numbered 1. The attacker then spins around the defender with a run numbered 2 and at the same time the supporting attacker returns a pass to the white attacker with a pass numbered 2.

Since this is a non-directional exercise it allows the attackers to see support from all angles; forward, backwards and from the side. For players to reach their maximum in creativity it is important that they learn to look all around themselves so that they can find multiple solutions to the problems that they face and use teammates from all angles and from all areas of the field.

It is important to remember that this is a timed exercise and that who the attacker in the middle is at any given time is determined by possession of the ball. Score can be kept by the number of successful movements created by each player in the center of the grid during the timed period. Don't forget to reward attackers for using False Patterns to keep the ball and penetrate past the opponent.

Diagram 18 B: 1 versus 1 with Side Support on all Sides: Wall Pass Example

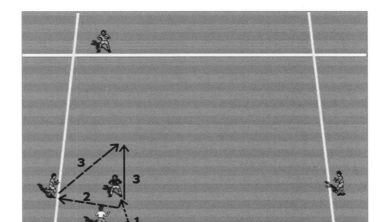

In Diagram 18 B, page 69, the white attacker commits the defender with a dribbling move numbered 1 and passes the ball as closely as possible to the defender without the defender being able to cut the pass out. This pass is numbered 2 in this diagram. The return pass should be in one touch behind the defender into the space that the attacker is making their run. The run by the white attacker is numbered with a 3 and the return pass by the support player is numbered with a 3 also.

Diagram 18 C: 1 versus 1 with Side Support on all Sides: False Wall Pass Example

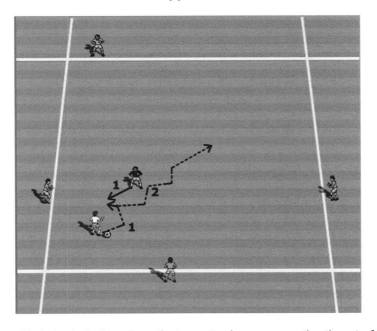

Diagram 18 C, page 69, is included to show that an attacker can use the threat of a wall pass to create a dribbling situation as a solution if the defender has taken away the passing lane. The white attacker starts to dribble at the defender. The start of the dribble is numbered with a 1. Then the

white attacker feints a pass to the support player which causes the defender to step into the passing lane. This run into the passing lane by the defender is numbered with a 1. The dribble past the defender by the white attacker is numbered with a 2.

Diagram 18 D: 1 versus 1 with Side Support on all Sides: High Wall Pass Example

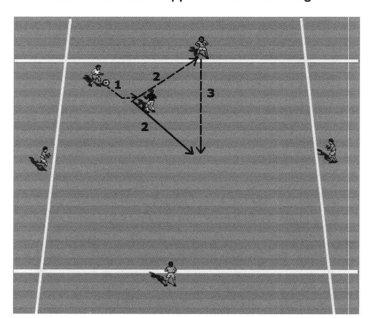

Diagram 18 D, page 70, the last diagram in this series shows the white attacker making a diagonal dribble, numbered with a 1, across the grid at the defender, and then uses a supporting player who is "up" field from them to create a High Wall Pass pattern. The pass to the supporting player is numbered with a 2. The run in behind the defender is diagonal and is marked with a 2. The return pass is almost straight down field and this pass is numbered with a 3.

Exercise 3: 2 versus 2: Inside a Square with Supporters on All Sides
(Grid 12-18 x 12-18 yards)
(See Diagrams 19, 19 A, 19 B, 19 C, 19 D, 19 E, 19 F, pages 72, 73, 74, 75, 76, 77 and 78.)

Keys to Exercise Three

1) A point is awarded for each completed 2 versus 1 pattern. This includes all patterns and the threatened use of them so that a dribbling solution is successful because of the deception.
2) Players playing in the middle compete until the time has expired. Games are won by the total of points awarded for 2 versus 1patterns.
3) The game lasts 2-5 minutes, depending on age and fitness level.
4) There are two teams of two players each working together in the center of the grid. The team in possession of the ball has the attacking role and the players without possession have the defending role. Which team attacks or defends is predicated by possession of the ball. The roles will swap back and forth through-out the time period allotted for the exercise.
5) The neutral players switch roles into the center of the grid to take their turn when time has expired for the group that was just working. (This is a work to rest ratio of 1 to 2)
6) The two attackers with the ball in the middle of the square are trying to learn to see any 2 versus 1 pattern that the support gives to them. This support is in all directions, forward, backward and sideways at any time that pressure has become high enough to react to it.
7) Passing from support player to support player should not be allowed.

8) To create 2 versus 1patterns attackers should commit the defender as quickly as possible. This is usually done by the attacker dribbling at the defender. The timing of the pass is critical to the success of the movement. There are two possible errors.
   a. If the pass is sent to soon then the attacker will not be able to run explosively past the defender into the space behind them to receive the pass. The defender will have time to recover and intercept the return pass.
   b. If the pass is sent to late the defender will be in position to intercept the pass as it leaves the attackers' foot.
9) The neutral players should return the pass in one touch. Allow two touches if there isn't a good return pass and the runners have to rework their runs to receive the ball back. Do not let the supporting players on the side dawdle with the pass.
10) The neutral players can return the ball to the attacker who gave it to them or to the attackers' teammate in the middle. This rule may cause the beginning of combination play to occur within the exercise.
11) The pair of attackers in the middle should try to use each other for creating 2 versus 1patterns. More 2 versus 1patterns are possible than when there were when there was just one attacker in the middle of the grid. This is because there are two attackers who can move in any direction to support each other. Patterns such as the Take Over, False Take Over, Curved Runs, False Curved Runs, X Patterns, False Wall Passes are all options that can occur because of the two players in the middle of the grid. These options were not available in the 1 versus 1 with Side Support Exercise because the availability of the second attacker in the middle of the grid kept these patterns from occurring.
12) Dribbling past defenders who try and jump the passing lanes should still be encouraged as a solution for the attackers.
13) Technical solutions that are creative should be encouraged if they are solutions needed to be successful.
14) Color differentiation should be accomplished for each group of two with scrimmage vests. The players can wear them which makes it a little easier for everyone to discern who is playing with whom.
15) Have four to six spare balls beside the grid to keep the exercise flowing.
16) The work to rest ratio is 1 to 1.
17) A good "first touch" is necessary to prepare the ball for the next move the attack wants to make. This relates to the mental thoughts that can only be seen when a concrete decision is made with a touch of the ball. Without a good touch showing mental decisions the instructor is left with players who do not start thinking about what the next action should be. Instead the attackers will take several touches that are tentative and lack purpose which in the game will lead to a slower rate of play.
18) Defenders still need to be aggressive in trying to win the ball back. Encourage intelligent use of pressure but defenders must pressure attackers so 2 versus 1patterns can take place. Passive defenders can not be allowed or the exercise will not be effective.
19) A coach should select a grid size that allows enough success to encourage the players to work hard but enough failure to force improvement.

Diagram 19: 2 versus 2 with Side Support on All Sides: Low Wall Pass

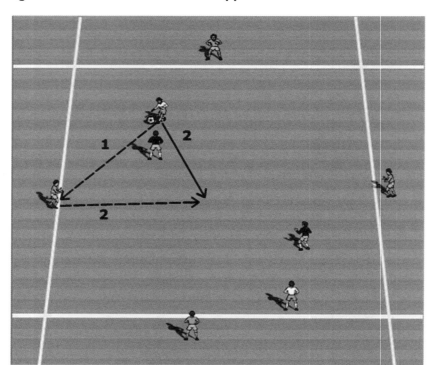

In Diagram 19, page 72, the exercise is essentially the same as the one before it. The difference is that there are two players for each team in the middle of the square. This allows for a little more freedom and some patterns to occur, like a Curved Run that could not happen before the second attacker was added.

In Diagram 19, page 72, the white attacker who is in possession of the ball combines with the supporting attacker on the left side of the grid. The pattern is a Low Wall Pass which keeps the return pass square and out of the reach of the second defender. The first pass by the white attacker is numbered 1. The run to penetrate behind the defender is numbered with a 2 and the return pass by the supporting player is also numbered with a 2 because the run and pass are really done almost at the same time.

Diagram 19 A: 2 versus 2 with Side Support on all Sides High Wall and Wall Pass Example

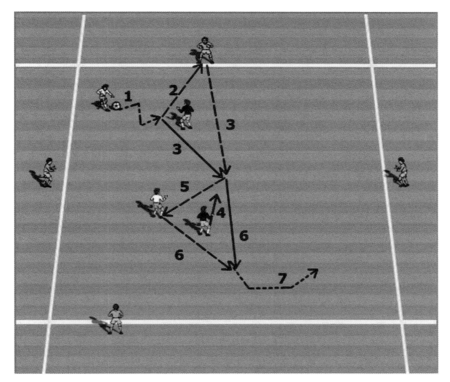

In Diagram 19 A, page 73, both of the white attackers in the grid and the supporting player at the top of the grid are involved in creating two patterns. The first pattern is started by the white defender with the ball near the top of the diagram. This attacker commits the defender with a dribble numbered 1. The white attacker then sends a pass back up field from the direction of the penetration with a pass numbered 2 and makes a diagonal run to penetrate behind the defense that is numbered with a 3. The return pass by the supporting attacker is also numbered with a 3.

A second pattern then occurs between the white attackers in the middle of the grid. The first white attacker who has just received the ball back now avoids the defender coming to pressure them. The black defender steps forward with a run numbered 4. The white attacker avoids the pressure with a pass numbered 5 to the second white attacker in the middle of the grid. The white attacker who just passed the ball continues with a run numbered 6 and receives a pass back from their teammate that is also numbered 6. The sequence that was started at the top of the grid by the white attacker is finished by the same white attacker at the bottom of the grid with a dribble numbered 7.

Diagram 19 B: 2 versus 2 with Side Support on all Sides: High Wall Pass Example

Diagram 19 B, page 74, is really just the first part of Diagram 19 A, a High Wall Pass. The white attacker with the ball commits the defender with a dribble numbered 1. They then pass the ball back up field from the direction they are penetrating with a pass numbered 2. The white attacker now makes a run in behind the defender numbered 3 and the supporting player returns a one touch pass numbered 2 that allows possession of the ball behind the defense. In the Diagram 19 A, page 73, the next sequence was diagramed out but as the coach it is important to recognize that there are now a myriad of other choices and patterns that can be used from the first movement. If the reader wants they can diagram other choices to see that the choices are almost limitless.

Diagram 19 C: 2 versus 2 with Side Support on all Sides: Curved Run Example

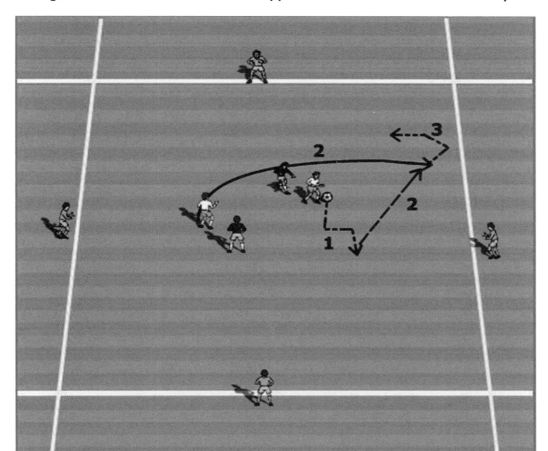

Diagram 19 C, page 75, shows a Curved Run Pattern created by the white attackers in the middle of the grid. The white attacker with the ball starts the pattern by dribbling, numbered 1, to draw their defender out of the space that the second white attacker will want to use. The second white attacker then makes a Curved Run around their teammate and the defender which is numbered with a 2. As the white attacker with the ball sees the run develop they pass the ball into the space in front of their teammate. That pass is numbered with a 2. The move is finished with the white attacker who did not start with the ball ending up with the ball and dribbling to create some space for the next sequence. The dribble is numbered with a 3.

Diagram 19 D: 2 versus 2 with Side Support on all Sides: X Pattern Example

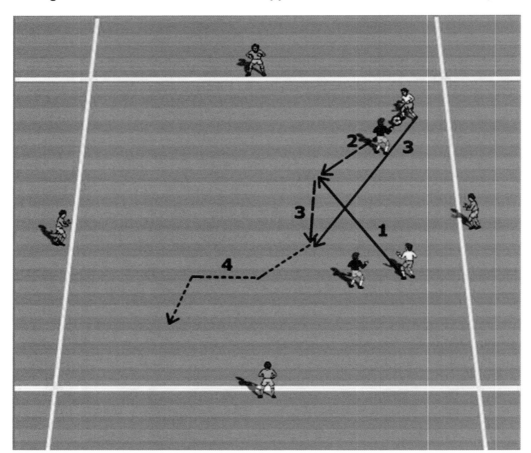

In Diagram 19 D, page 76, the pattern to see is the X Pattern. The white attacker without the ball makes a diagonal run in behind the defender pressuring the ball; the run is numbered with a 1. The black defender marking the white attacker making the run also makes a run to mark the attacker which is numbered with a 1.

The white attacker with the ball makes a pass numbered with a 2 to the white attacker without the ball. The white attacker who just made the pass now makes a run, numbered 3. The attacker receives the ball back from their teammate with a pass also numbered with a 3. Upon receiving the ball the white attacker starts dribbling which X's over the run just made by their teammate. The dribble is numbered with a 4. To create some time and space the white attacker now in possession of the ball dribbles away from pressure.

Diagram 19 E: 2 versus 2 with Side Support on all Sides: Using Second Player Combination Example

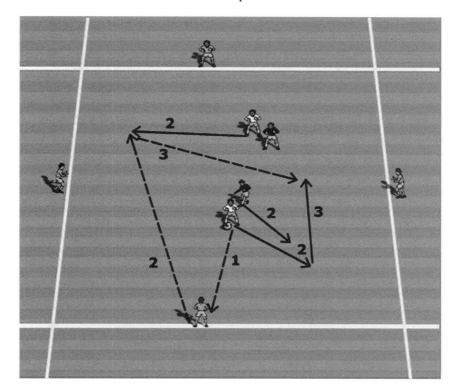

Diagram 19 E, page 77, shows that because of two attackers inside the grid combination play can start to occur. The white attacker with the ball, in the center of the grid, makes a pass numbered 1 to the supporting player at the bottom of the grid and then makes a run designed to either pull the defense out of the way or to have the defender not track them and receive the ball back. The run is numbered with a 2. The defender tracks the white attacker with a run also numbered 2 which forces the supporting player to pass the ball to the other white attacker who has moved into a wide space opposite of their teammate's run. The pass by the supporting attacker at the bottom of the grid is numbered with a 2 and the run to receive it by the other white attacker in the center of the grid is also numbered 2. The white attacker who started the whole sequence makes a run numbered with a 3 in behind the defender tracking them and receives a pass from their white attacking teammate that allows all three players to have combined create possession of the ball that was not available without the three players cooperating on the same wave length. The pass is numbered with a 3.

Diagram 19 F: 2 versus 2 with Side Support on all Sides: Flick and Spin Example

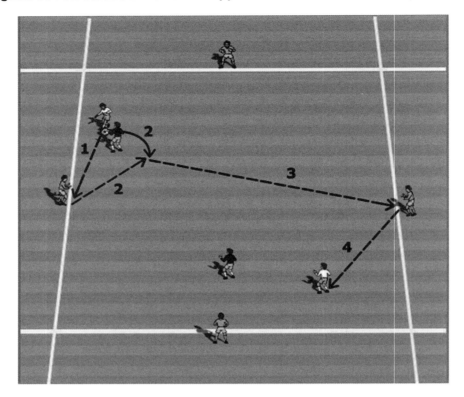

Diagram 19 F, page 78, is a Flick and Spin pattern that relieves pressure on the ball and allows the ball to change sides of the grid. The white attacker in the middle of the grid on the left hand side with the ball makes a pass numbered 1 to the supporting player on the left side of the grid. The white attacker then spins away from the pass and makes a run, numbered 2 to penetrate the space behind the defender and receives a return pass numbered 2. The white attacker then plays the ball all the way across the grid to the supporting player on the right side of the grid. The pass is numbered with a 3. The supporting player then plays a one touch pass back into the grid to the other central white attacker nearest them. That pass is numbered with a 4.

One of the most important concepts in this sequence is that if the white attacker passing the ball across the grid had hit the pass directly to their white teammate in the middle of the grid the other defender might have intercepted it. By playing the ball with the pass numbered 3 the white attacker was able to get the ball where they wanted it to go without the risk of interception. They did this by passing the ball to the supporting attacker on the edge of the grid which allowed them to make a safe pass from the support player to the other white attacker without the threat of interception. This concept of selecting one pass to actually get to another opportunity is a subtle one that is often missed by players and sometimes coaches. Direct solutions are not always the successful ones. It may take two passes or three passes to move the ball to where the team wants and thereby set up the opportunities they are looking for in the game.

Exercise 4: 2 versus 2 with Side Support for Each Team
(Grid 12-15 x 16-25 yards)
(See Diagrams 20 A, 20 B, 20 C and 20 D pages 81, 82, 83 and 84) (This exercise will easily expand into exercise 5.)

Keys to Exercise Four

1) The "game" lasts 5 to 15 minutes depending on the fitness level of the players and the

age group. The two players in the middle keep playing until time has expired. (The game can be longer if side players are allowed to enter the game. See variations)

2) Score is kept by the number of times a team reaches the end line and successfully steps on the ball when it is on the end line.

3) The coach can also award points for successful 2 versus 1patterns if extra incentive to execute the patterns is needed. Or if the coach wants a particular pattern they can award points for just that particular pattern.

4) Score can be kept through-out the game or as a set of mini-games. Mini-games require a predetermined number of points to be reached to produce a winner of the game. (To achieve fitness the game should continue to flow until the time period has elapsed.) If fitness is not a consideration the coach can stop the exercise when the score for winning a mini game has been reached.

5) Possession is continuous. A team turns and attacks the other end without interruption when ever a point is scored. The defense must gain possession of the ball back to become the attackers. Scoring a point does not turn the ball over to the other team.

6) Possession of the ball determines who is attacking and who is defending.

7) Defenders do not need to give room for the attacking players when they "turn" to attack the other end line after scoring on the end line. (Younger players may need a rule that allows them to have a free turn to attack the other end of the grid.)

8) Turn over of the ball occurs when the defending players takes the ball away. Their team now attacks from end to end. They may start by attacking either end to start. Once they have scored on one end line they must attack the other end of the grid.

9) A turn over of possession also occurs when a pass is so poorly hit that it leaves the area of the grid. If the pass is missed by an errant first touch then that is also a turn over. Any loss of the ball outside the grid will cause possession to change.

10) Side players need to "sharpen" their angle of support along the sideline to be available for passes.

11) Side players should be playing the ball back in one touch. The coach can let the support players use two touches at the coaches' discretion. Do not let the support players hold the ball for long periods of time trying to find a pass. The coach can make this a loss of possession if the ball id not played quickly enough.

12) Side players do not play defense against each other. Because the side players can not defend this will create 2 versus 1situations that are easily exploited. The 2 versus 1patterns are both on the inside of the grid and in combination with the support players on the edge of the grid.

13) The attacking players in the middle should be sure to knock the first pass into the "top" foot of the side players. Remind them to keep in mind where the players' top foot, the one away from defender that would exist in the game. Since there is no defense being played by the support players on the side of the grid this point needs to be a mental focus for the players.

14) Have four to six extra balls by the grid so the game does not have to stop every time the ball is accidentally played away from the immediate grid area.

15) If the defenders do nothing but back up to defend the coach must not allow this behavior from the defenders. The defenders need to try and regain possession of the ball. (Delay is appropriate when playing defense in the real game but is counter productive to the intent of this exercise.) Do encourage the defenders to work in conjunction and with intelligent pressure but do not let them be passive for prolonged periods of time.

16) It is alright for the attacker to dribble by a defender. This is because a defender can take away the dribble or they can take away the pass but they can not take away both options. If the option of creating a 2 versus 1 pattern is taken away by the defenders' positioning the attacker should learn to dribble in that situation. This will be what the player should do in the game and the exercise should imitate that point.

17) Encourage the use of the outside of the foot to make the wall pass as late as possible, disguised as possible and keeping the player in stride to make an explosive run past the defender an easier task. The coach can also encourage a toe poke to keep the pass disguised, avoid intense pressure and/or to keep the run in stride. All technical solutions

are appropriate.

18) A coach should select a grid size that allows enough success to encourage the players to work hard but enough failure to force improvement.

19) A good "first touch" is necessary to prepare the ball for the next move the attack wants to make.

20) The coach can add large goals about 20 yards from the ends of the grid so that keepers can train. The attackers should shoot in one touch as quickly as possible after leaving the end of the grid. Keepers would give the ball back to the team that shot at them and a larger number of balls should be kept around the exercise near the goals to avoid long delays in playing.

Variations:

21) Side players enter the grid when they receive a pass from teammates who has been in the center of the grid. (See Diagram 20 B, page 82.)

22) The attacking player who passes the ball must replace the support player from the side of the grid that enters the center of the grid upon receiving the ball.

23) The support player enters the grid and either carries the ball in by dribbling into the grid or passing to the second attacking player in the middle. In either scenario the side supporting player enters the grid and becomes an active attacker in the center of the grid.

24) Occasionally, the supporting player who is just entering the grid sends a pass to the opposite side of the grid to the other support player. This forces the player making that pass to run across the grid and replace the support player that they just passed too on the opposite side of the grid. This would seem obvious because as they entered the grid they became one of the center players who must leave the grid if they pass to the support player. However, the players sometimes get confused over this pattern and need reminding. The concept is the same as the replacement pattern in Diagram 20 B. (See Diagram 20 B, page 82)

Variation: Curved Run on the Edge of the Grid

1) The side player can dribble in and have the passer make a curved run around them. If the player just entering the grid returns the ball to the curved runner then they step back to the line and resume the supporting position. The replacement pattern is the same concept shown in Diagram 20 B. (See Diagram 20 B, page 82.) If the attacker making the curved run does not receive the ball then they must then step into the support position on the side of the grid.

2) All the 2 versus 1 patterns can and do occur in this exercises. As the game flows the coach should not be hesitant to freeze the play and show how a pattern would work. The more experienced the players and comfortable they are with the exercise the less instruction should be necessary.

3) It is hard for the double pass pattern to occur. The coach needs to point out when this pattern is possible. It is only possible if the two central players are at opposite ends of the grid. (See Diagram 20 C, page 83.)

4) A player who has just entered the grid from a supporting position may turn and pass the ball back to the player who just replaced them on the side of the grid if that is the best option. The players would just swap roles again as to who was in the center of the grid and who would be supporting on the side of the grid.

Diagram 20 A: 2 versus 2 with Free Support Players on each Side: Side Players do not enter.

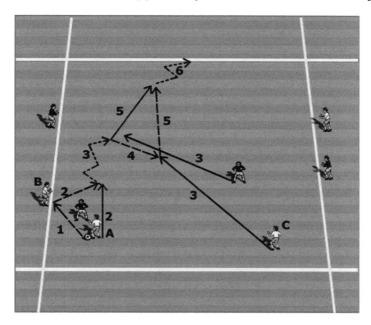

In Diagram 20 A, page 81, the reader can see that the ball is passed by the white attacker A (lower left grid) to support player B. This pass is numbered with a 1. In the initial stage of this exercise the supporting player does not enter the grid. What occurs inside the grid is that attacker A combines with the supporting player B to use a wall pass to penetrate. Attacker A makes a run numbered 2 behind the defender and the pass from the supporting attacker is sent back with a pass numbered 2.

Attacker A then dribbles forward to commit the second defender. This dribble by attacker A is numbered with a 3. Attacker C makes a run to support attacker A and create another Wall Pass. This run by attacker C is numbered with a 3. Player A takes advantage of this support and combines with attacker C using a wall pass to penetrate to the line and score a point. The Wall Pass pattern is shown with attacker A sending a pass to attacker C numbered 4. Then attacker A makes a run behind the defender that is numbered with a 5. Attacker C sends a return pass to attacker A that is numbered with a 5. Attacker A finishes the move with a dribble that is numbered with a 6. The players would now turn to attack the other end of the grid.

Remember that the game can either be a pre-set period of time or a set number of points scored by reaching the end line and stopping the ball on the end line. The exercise can also have points given for performing 2 versus 1 patterns. In this variation where the side players can not enter it is best to use a set period of time to produce fitness but not fatigue.

What is extremely appealing from the coaches' point of view is that in this exercise the 2 versus 1 patterns are all available. Players also usually find the exercise extremely enjoyable. This is because it so closely replicates the game with the exception of shooting to score. Remember to remind the supporting players on the edges of the grid to sharpen into positions that provide support. The support players are not just statues waiting for the pass to be made to them.

The coach can place two large goals and keepers at the end of the grids for a one touch shot for passing the grid line at one end or the other. The problem is that a lack of keepers will most likely limit the number of grids that can use this solution. The advantage is that the coach can keep the keepers practicing shot blocking in a more real situation that requires timing and the reading of the game.

Diagram 20 B: 2 versus 2 with Free Support Players on each Side: Side Support Players May Enter the Grid when Receiving the Ball

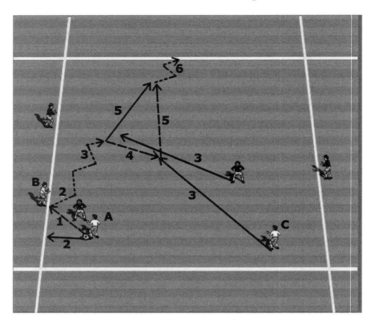

In Diagram 20 B, page 82, shows the variation of the exercise where the support player enters the grid upon receiving the ball. Attacker A passes the ball to the support player on the side, player B. The pass to player B is numbered with a 1. Player A then exits the grid with a run numbered with a 2. Because this is one of the variations of the exercise player B can enter the grid and attacker A now replaces them on the end line. Player B carries the ball into the grid, which is numbered with a 2 and then dribbles forward towards the end line which is numbered with a 3.

As the opposing defender from the far side of the grid comes to prevent B from dribbling to the end line attacker C runs to a good support position for player B. Both the defenders run to pressure and the supporting run by attacker C are numbered with a 3. Attackers B and C then complete a Wall Pass. Attacker B makes a pass numbered 4 and then makes a run in behind the defender that is numbered 5. The return pass by attacker C to attacker B is numbered with a 5 and the whole move is finished to the end line with a dribble that is numbered with a 6. The attacking and defending is continuous from one end of the grid to the other as a team losses or gains possession of the ball. This pattern sends player B to the end line and allows the team to turn and attack the other way.

Diagram 20 C: 2 versus 2 Free Support Players on each Side: Double Pass Set-up

The coach can divide the grid with cones or tell the players to use their judgment regarding the approximation of players being at each end of the grid. Diagram 20 C, page 83, shows the grid divided artificially so the players can see and create the opportunities for performing Double Pass Patterns. This is a great pattern to demand if there are large goals set up with keepers about 20 yards beyond the edge of the grid. The Double Pass Patterns are most frequently used near the edge of the penalty box in games. The pattern is not exclusive to that area but is most useful in penetrating this area.

This dividing of the grid can be done with either the side support players being held on the side lines and not entering the grid. Or in the variation they supporting players can enter the grid. The side support players are not held to any area of support along the side line. They can move up and down as they need to for support of the ball during any time in the exercise.

If the pass from attacker A is sent straight back by attacker B to attacker A then the pattern is a Double Pass Straight Return pass pattern. If the return pass from attacker B to attacker A who is moving forward to receive the return pass is diagonal then the pattern becomes a Double Pass Diagonal Return pass pattern.

If the initial Double Pass Pattern is changed up by the use of side support players but the movement of the central strikers continue to be in the Double Pass Pattern then the play essentially becomes a form of combination play.

Diagram 20 D: 2 versus 2 with Free Support Players on each Side Double Pass Pattern Diagonal

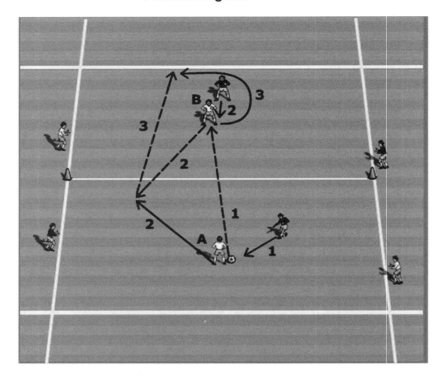

Diagram 20 D, page 84, shows the Double Pass Pattern executed with a return pass that is diagonal. Attacker A in the bottom of the grid sees the pressure coming from the defender nearest them. The run by the defender is numbered 1. The response is a pass numbered 1 by attacker A to attacker B to the top of the grid. Attacker B and A realize that to keep the pressure of the defender marking attacker A as little as possible the run and pass should be played to the left side of the grid. Attacker A's return pass is diagonal and numbered with a 2. Attacker A's run is also numbered with a 2. The run and the pass are essentially simultaneous.

When the pass from attacker A first arrives towards attacker B the defender marking attacker B makes a run to put more pressure on attacker B. This run is numbered with a 2. The pressure by the defender is actually advantageous to executing the pattern because it makes it easier for attacker B to spin away and get in behind the defender. The run that divides the vision of the defender between the ball and attacker B is numbered with a 3. Attacker A then makes a penetrating pass behind the defender to attacker B which is numbered with a 3.

Diagram 20 E: 2 versus 2 with Free Support Players on each Side Double Pass Pattern Straight

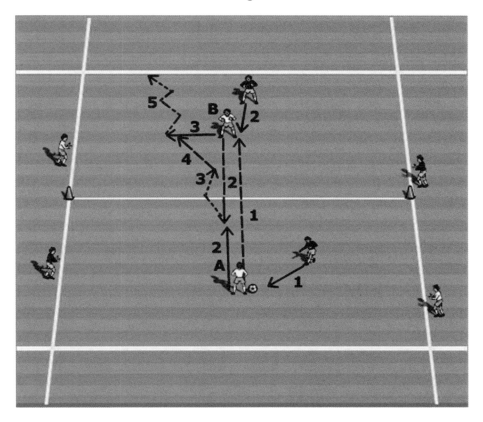

In Diagram 20 E, page 85, attacker A passes the ball forward to player B with a pass numbered 1. Attacker B returns a straight pass back to attacker A which is numbered with a 2. The straight returning pass forces a different run by attacker B so that they can penetrate forward. The first pass from attacker A to attacker B is in reaction to the pressure arriving from the defender at the bottom of the gird whose approaching run is numbered with a 1. After the initial pass attacker A then makes a straight run forward that is numbered with a 2 and receives the return pass from attacker B which is also numbered with a 2. These movements occur almost simultaneously.

Attacker B then slides to a position even with their defender which is numbered with a 3 (this is most important when trying to stay onsides.) Attacker B should keep their chest on the defender so that they can see what the defender is doing. This means that the run is made in a backwards or sideways sliding motion that allows attacker B's eyes to be on the defender marking them. At the same time attacker A who has just received the ball starts with a short dribble to try and commit the defender in the top part of the grid. The dribble is numbered 3. As soon as attacker A can see enough of a gap form between attacker B and the defender closest to them open up attacker A will slip the ball to attacker B with a pass numbered 4. Attacker B finishes off the move with a dribble numbered 5. (A Wall Pass can easily by created by attackers A and B out of this situation instead of the Double Pass Pattern that slides attacker B into the back of the defense.) While the support players appear to be permanently positioned on the side they are not and can move anywhere along the edge of the grid through-out the exercise.

Diagram 20 F: 2 versus 2 with Free Support Players on Each Side Double Pass Pattern Set Up Then Not Used

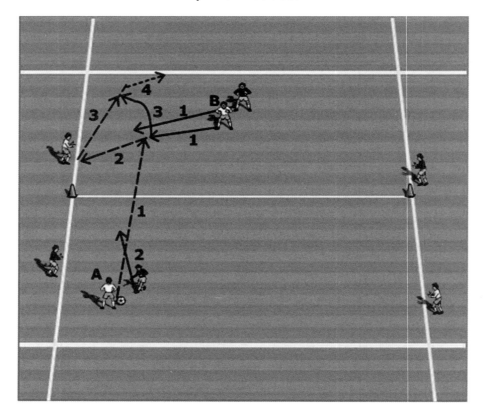

Diagram 20 F, page 86, Double Pass Pattern is disrupted after the initial pass by attacker A to attacker B which is numbered with a 1. The defender makes a return pass impossible with their run numbered with a 2 into the space that attacker A would need to run forward into to receive the return pass. Attacker B who received the pass from attacker A, numbered 1, makes a run to receive the initial pass that is also numbered 1. Attacker B is tracked by the defender's run which is also numbered with a 1. All of these actions are essentially simultaneous.

Attacker B then makes a pass to the supporting player on the left side of the grid, numbered 2 and slips around the defender with a run numbered 3 to receive the pass back from the support player that is numbered 3. Depending on the position and momentum of the defender the pattern used to penetrate to the end line could be a Wall Pass or a Flick and Spin. The move is finished with a dribble to the line numbered 4. This is essentially combination play started by attacker A and finished by attacker B and a support player..

The diagram is placed in the book to show that even the attempt to create Double Pass Pattern will change and the adjustments can still be effective in penetrating the defense. Remember that ball possession can flow back and forth in this exercise for a determined time period or until a point total is reached.

Exercise 5: 3 versus 3 / 4 versus 4 with Each Team Having a Side Support Player
(Grid 18-35 x 25-45 yards)
(See Diagrams 21, 21 A, 21 B, 21 C, 21 D, 21 E, pages 89, 90, 91, 92, 93 and 95.)

The reason for Exercise 5 being separate from what is essentially the same game as exercise four is because the numbers of players not only allows 2 versus 1patterns but also provides the small group shape of left/right/split support to occur. The players are now playing possession soccer (left/right/split support) with 2 versus 1 patterns being used to penetrate the defense from one end line back to the other. The concept of left/right/split support can be reinforced during this exercise. This is not possible before these numbers of players became involved in the exercise. It allows the coach the luxury of reinforcing the basic shape of left/right/split around the ball, then instruct the players on how to exploit the penetration achieved with the 2 versus 1. The coach can help the players understand how to form and reform the shape of left/right/split around the ball. This is a fast, flowing game that is emblematic of soccer in all of its' twisting variations on the same themes. (See the book: **Improving Your Team's Possession Play)**

Keys to Exercise Five

1) The exercises' "game" lasts 5 to 20 minutes depending on the fitness level of the players and the age group.
2) The players in the middle keep playing until time has expired.
3) Score can be added up until the time has expired or be a series of mini games that reach a predetermined number of points. A game is won by itself or as a part inside of a set of games the way tennis is scored. If fitness is desired or of concern the exercise should still continue to flow for the set time period.
4) A team scores a point when one of its' players steps on the ball as it reaches an end line. The game is continuous as the team now turns and attacks the other end line. There is no free zone so attackers who are stuck on the end line by a pressuring defender need to be able to solve the problem. Younger players may need a free zone to turn and attack the other end.
5) If the players are still having problems executing or identifying the 2 versus 1patterns then the coach can give points for the 2 versus 1patterns. If there is a specific pattern that needs reinforcing then points can be awarded for that particular patterns' execution during the exercise.
6) When the defending player takes the ball away their team keeps possession and attacks from end to end. Transition is immediate for both teams. When first winning the ball in the middle of the grid a team may attack either end to begin their possession. After they reach one end they must turn and attack the other end line.
7) When a player reaches one end of the grid they "turn" and attack the other end of the grid.
8) Side players need to "sharpen" their angle of support along the sideline to be available for a 2 versus 1 pattern or to release pressure on an attacking player. The side support players may need to get completely square in support of players who have reached and end line to score and have a marking defender on their back. Without the side support players coming to support the only solution for the attacker with the ball would be to use a turning dribbling move. With only the dribbling solution possible and no passing options it will be much easier for the defender to dispossess the attacker with the ball. Side support players must "sharpen" up and down the length of the field.
9) Side support players should be playing the ball back in one touch. The coach can allow two touches if necessary. Do not let the support players slow the game down by standing over the ball looking for a passing opportunity. If the support players hold the ball to long the coach can make that a turn-over.
10) The support players on the side can decide that the attacker who gave them the ball is not the right passing choice and pass the ball to another attacker who is inside the grid.
11) Side support players do not play defense against each other. Because the side players can not defend this will create 2 versus 1situations that are easily exploited within the game.
12) The attacking player in the middle of the grid should be sure to knock the first pass into the "top" foot of the side support players. Remind the attacker to keep in mind where the support players' top foot would be, the one away from a defender that would exist in the

game but does not exist in the exercise.

13) Have four to six extra balls by the grid so the game does not have to stop every time there is a ball from the immediate grid area

14) If the defenders do nothing but back up to defend the coach must not allow this behavior from the defenders. The defenders need to try and regain possession of the ball. (Delay can be a good defensive solution in the game but is counter productive to the exercise.)

15) Most if not all of the 2 versus 1 patterns can and do occur in this exercises. As the game is played do not be hesitant to stop and show how a pattern could be used. Double pass patterns are the hardest to recreate for this game. However, the increased number of players in the center of the grid allows this particular pattern to occur much more often and without special conditions being enforced to create the situation. "Target" attackers will appear in each end of the grid in a natural way. Remember to remind the top attacker in the pattern to either open up for a straight back pass pattern, or spin away from the ball into a diagonal run to penetrate for a return pass behind the defender.

16) An attacker can dribble by the defender. This is because a defender can take away the dribble or they can take away the pass but they can not take away both options. If the passing lane for the wall pass is taken away by the defenders' positioning what the coach wants the attacker to learn is to dribble in that situation in the game. The exercise must reflect this idea.

17) Encourage the use of the outside of the foot to make the wall pass as late as possible, disguised as possible and keeping you in stride to make an explosive run past the defender an easier task. The coach can also encourage a toe poke to keep the pass disguised or to avoid intense pressure. All technical solutions are acceptable.

18) A good "first touch" is necessary to prepare the ball for the next move the attack wants to make.

19) Players should maintain an "open" body shape to increase their vision of the game which will allow a faster speed of the game to occur.

Variations:

a) **3 versus 3 / 4 versus 4 with side support that stays on side (Keys are above)**
b) **3 versus 3 / 4 versus 4 with side players entering the grid upon receiving a pass**
(This is the form of the exercise I use most often. It is the most dynamic and game like for of the exercises. See the keys to the variations below.)

Keys to the Variations:

20) Side players can enter the grid when they receive a pass. (See Diagram 21 A, page 90.)

21) The attacking player who passes the ball must replace the side player when the side support player receives a pass and carries the ball in with a dribble or passes to another attacking player inside the grid. (See Diagram 21 A, page 90.)

22) The side player can dribble in and have the passer make a curved run around them instead of just moving to the side of the grid. If the ball is returned to the curved runner then the passer now steps back to the line. (See Diagram 21 A, page 90.)

23) Passes across the entire width of the grid to the opposite support player made by a player just entering the far side of the grid are treated just like any other pass from inside the grid to the support players. The player exits to the side of the grid where they just passed the ball.

24) All of the 2 versus 1 patterns can and do occur in this exercises. As the game is played do not be hesitant to stop and show how a pattern could be used. Double pass patterns are the hardest to recreate.

25) "Open" body shape should be reinforced by the coach. The players can maximize their vision of the field by positioning their bodies shoulder on the ball carrier and by backing out of the space they occupy. This allows them to see most if not all of the grid.

26) All players in the grid and on the side lines supporting the play should be "sharpening" to create good passing lanes for their teammate who is in possession of the ball.

27) All the players should understand and provide left/right/split support through-out the flow of the exercise. It is the constant shaping and reshaping of this tactical unit that provides insight into all the runs needed for both support and penetration. (For a complete explanation see the book: Improving Your Team's **Possession Play: Tactics, Drills and Small-Sided Games to Teach Possession Soccer.)**

28) Be sure to reinforce the concept of a good first touch. A good first touch does not carry with it any notion of direction. What a good first touch does is gain an advantage for the team in possession of the ball whether the advantage is a shot on goal or continued possession of the ball.

Diagram 21: 3 versus 3 with Free Side Support Players on the Side

Diagram 21, page 89, shows the set up of 3 versus 3 with two side support players for each team. The exercise is scored by reaching an end line and stepping on the ball. Possession of the ball is kept by the scoring team and they then attack the other end of the grid. This exercise allows all of the 2 versus 1 patterns to occur. The coach may need to "freeze" the players and show in a slow walk through how some of the patterns can be created. **("Freezing"** the play is telling the players to stop **exactly** where they are so that they can see the situation and then walk through what tactical possibilities there are in that situation. If the coach allows the players to wander after the freeze command is made the picture will not be accurate and the teaching will not be as effective.)

The small group shape that is critical to possession soccer, Left/Right/Split Support, can be seen by players A, B, C and E. Player A has the ball and support for them can be seen on the left from player B, on the right from player E and in the split position the support is supplied by player C. This shape should be supplied constantly through out the exercise. Using 2 versus 1 patterns will sometimes supply the shape and sometimes temporarily disorganize the shape of left/right/split. The important issue is as the ball moves the players should also move to reform the shape and support the ball. Which player supplies what support position is constantly changing and shows the dynamic nature of soccer. (See Diagram 21, page 89.)

Diagram 21 A: 3 versus 3 with Free Side Support Players on the Side: Rule Example

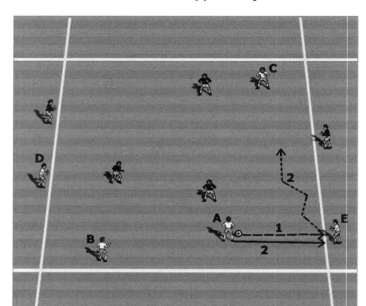

In Diagram 21 A, page 90, attacker A passes the ball to attacker E. This pass is numbered with a 1. Attacker E then dribbles into the grid while player A replaces the side support position. The dribble by attacker E is numbered with a 2 and the run by attacker A to replace the support position on the side of the grid is also numbered 2. It is a good mental exercise for the reader to readjust the players into left/right/split support to provide that shape to the new position of attacker E as they dribble.

Interestingly the support on the left is supplied by the movement of player A to the side of the grid. Support on the right is supplied by player C's position. In this instance only one player needs to sharpen and that is player D who needs to move to their left or up the grid to assume a good split position.

This readjustment of positioning by "sharpening" can not be emphasized enough if the coach wants to teach the players how to possess the ball. Passing lanes must be created by three players in support of the ball at all times. The players also need to keep their body shape "open" so that they can see the field of play before they receive the ball. This allows for better decisions when receiving the ball and for a much higher speed of play since decisions can be made before the ball arrives and not after a ball is received. Diagram 21 B, page 91, illustrates another set of runs creating left/right/split support by players "sharpening." Notice that the body shapes are "open" to the field and their teammates. This will allow for that all important first touch and speed of play.

While Diagram 21 A , page 90, does not show a specific 2 versus 1 pattern it is easy to see that if attacker E continues to dribble straight at the defender next to attacker C in the upper end of the grid that attackers E and C can create a Wall Pass to penetrate to the end line.

Diagram 21 B: 3 versus 3 with Free Side Support Players on the Side: Movement of Players to Support Player in Possession of the Ball

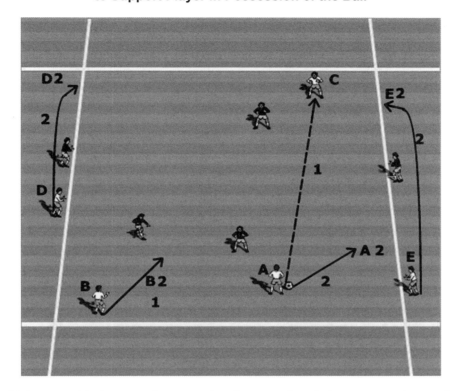

In Diagram 21 B, page 91, the pass from attacker A to attacker C does not produce a 2 versus 1 pattern. To produce good support it does produce a set of runs. It forces players E, D and A to "sharpen" into good supporting positions. The shape is left/right/split. The second that A strikes the ball towards player C then player E and D must slide down the outside of the grid to supply support on the left and the right of player C. Player A moves to their right to supply a possible split pass back from player C if it is required or desired. Attacker B makes a run to try and provide support in another split position.

Remember, there are only two reasons to pass a ball to a teammate in a match

  a) Because the teammate has a superior position if they are in possession of the ball;
  b) Because there is too much pressure on the player with the ball and passing it will relieve that pressure.

The work by players to create the shape is critical. Out of the shape comes the ability to create and use 2 versus 1patterns to penetrate. The ability to use 2 versus 1 and create the left/right/split support shape allows the team to move the ball both cohesively and creatively with possession to penetrate against opposing teams. Having all the players interested in receiving the ball is a positive for the team. There are any numbers of 2 versus 1patterns that can be created out of the position of the players shown in Diagram 21 B, page 91. This is particularly true if the variation that allows the side support players to rotate into the grid as they receive the ball is being used. Diagramming some solutions on a piece of paper can help in seeing them so that the ideas can be passed on to the players. In Diagram 21 C, page 92, there is another set of runs from the same supporting positions to allow the reader to see the concept in motion.

The coach must be able to mentally see the shape of left/right/split all the time. This requires off the ball coaching. This is a coaching skill that needs to be constantly used. It not only drives the shape of the small group it also is a critical skill for the organization of the entire team as it moves to prepare properly to the movement of the ball and any potential moves will be required next. Teams that are well prepared regarding off the ball movement have a higher speed of play because their anticipation has been honed. Coaching off the ball can be defined as assessing and teaching movements by players who are not in possession of the ball. Many coaches just coach the ball carrier and/or the one or two players in the immediate vicinity of the ball. However, for team success, the players off the ball need to understand their roles and the possible situations that they may be suddenly faced with in a game.

Diagram 21 C: 3 versus 3 with Free Side Support Players on the Side Wall Pass and Curved Run

In Diagram 21 C, page 92, attacker A combines with player B to create a wall pass. The pass from attacker A to attacker B is numbered with a 1. The run by attacker A to receive the ball back from attacker B is numbered with a 2 and the return pass that creates the Wall Pass from attacker B is also numbered with a 2.

Attacker A then dribbles forwards, numbered with a 3, to commit the defender before passing the ball to player C. The pass by attacker A to attacker C is numbered with a 4. Attacker E in the side support position on the right of the grid has made a run to support attacker A on the right side. This initial run to support by attacker E is numbered with a 3. Attacker D on the left side of the grid has also made a run to supply support and the initial run is numbered with a 3.

Attacker A then makes a Curved Run around player C so as to receive the ball on the end line. Attacker C has dribbled into the upper middle of the grid to help create space for the Curved Run by attacker A. The dribble by attacker C is numbered with a 5. Player D "sharpens" on the left again to supply support for attacker C. This run is numbered with a 4. As attacker A reaches the end line with the ball attacker E needs to "sharpen" up the grid again to give support on what now becomes the left as attacker A scores on the end line and turns to attack the other end of the grid. That run by attacker E is numbered with a 4. Attacker C will supply the support for attacker A on the right and attacker B must sharpen to supply a split position for attacker A to utilize. Attacker C does not have to make a move to supply the support but attacker B needs to make a run into a good split position and that run is numbered with a 5.There are other ways for the attackers to recreate the starting position of Left/Right/Split support but what is written is probably the most efficient way for the attackers to reshape.

Essentially this is a cycle of shaping and reshaping the game. It was started from the shape of Left/Right/Split and then exploited by the use of two different 2 versus 1patterns; a Wall Pass and a Curved Run. A new set of decisions will set off another cycle trying to exploit the defense with 2 versus 1 penetration and the shaping of possession through Left/Right/Split support around the ball.

Diagram 21 C, page 92, is an example of how the exercise might flow in a given "cycle." The permutations are endless. Because they are endless the coach needs to teach the players to think within the patterns that constantly repeat themselves in the game. This book concerns 2 versus 1 and the patterns that repeat themselves so that the coach can teach and instruct their players to use them. In this exercise the issue of support becomes equally important and the use of left/right/split shape to support the ball now becomes essential to both understand and use. (See the book; **Improving Your Team's Possesion Play)**

Diagram 21 D: 3 versus 3 with Free Side Support Player on the Side: Several Cycles of Play

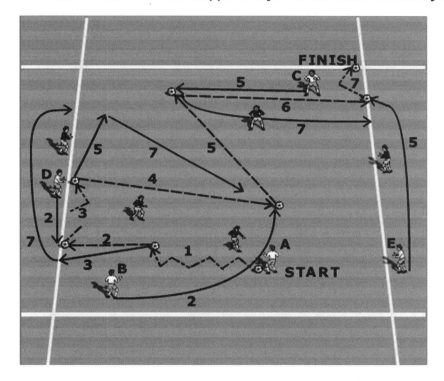

To read and understand Diagram 21 D, page 93, the reader must simply follow the sequence of numbers by each line. The reader can line it out one step at a time on a piece of paper if, as I do, they have problems abstracting the runs and the sequences. My personal response if I saw this diagram would be along the lines of; "Holy scrud monkeys."

    a.   The initial start point is in this diagram is attacker A in the lower central part of the grid and the dribble towards the left of the grid. The dribble is numbered 1.

    b.   Attacker B starts a Curved Run around attacker A, who instead of using the run of attacker B, passes the ball to attacker D who has sharpened down the side line on the left side of the grid to support attacker A. The Curved Run by attacker B is numbered 2. The support run by attacker D is numbered 2. The pass by attacker A to attacker D is numbered 2. All the movements numbered 2 are essentially happening at the same time.

c. Attacker A immediately starts to exit the grid with a run numbered 3 and replace player D on the side line. Attacker D enters the grid with a dribble that is numbered with a 3.

d. Attacker D passes the ball to attacker B who has stopped their Curved Run and "sharpened" into a position to receive the potential split pass from attacker D. The pass from attacker D to attacker B is numbered with a 4.

e. Attacker D "sharpens" up field in the direction of the attack without letting a defender get in a position to cut out a pass. This allows attacker D to support attacker B if it is needed. This run is numbered with a 5.

f. Attacker C now makes a run towards the middle of the field to provide support in a "split" position. This run is numbered with a 5. The run is rewarded with a pass from attacker B that is numbered with a 5.

g. Attacker E recognizes the need to "sharpened" and makes a long run up the right edge of the grid to supply support to attacker C. This support run to supply support on the right is numbered with a 5. Early recognition of the lack of support for attacker C when the ball is first passed by attacker B makes the run almost simultaneous with the pass from attacker B to attacker C.

h. Attacker C chooses pass the ball to attacker E with a pass numbered 6. Attacker E then dribbles into the grid to score on the end line. The dribble is numbered with a 7.

i. Attacker C then exits the center of the grid to replace the support position on the right side of the grid with a run numbered 7. This run is dictated by the rules that require that each group of players have one player on each side of the grid.

j. As attacker E turns to attack the other end of the grid they have support on the left from attacker C, support on the right from attacker A who has made a run numbered 7 up the left side of the grid and support in the split position from attacker D who has made a run in the center of the grid numbered 7 to supply it.. Since attacker D has made the run into a split support position attacker B can stretch the field by pushing towards the other end of the grid.

The cycle of 2 versus 1, the tactical unit of left/right/split support and Combination Play supply all the attacking decision making needed. This is true in almost all situations. The only issue left is the skill with which the players can use 1 versus 1 tactics and abilities. In other words can the player beat a single opponent off of a dribble, shield the ball and dribble to gain time for tactical opportunities to be created. Diagram 21 D, page 93, is another example of showing a possible series of patterns inside of 2 versus 1 patterns and left/right/split support structure.

The decisions that a group of three players much less five players can make rise exponentially into the billions in just 3 to 5 possible passes or dribbles. Teach players to understand the game components, allow them to think, provide some team structure based on the abilities of the players and let the magic of technique create the game. Coaching is of course a complex art and the last sentence would seem to minimize the art form. But in many ways the game is still simple in its elements but difficult to do. Technique, technique, technique is a mantra that all coaches should preach to them selves and to their players if the game is to reach its' most beautiful levels.

Diagram 21 E: 3 versus 3 with Free Side Support Players on the Side:

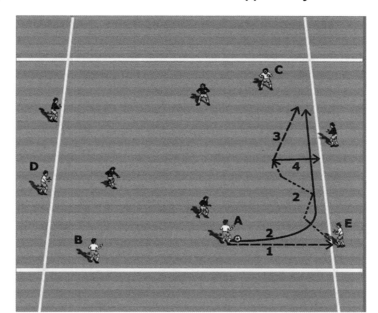

Diagram 21 E, page 95, shows the reader how a pass from inside the grid followed by a Curved Run around the entering side support player can occur. Players often have trouble seeing that this option exists when they first start doing the exercise. This is the reason for Diagram 21 E.

Attacker A makes a pass, numbered 1 to support attacker E who is supporting on the right edge of the grid. Attacker E then starts entering the grid with a dribbling movement that is numbered with a 2. Attacker A starts to run to the right side of the grid to replace attacker E but turns that movement into a Curved Run around attacker E along the right side of the grid. This run by attacker A is numbered with a 2. In this instance attacker E chooses to pass the ball to attacker A when the Curved Run occurs. The pass by attacker E to attacker A is numbered with a 3. Attacker E then replaces attacker A, who is actually making their run as the right support player on the right side of the grid. Attacker E's run onto the right side of the grid is numbered with a 4.

It is optional for attacker E to return the pass to attacker A. If attacker E continues on with their dribble or passes the ball to another attacker then attacker A exits the interior of the gird and takes up a position on the edge of the grid. Attacker A would simply continue to work at supplying good support for the who ever has the ball. This additional flexibility to make a Curved Run around the entering support player makes the exercise more fluid and game like. A little instruction by the coach will help the players see the possibility and the solution so that they can solve the problem and use the solution.

Exercise 6: Warm-Up Patterns down the Length of the Field
(10 x 10 yards imaginary grid or side line grids)

(See Diagrams 22, 22 A, 22 B, 22 B1, 22 C, 22 C1, 22 D, 22 D1, 22 E, 22 F 22 G, pages 97, 98, 99, 101, 102, 103, 104, 105, 106, 107 and 108.)

Keys to Exercise Six

1) Since there is no pressure on attackers or just limited amounts of pressure the coach should expect execution to be as nearly perfect as possible. The accuracy of the pass, the speed of the pass, the quality of the run, and the timing of the run should all be as cleanly executed as possible.

2) The coach can use the touch line on each side of the field as one boundary edge and have the players estimate a ten yard width as they jog to the end lines to make the grid as the players go up and down the length of the field executing the patterns. The other way to set up the grids is to cone them out into clearly discernable grids. Some players will need to have the area sectioned out by cones into discernable grids while others will be able to perform the exercise without any cones.

3) If the coach wants to keep the exercise under a closer eye to make corrections during the repetitions the coach may want to set up two or three squares for the players to work through and then return to the starting spot to repeat the exercise. This will keep the players within twenty to thirty yards of the coach and allow instruction to be more easily communicated.

4) Players can stretch at each end of the line until fully warm and as they warm up they can pick up their tempo of execution. (See Diagram 22 B, page 99.)

5) When there are no defenders it is important to make sure the players are rehearsing in their minds and then performing the tactical and technical execution to be done to be successful in match conditions. They should make their moves, runs and passes as if there were defenders in the grids.

6) Be sure to start the players from positions inside the grids that allow the 2 versus 1 pattern desired to emerge. (See Diagrams 22 – 22 G, pages 97, 98, 99, 101, 102, 103, 104, 105, 106, 107 and 108.)

7) A defender can be added to each square to put on limited pressure.

8) A good "first touch" is necessary to prepare the ball for the next move the attack wants to make. This touch in this exercise is much more predictable because there are specific objectives in mind.

Diagrams 22: Warm-Up Patterns: Set Up

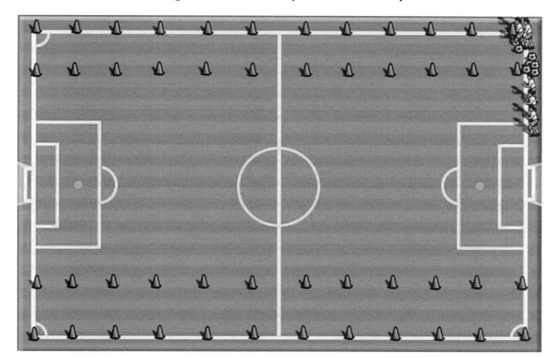

In Diagram 22, page 97, cones are set up in approximately 10 yard grids from one end to the other on the field. Players start working through the cones on one side of the field and work their way back through the cones on the other side of the field. The coach can have the players change patterns from one side of the field to the other or keep repeating the pattern up and down the field. If the coach uses ten yard grids, a reasonable amount of space for experienced players since there is no pressure, then players will perform a pattern 11 times each repetition down the field. The grid size should vary based on age and experience. The younger the age and the less the experience level the larger the grid.

Diagram 22 A: Warm Up Pattern

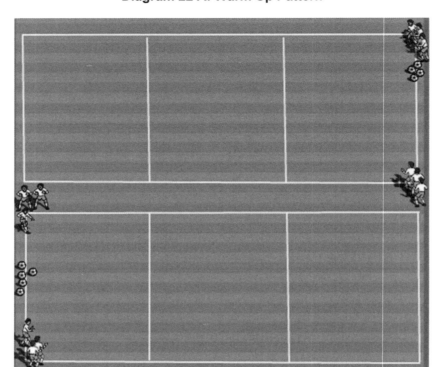

In Diagram 22 A, page 98, the area of the field can be marked out with actual cones or the players, particularly after experiencing the exercise, can simply imagine the grids and perform accordingly.

This grid area is slightly larger than 10 yards long. Each grid in this diagram is approximately 14 yards long. Grid size will vary with age and ability. The younger the age of the player and/or the less experience the player has the larger the grid area should be for the exercise.

It is not recommended that the coach do all of the patterns in a single session. This will tend to bore the players to death and lose concentration for the practice. Instead pick two to four of the patterns to reinforce the relative positioning and movements required to perform a 2 versus 1 pattern. The coach must demand concentration, effort and an attempt at perfect execution for this exercise to be useful. This demand on the mental aspect of training even in a warm-up exercise is very useful in training teams to perform at higher levels. Concentration and focus are elements that are always needed to be successful. However, yelling at them for a poor pass is not necessarily a good enforcer of concentration. Just point out the good passes and touches while demanding the effort to make the passes and touches good ones.

Diagram 22 B: Curved Runs and Wall Passes Warm-Up

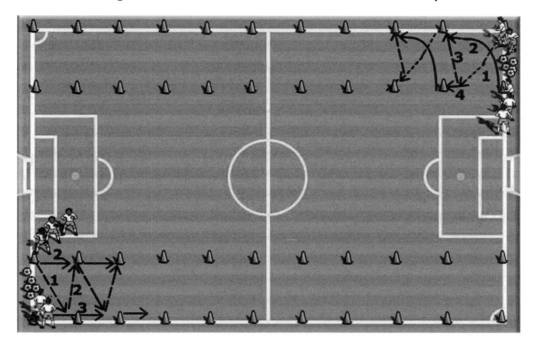

In Diagram 22 B, page 99, along the top row the first player dribbles into the grid with a dribble numbered 1. Once the space on the outside of the field is open the player on the inside makes a Curved Run around the dribbling player. That run is numbered with a 2. The pass from the dribbling player to the runner making the Curved Run is numbered with a 3 and both player end up at the next set of cones. The dribbling player will have to take a couple of steps forward and that run is numbered with a 4. The pattern is then repeated through out the coned areas.

The pattern on the lower edge of the grid is a Wall Pass. The player on the lower edge of the grid moves up to the middle of the grid and waits for the pass from the player on the other edge of the coned grid. The pass that starts the Wall Pass is numbered with a 1. The return pass and the run to receive it are both numbered with a 2 since the action is simultaneous. Then the player who served as the wall runs up to the middle of the next grid to set up another wall pass. That run is numbered with a 3. The two players move up the length of the field this way.

All of the teams' players start at the end of the field. This will allow them to repeat the pattern they are working on at least ten times down the length of the field. What it will also teach the players is that to create certain patterns of play there needs to be positions of relative placement by the players for the pattern to occur. The exercise is an excellent warm-up in that it uses a physiological movement while demanding both technical and tactical use of the ball. The coach needs to make sure that the players keep mental focus while executing the patterns. The USSF concept of economical training taught in the coaching schools is exemplified even in this exercise. There is no pressure and the physical work rate is not high enough to create a higher fitness level.

A quick review of the concept of **economical training** would be useful. Soccer is a complex use of the physical, psychological, technical and tactical aspects of the sport. With the limited amount of time that is available to coaches in teaching the game to youth or preparing their teams it is critical to avoid training just one aspect of the game at a time. Economical training is the use of multiple aspects of the game at once and not the isolation of just one element.

Pure fitness drills are examples of not using the economical use of a players' or teams' time. When doing just physical work the coach leaves out any other aspect that can be taught. If a coach uses twenty minutes to work on fitness at the end of practice out of ninety and uses ten minutes at the start of a practice to just jog and stretch the players then the coach will have used 33% of the time available for a player to learn on only the physical component of the game. This is not as the USSF puts it "economical" in nature. Incorporating the ball with the players' warm-up besides physiologically warming up the team at the start also demands at least using one other area, technical touch, of the four categories a coach needs to train. Add a tactical element as this exercise does and the coach is adding economy to the training structure.

The stress on small sided games to train players is in essence the epitome of economical training. The physical work rate is higher than a large match because players must be involved all the time. The numbers of touches a player will be forced to receive and use are significantly higher allowing an opportunity to improve technical issues faster. The number of tactical decisions a player is making are arithmetically increased and the psychological focus, effort, involvement, concentration etc for the players are also being constantly used. Small sided games or exercises that most closely resemble the game itself are superior teaching tools because they automatically use the concept of economical training.

These warm-ups require technical and tactical learning or work while demanding psychological concentration and a physical warm-up that uses the previous three aspects rather than running a lap to warm up physically.

Diagrams 22 B1 through 22 G

The following diagrams are set up to show only a couple of squares rather than the entire length of the field. It is left to the imagination of the reader to continue the exercises' movements down the whole length of the field if they are set up that way. The coach can just set up a couple of squares so the players perform the exercise with just a quick couple of repetitions. That way if space is limited or the coach wants to be closer to the repetitions than the 110 yard grid will allow to make corrections the exercise can be set up with only a couple of grids. The coach can just make three or four squares and have the players return right back. This allows for more constant oversight of the players efforts.

Diagram 22 B1: Curved Runs and Wall Passes in 3 Squares

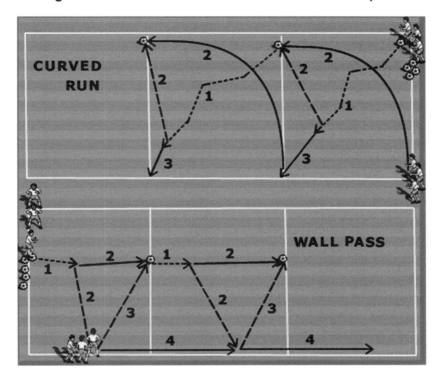

Diagram 22 B1, page 101, is a clearer illustration of the Curved Run and Wall Pass patterns shown in Diagram 22 B, page 99, and how they are set up for the exercise. In the top half of the diagram the Curved Run pattern is shown. The player with the ball dribbles diagonally across the grid. This dribble is numbered with a 1. As space is created in the area that the dribble has just gone through the second player in the pattern makes the Curved Run around the player with the ball. That run is numbered with a 2. As the player making the run comes around the player with the ball it is possible for a pass to be given back from the direction that the dribble came from or to make a pass that leads the runner forward. That pass is numbered with a 2 and changes ball possession by the players. The player that was dribbling the ball then runs to the cone they were moving diagonally at to finish the sequence and get ready to start again. That run is numbered with a 3. Both players are now at the next set of cones and start that pattern over again.

In the lower half of Diagram 22 B1, page 101, the Wall Pass pattern is illustrated. The starting spots for the players are significantly different. One player must start on the side of the grid in the middle and the other player starts from the beginning edge of the grid. The player on the beginning edge of the grid starts the pattern by dribbling into the square. That dribble is numbered with a 1 and replicates the need for the attacker with the ball to commit a defender to set up the Wall Pass pattern properly. The player dribbling the ball then sends a pass to the supporting player that is numbered with a 2. It is suggested that the players learn to make this pass with the outside of the foot because it is a more deceptive surface, keeps the player in a running motion and allows the attacker to get a little closer to the opponent before releasing the ball with a flick of the ankle and a minimum of warning that the pass is going to be made. The player who just made the pass now makes a run that in the game would be on the far side of the defender. That run is numbered with a 2 and the supporting player sends a pass back that is numbered with a 3. The supporting player now needs to run forward to get into the middle edge of the next grid to start the pattern over again. That run is numbered with a 4.

Diagram 22 C: Take Over and X Pattern

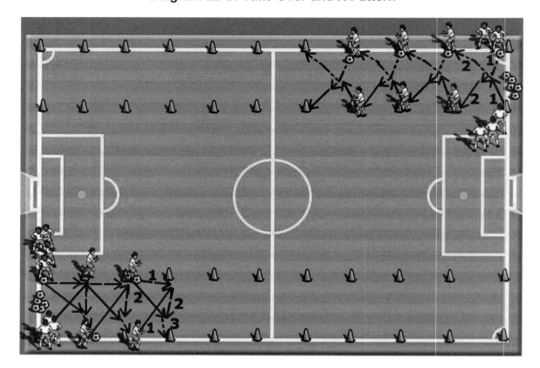

In Diagram 22 C1, page 102, the players are working on two patterns. In the upper half of the diagram illustrates the players working on the Take-Over Pattern. The coach can also ask the players to use a False Take Over as well so that the element of communication has to take place inside the warm-up exercise. Letting the players choose the pattern will help them read the game and communicate it.

The top half of Diagram 22 C1, page 103, is the Take-Over Pattern. The player with the ball dribbles across the grid and their teammate makes a run straight at them. Both the dribble and the run are numbered with a 1 since the moves are simultaneous. The ball changes possession and the pattern finishes with the player who now has the ball dribbling to the cone and the other player making a run to the opposite cone. Both the dribble and the run are numbered with a 2. Remember to stress to the players that the exchange of the ball is done right foot to right foot or left foot to left foot or the players will collide.

The bottom half of Diagram 22 C 1, page 103, illustrates how players would move, pass and dribble the ball to execute an X Pattern. Since there are a couple of ways to create the X Pattern this one shows how to create it using a diagonal run and pass. The player on the lower half of the grid makes a diagonal run, numbered 1, to receive a straight pass from the other attacking player which is also numbered 1.

The attacking player who passes the ball then cuts into the space behind where the first runner ran. This run is numbered with a 2. The player receives a pass sent slightly backwards and in front of them from the player who has just received the pass. This slightly backwards pass is numbered with a 2. The player now receiving the ball (the player that started the exercise) dribbles the ball forward to the edge of the grid to start the sequence over again. That dribble is numbered with a 3. (If you want to alternate the roles that each player takes after each repetition then the ball needs to be passed square at the top of the grid after each repetition to create a change in roles. Personally, I just let the players make sure that the next time around the exercise they change the passing and running roles for the X pattern.)

Don't forget that the X Pattern can be created in a second way with a diagonal dribble and a run that cuts back behind and across the dribble. A third way to create an X Pattern is to have the player dribbling the ball at high speed just step on it and leave the ball for the cutting runner to pick up as they cut behind their teammate. (See X Pattern, explanations on page 29.)

Diagram 22 C1: Take Over and X Pattern in 3 Squares

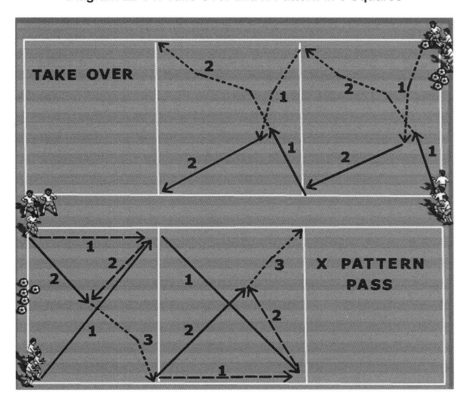

In Diagram 22 C1, page 103, the players are working on two patterns. In the upper half of the diagram illustrates the players working on the Take-Over Pattern. The coach can also ask the players to use a False Take Over as well so that the element of communication has to take place inside the warm-up exercise. Letting the players choose the pattern will help them read the game and communicate it.

The top half of Diagram 22 C1, page 103, is the Take-Over Pattern. The player with the ball dribbles across the grid and their teammate makes a run straight at them. Both the dribble and the run are numbered with a 1 since the moves are simultaneous. The ball changes possession and the pattern finishes with the player who now has the ball dribbling to the cone and the other player making a run to the opposite cone. Both the dribble and the run are numbered with a 2. Remember to stress to the players that the exchange of the ball is done right foot to right foot or left foot to left foot or the players will collide.

The bottom half of Diagram 22 C 1, page 103, illustrates how players would move, pass and dribble the ball to execute an X Pattern. Since there are a couple of ways to create the X Pattern this one shows how to create it using a diagonal run and pass. The player on the lower half of the grid makes a diagonal run, numbered 1, to receive a straight pass from the other attacking player which is also numbered 1.

The attacking player who passes the ball then cuts into the space behind where the first runner ran. This run is numbered with a 2. The player receives a pass sent slightly backwards and in front of them from the player who has just received the pass. This slightly backwards pass is numbered with a 2. The player now receiving the ball (the player that started the exercise) dribbles the ball forward to the edge of the grid to start the sequence over again. That dribble is numbered with a 3. (If you want to alternate the roles that each player takes after each repetition then the ball needs to be passed square at the top of the grid after each repetition to create a change in roles. Personally, I just let the players make sure that the next time around the exercise they change the passing and running roles for the X pattern.)

Don't forget that the X Pattern can be created in a second way with a diagonal dribble and a run that cuts back behind and across the dribble. A third way to create an X Pattern is to have the player dribbling the ball at high speed just step on it and leave the ball for the cutting runner to pick up as they cut behind their teammate. (See X Pattern, explanations on page 29.)

Diagram 22 D: Low Wall Pass and High Wall Pass with Curved Run to Move Forward

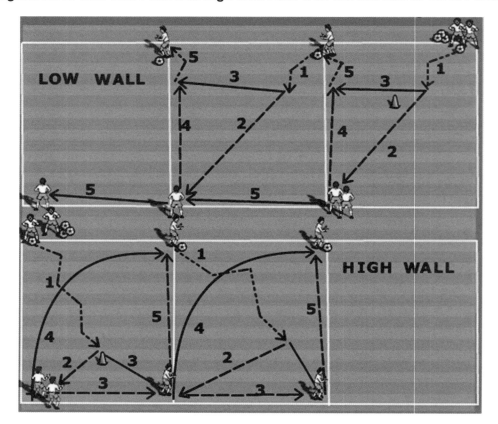

In Diagram 22 D, page 104, the starting position must change for the Low Wall Pass Pattern to emerge. The players need to start at opposite diagonal corners of the grid. The player with the ball makes a short dribble into the grid. This dribble is numbered with a 1. Then the player passes the ball to the attacker up field in the grid. The pass numbered with a 2 is forward and diagonal in nature. Then the player making the pass must make a hard committed run forward which is numbered with a 3 in the diagram. The player receiving the ball then returns the ball with a square pass, numbered 4, to the attacker who first passed. This creates a Low Wall Pass Pattern. If the players are having a hard time conceptualizing the pattern the coach can set out a cone or a passive defender in the grid to show that the pass needs to be made sooner and the run may need to be more explosive to execute this Low Wall Pass Pattern. The player laying off the wall pass needs to make a run forward into the next grid so that they can now execute the pattern over again. This run is numbered with a 5. (Don't forget the other relative positioning of players that can be used as shown in the Low Wall Pass Patterns on page 21.)

In the lower half of Diagram 22 D, page 104, the pattern is a High Wall Pass. There is a cone set up in the first grid to show how the pattern should work. The attacker with the ball makes a diagonal dribble at the cone, which is numbered with a 1, while the supporting attacker is simply holding their position. Because the supporting attacker is now up field of the player with the ball relative to the direction that the play is going, the first pass is backwards to the feet of the supporting player. This pass is numbered with a 2. The dribbling attacker, now without the ball, makes an explosive diagonal run forward to receive the second pass, numbered with a 3, of the wall pass. The run forward is also numbered with a 3 because the action is essentially simultaneous. To get the supporting attacker forward they make a curved run forward to the edge of the next grid. This run is numbered with a 4. A square pass sent across the grid lets the roles reverse and the players can practice both roles while using the pattern over again. The pass to change roles is numbered with a 5.

Diagram 22 D1: Double Pass Straight and Double Pass Diagonal

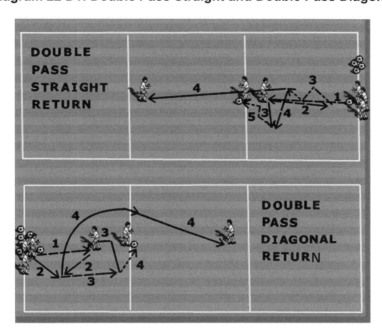

Diagram 22 D1, page 105, shows both the Double Pass Patterns. In both the upper and lower parts of the diagram the starting points for the players need to be at opposite ends of the grid. The pattern shown in the upper half of the diagram is a Straight Double Pass that demands that the attacking player at the end of the grid slid open with their chest showing to where the defender would be in a game. (If players are confused as to where the defender would be the coach can place a cone in the grid to simulate the defenders' position.) The first pass is made by the player at the start of the grid into the forward attackers' feet. This pass is numbered with a 1. The ball is returned straight back, the pass is numbered with a 2, which forces the attacker at the top of the grid to slide sideways out of the path of the ball and force the defender to choose between tracking the attacker or the ball.

The run by the forward attacker sideways is numbered with a 3. The player with the ball, the player that first played it forward, now dribbles forward to commit the defender as their teammate slides to the side of the defender. The dribble is being made at the same time as the sideways run so it also is numbered with a 3. The attacker dribbling forward sends the ball into their teammates' feet with a pass numbered 4. This allows the attacker to dribble forward to the end line of the first grid. This dribble is numbered with a 5 and the other player makes a hard run into the far end of the next grid to set up the pattern again. This run is numbered with a 4 because it starts the moment that the pass numbered 4 is made to the feet of their teammate.

In the bottom half of Diagram 22 D1, page 105, the Double Pass Pattern using the diagonal return pass is shown. This pattern allows the attacker receiving the first pass to spin away to receive the return pass in behind the defender. The first pass is made by the player at the starting edge of the grid to the feet of the player at the far end. This pass is numbered with a 1. The return pass, numbered with a 2, is passed back and laid off diagonally. The player who started the sequence then makes a run forward to the ball numbered with a 2. The player in the top half of the grid now spins around the defender and makes a diagonal run numbered with a 3 that will allow a penetrating pass to be sent forward. This penetrating pass is numbered with a 3 in the diagram. After receiving the pass behind the defender the attacker dribbles to the line. This move is numbered with a 4. While the player with the ball dribbles they are waiting while their teammate makes a Curved Run forward, numbered with a 4, to reach the end of the next grid and start the pattern over again.

Diagram 22 E: Flick and Spin Wall Pass and False Wall Pass

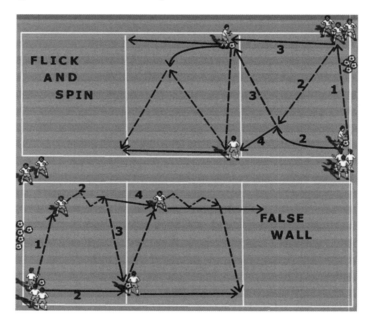

In the upper half of Diagram 22 E, page 106, the Flick and Spin Wall Pass is shown. The players starting position in this case is even with each other. This allows them to support the player with the ball. The attacker with the ball should mentally see them self shielding the ball. The support player can be slightly up or down field and still successfully perform a Flick and Spin Pattern. (See variations of the Flick and Spin on pages 28, 29 and 30.)

The initial flick pass is made to the support player and the passing player spins in the opposite direction to make a run behind where the defender would be in a game. The flick pass is numbered with a 1. The run spinning around the defender is numbered with a 2 and the return pass by the supporting player is also numbered with a 2. The supporting player makes a run forward to the next cone. That run is numbered with a 3. At the same time the ball is sent to the player making the run forward with a pass numbered 3 and the player who executed the spin move makes a run numbered 4 to the opposite cone. This allows for the swapping of roles as the players move through the grids. (See Diagram 22 E, page 106.)

The lower half of Diagram 22 E, page 106, is a False Wall Pattern that turns away from the initial passer and then sends the ball back to the first attacker from a later dribbled position. The starting position is one player forward in the grid and the other starting on the end of the grid. The player starting with the ball starts at the end of the grid. The attacker with the ball makes a pass numbered 1 to the player up field. The player receiving the initial pass instead of returning it in a Wall Pass Pattern turn away from where the pass would have gone and dribbles in the opposite direction. This illusion of a Wall Pass is how the pattern gets its' name: False Wall Pass. The dribble away is numbered with a 2. The player making the initial pass makes a run just as they would in a Wall Pass and that run is numbered with a 2. The player with the ball that is dribbling now plays a late pass back to their teammate. This pass is numbered with a 3. Both players then run and/or dribble to the start of the next grid and start the sequence again. The player who will dribble away from what looks like a Wall Pass has to make a run forward into the next grid. This run is numbered with a 4. Remember that the initial pass to the player in the grid should be made to the top foot of the player to help shield the ball naturally. The coach should also point out that the reason for the player using the False Wall Pass is because the defender that is imaginary in this exercise would be jumping the passing lane for a return pass. This jumping of the passing lane is essential to understanding when to use a False Wall Pattern.

If the coach wants the roles to reverse after each repetition the players need to exchange a square pass at the top of the grid. This will start the sequence again. Otherwise the coach can just instruct the players to make sure that the roles of the pattern be exchanged the next time they run through the grids.

Diagram 22 F: Diagonal Run/Straight Pass and Diagonal Pass/Straight Run

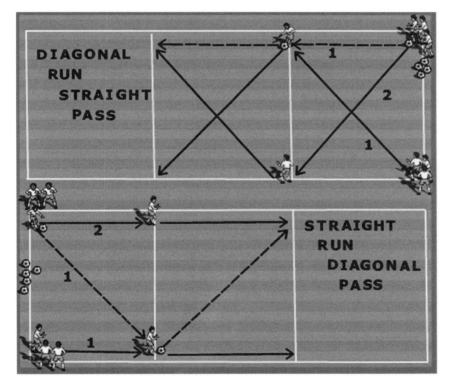

The two patterns in Diagram 22 F, page 107, are very straight forward in nature. The upper half is a straight pass made to a diagonal run. The sequence starts with both players at the edge of the grid. The player without the ball makes a run diagonally across the grid out in front of the player with the ball. This run is numbered with a 1. The pass is then made straight forward to the runner. This pass is also numbered with a 1 because the run and pass are almost simultaneous. The passer then runs diagonally across the grid to start the sequence over at the edge of the next grid. This run is numbered with a 2. The roles automatically reverse this way.

In the lower half of Diagram 22 F, page 107, the run is made straight to a diagonal pass. The players both start at the edge of the grid. Both attackers in this pattern never leave the side of the grid that they start on. The player without the ball makes a straight run forward in the grid which is numbered with a 1. A diagonal pass is sent across the grid to the runner and that pass is also numbered 1. Then the player who passed the ball makes a run forward to the next cone to start the sequence over again. That run is numbered with a 2. Only the ball moves back and forth not the players. The pattern automatically reverses the roles after each sequence. These patterns also give rise to the old saying; "Diagonal Run, Straight Pass and Straight Run, Diagonal Pass." This does not account for the Diagonal Run to a Diagonal Pass.

Diagram 22 G: Curved Run Late Pass and Dummy Pattern

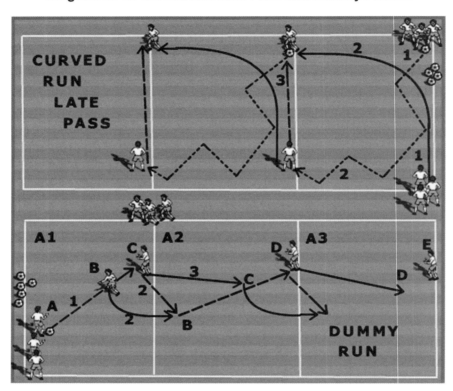

In Diagram 22 G, page 108, the patterns using a late run in a Curved Run Pattern to surprise the defense is shown. In the lower half of the diagram the use of Dummy moves is explored. In the top half of Diagram 22 G, page 108, is the Curved Run with a late pass.

The attackers start even with each other in the Curved Run Late Pass Pattern. The player with the ball makes a diagonal dribble to clear space for their teammate to run around in the typical Curved Run Pattern. The dribble is numbered 1 at the start. The Curved Run around the ball and teammate is started with the number 1 and ends numbered with a 2. What is different about this pattern is how long the dribble is held and the mental picture that the dribbler has beaten the defender and has moved past the defender but then chooses to play the ball late as another defender steps up to pressure them in a game. The second half of the dribble, which would be after the player beat their defender, is numbered with a 2. Then as the player dribbling ball reaches the line this would be an arbitrary point for the defense to have had another defender slide over which would let the player with the ball now play the pass late to their teammate making the Curved Run. The pass is numbered with a 3. In a game this pass is often slipped in between the recovering defender and the defender stepping up into pressure.

In the lower half of Diagram 22 G, page 108, a Dummy Pattern is shown. While all the other patterns only take two players a Dummy Pattern requires three players. One to pass the ball, one to dummy it and one to receive it after the ball is dummied. Therefore, to do this pattern the coach must have a player in each grid waiting at the far end. The players are all lettered to help in the explanation.

Player A sends a pass to the feet of player B who is positioned approximately half way up the grid. Player C is positioned at the far end of the grid. The pass is numbered with a 1. Player B lets the ball run by them or through their legs to player C and then makes a run forward, numbered with a 2. Player C passes the ball to player B with a pass numbered 2 and then player C makes a run, numbered 3, into the next grid to get in front of player D so that the sequence would start again. What is not shown is how to get the other grids ready.

As soon as player B starts the next grids' Dummy Pattern they step back to the top of the first gird where player C used to be. Player A steps forward to where player B used to be and a new player will start the sequence again from the starting edge of the grid. This keeps the exercise moving forward with players in every grid taking every role. It is somewhat confusing so if the players are little lost at first do not be surprised.

Exercise 7: Pattern Warm-Ups:
(Free space or ten yard grids) (See Diagrams 23 and 23 A, pages 110 and 111.)

Keys to Exercise Seven

1) The warm-up period should be no longer than 10 to 15 minutes. The time period can be shorter than that and still be an effective technical, tactical and physiological warm-up. The physical pace is not high but attention to detail is crucial.
2) Be sure to have at least one full sized goal set up on a field size of the coaches choosing to give the players a sense of direction. The goal can also be used to warm up the keeper. The field size should be large enough to avoid groups of players running into each other as they warm up.
3) Players split up into groups of 3; each group with a ball. Two players will replicate patterns. The third player becomes a limited pressure defender. The roles rotate.
4) Who works as the defender after each repetition is a bit random by nature. Players need to adjust to make sure that they all take the roles of attackers and defender. (See Diagram 23, page 110.)
5) The coach can grid out the playing space into ten yard grids if they like but I prefer to leave the space open and let the players work out in their heads what their pattern should look like based on the area of the field that they are working in and their relationship to the goal. (The coach may have to spend time working with the players in the groups to get them to properly visualize where they are on the field, what would work and what it would look like properly executed.)
6) When there is limited pressure from defenders it is important to make sure the players are rehearsing in their minds and then performing the tactical and technical execution as near to perfectly as can be done so that they can be done successful in match conditions.
7) Even though the pressure is limited the defenders can not just back up to defend. The coach must not allow this behavior from the defenders. Instead the defender needs to help the attackers rehearse by moving to close them in a realistic way without full pressure.
8) The players are permitted to work on the patterns they want unless the coach has requirements for them regarding specific patterns during the warm-up.
9) Dynamic stretching periods should be held periodically during the warm-up.
10) A good "first touch" is necessary to prepare the ball for the next move the attack wants to make.
11) Players should always make sure they are "sharpening" to make themselves available to

their teammate who possesses the ball. Defenders, even with limited pressure, can move through the passing lane for a 2 versus 1 pattern. This fact requires attacking players to move their supporting positions by sharpening.

12) Keepers can be warmed up separately on any topic from catching to shot stopping to dealing with crosses.

Diagram 23: Groups of Three: Warm-Up Full Field

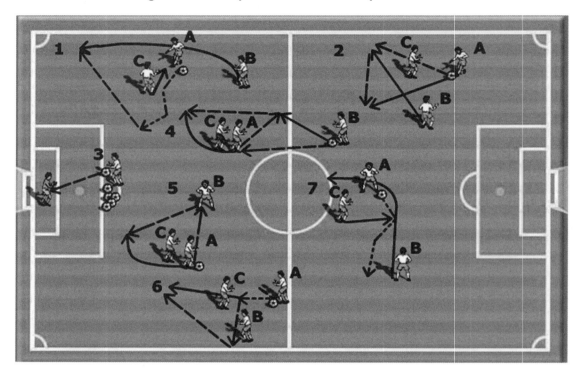

Diagram 23, page 110, shows several patterns of 2 versus 1 play being used to warm-up. A full field or half field is used for the players to create 2 versus 1 patterns as they warm-up. It is clear that all the patterns can be used including all the false 2 versus 1 patterns. Each group is numbered and an explanation of the pattern being used follows.

1) The three players in the upper left corner of this diagram, labeled number 1, use a False Curved Run that includes a dribble by the attacker past the defender. The dribbling attacker then plays the ball back in behind the defender that they had just beaten. The pass is to the player making the curved run that kept the run alive and was rewarded with the late pass. The pattern is one that can be witnessed in high level professional matches.

2) The group of three in the upper right corner of the grid, labeled number 2, an X Pattern from two passes.

3) The keeper is being worked out and warmed up by another player or coach in the goal box.

4) The group of three in the center of the field, labeled number 4, is working a Double Pass Pattern with a diagonal return pass.

5) The fourth group of three that is encroaching on the penalty box, labeled number 5, is using a Flick and Spin Pattern of play.

6) The group of three players located to the center and lower edge of the field, labeled number 6, are using a Wall Pass for their pattern.

7) The group of three players in the right part of the field, labeled group 7, is executing a False Curved Run.

Diagram 23 A: Rotation of Players for Groups of Three: Warm-Up

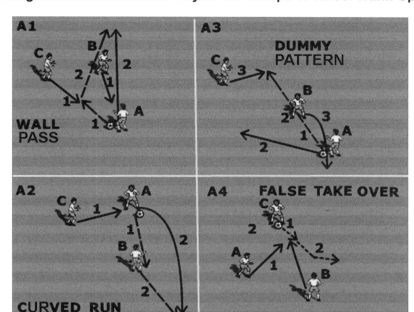

In Diagram 23 A, page 111, three players are rotating through the patterns. Each square shows the same three players changing roles and using different patterns to warm up. In section A1, a Wall Pass between players A and C is shown while player B plays the part of a low pressure defender. In section A2 player A has the ball and combines with player B for a Curved Run while player C takes the defenders' role. Section A3 shows all three players combining to create a Dummy sequence. In section A4 players A and C now combine for a False Take Over while player B becomes the defender again. Most likely in any next pattern players C and B would combine while A takes the role of the defender. The players in each group can make sure that everyone is working as the defender and that every one is getting the chance to work on 2 versus 1patterns.

Exercise 8: Lines of Four across a Grid
(Grid 10-15 x 15-20 yards)
(See Diagrams 24 A, 24 B, 24 C, 24 D, 24 E, 24 F, 24 G, 24 H and 24 I, pages 113, 114, 115, 116, 117, 118, 119,120 and 122.)

Keys to Exercise Eight

1) Start the exercise by using a total of eight players, four players facing each other on opposite sides of the grid. This would means that the two sides of the grid have 4 players each at the start of the exercise. The coach can use more but the repetition rate will drop down significantly. (See Diagram 24 A, page 113.)

2) Players must always continue across the grid in the direction they were going at the start of the exercise after each repetition is finished. This occurs whether the attack is successful or the attacking players lose the ball. This means that the attacking players end up on the side the defenders came from and the defenders ends up where the attackers started the exercise. Players always switch sides of the grid regardless of the outcome of the attack.

3) The ball always switches to the opposite side of the grid from one repetition to the

next. This means the ball must end up on the side of the grid that the defender came from to start the sequence. The ball ends up where the attackers end up whether the attack is successful or not. If the defender wins the ball they simple pass it to the grid line that they came from to start the movement. This causes everyone to get into a rotation that allows all players to play offense and all players to end up playing defense. (This is initially confusing to players.) (See Diagram 24 A and 24 B, pages 113 and 114.)

4) Two players from one side of the grid attack one defender coming out into the grid from the other side. The coach must encourage younger players or players with limited experience to use the patterns. Otherwise players will just make one well timed square pass and the receiving player will run the ball forward on the dribble. This is a good basic way to beat the opponent but not much use in teaching the 2 versus 1 patterns.

5) To encourage different patterns have the attacking players start from different areas in the grid. Have the support player start from the side, pushed up high in the grid, pushed up low in the grid or side by side with direct pressure on the player with the ball. This varying of the starting points for the attackers and the defender will allow for all the possible 2 versus 1 patterns. (See Diagrams 24 C, 24 D, 24 E, pages 116, 117 and 118.)

6) A good "first touch" is necessary to prepare the ball for the next move the attack wants to make.

7) Be sure to have plenty of extra balls available to keep the exercise flowing.

Variation Allowing 3 Attackers and 2 Defenders

8) Evolving the exercise to 3 versus 2 may mean a slightly bigger grid for less experienced or skillful players. If the players are skillful enough and understand the patterns well enough to use them quickly then the grid may not need to be adjusted. The coach must judge the skill level of the players to get the correct grid size.

9) Using 3 versus 2 means a higher work rate because it takes fewer repetitions before players must work again. The tactical lesson now is the need for the players to recognize where, when and how to create 2 versus 1 out of the 3 versus 2. (See Diagram 24 H, page 120.)

10) In a 3 versus 2 there are not quite enough players for left/right/split support but the basic concept of supporting shape can be addressed and that many of the runs that players make will be to supply support positions on the left, right or split positions.

11) Be careful not to let the attackers start to close together. They should be in realistic distances from each other at the start of each repetition. This does not mean that the attackers will not get close to each other in executing a pattern. Obviously a Take Over or False Take Over will require close proximity of the attacking players. It is also worth noting that the exact distance from one player to the next in not something that is set in concrete. The timing and spacing of each repetition will be a little different each time.

12) The coach should make sure that players display a good first touch.

13) The players will need to "sharpen" to help their teammates and set up possible 2 versus 1 patterns.

Diagram 24 A: Lines of Four: Rotation Example

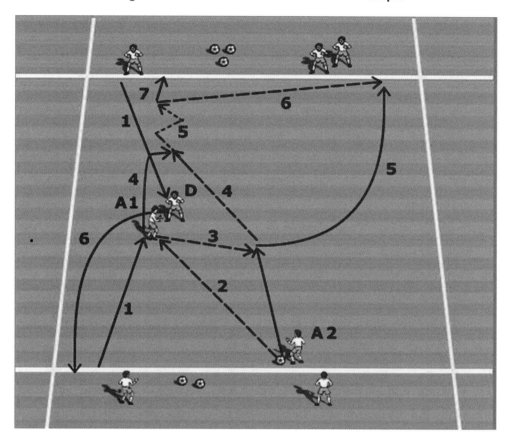

In the Diagram 24 A, page 113, the attacking players start at the bottom of the grid. Both attackers are labeled with an A1 and an A2. This exercise uses two attacking players against the one defender that stepped into the exercise from the upper edge of the grid. The defender is labeled with a D. The attackers use a Diagonal Double Pass pattern to commit the defender and then penetrate forward across the grid.

The attacker from the far left lower area, attacker A1 of the grid starts by pushing up high in the grid. The run is numbered as 1. As attacker A1 pushes up the field the defender runs forward, also numbered with a 1. The second attacker makes a pass to A1 which assures that the defender will commit to the attacker A1 who is receiving the ball. The pass is numbered with a 2. Attacker A2 then makes a run forward to a pass sent by A1 that is slightly backwards and diagonal. Both the run and the pass are numbered with a 3.

Attacker A1 now spins around the defender with a run numbered 4 and receives a pass from A2 in behind the defender. The pass is numbered with a 4. A1 dribbles towards the far end of the grid and then passes the ball to A2 who has made a run in wide support of the ball. The run to create wide support is numbered 5 and the dribble is numbered with a 5. The pass from A1 to A2 to finish the move is numbered with a 6. A1 reaches the grid line with a run numbered 7. All players must end up on the opposite side of the grid than they started from no matter the result of the attack. The defender leaves the grid with a run numbered 6.

Rotation Explanation:

No matter whether the outcome of the attack is successful or if it is a failure the attackers end up on the opposite side of the grid from where they started. The defender will also end up on the opposite side of the grid from where they started the exercise. The ball will now start on the side of the grid that the attackers were moving towards. In Diagram 24 A, page 113, the ball should end up on the lower edge of the grid. Another way to explain where the ball ends up is to tell the players that the ball must end up where the defender started. This rotation goes back and forth with the ball always starting on the opposite end of the grid from the last repetition.

This starting from opposite ends each time and the players ending up on opposite ends each time causes a rotation that will allow the players to be both attackers and defenders through-out the exercise. For some reason this is confusing to players at first. I believe that is because the players react as they would in a game. If a defender wins the ball in a game it should go in the direction the defender is moving towards. However, in this exercise the defender turns around after winning it and sends it back to the players on the edge of the grid that they just left. The Diagram 24 B, page 114, shows where the ball would start and how many players would be on each side after the first rotation from Diagram 24 A, page 113.

Diagram 24 B: Lines of Four: Player Alignment After First Rotation

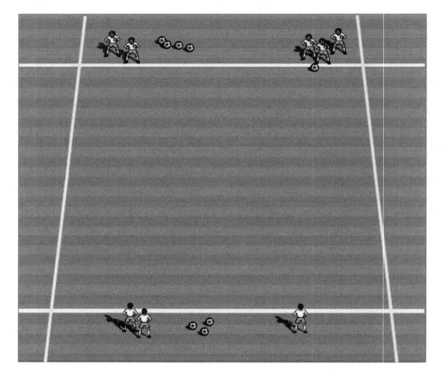

This Diagram, 24 B, page 114, shows what the start of the second repetition would look like after the exercises' first sequence is shown in diagram 24 A (See page 113.). In the direction that the attackers went, from the bottom of the grid to the top of the grid, there would now be five players on one side and in the direction that the defender went, top to bottom, there would be only three players. The attack now starts with the five players and a defender steps into the grid from the group with only three players. This rotation keeps the numbers balancing back and forth and allows all the players to end up playing offense and defense. It confuses players so be ready to be patient and prepared to restate the pattern for the repetitions more than once.

The next series of diagrams in the book show how the adjustment of the starting position for the supporting player will change the patterns that can be executed. In both the patterns diagramed the players have started wide of each other allowing the players to space apart from each other. This spacing allowed the Curved Run to occur.

Diagram 24 C: Starting One of the Attackers Higher in the Grid

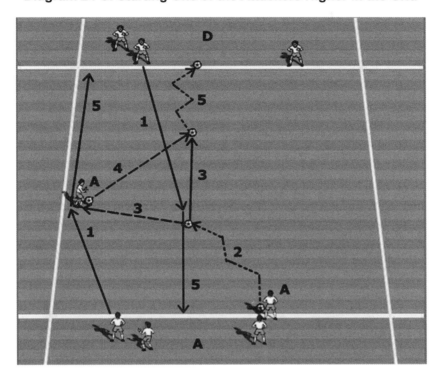

In Diagram 24 C, page 115, the attack starts from the bottom edge of the grid with the players marked with A's for attacker. This is not the first repetition for this exercise so one side, the one the defender comes from, has three players and the other side of the grid has five players to start. The side with five players is where the attack would start. Diagram 24 C, page 115, shows the attack starting from the bottom of the grid and the defense starting from the top of the grid.

One attacker has pushed up the grid and wide left to start the sequence. That attackers' run is numbered with a 1. The other attacker with the ball starts to dribble forward into the grid. The dribble is numbered 2. The defender steps into the grid and makes a run numbered 1 to deal with the attacker with the ball. As the defender runs to shut down the attacker with the ball the ball carrier lays off a pass, numbered 3, to the supporting attacker who sends it back in the form of a Wall Pass. The pass is numbered with a 4 and the run to get in behind the defender is numbered with a 3. The move is finished off as the attacker receiving the wall pass dribbles forward to the line. The dribble is numbered with a 5 and the run out of the grid by the supporting attacker is also numbered 5. The defender exits the grid with a run numbered 5. The sequence will put five players on the top of the grid and three on the bottom of the grid for the next repetition.

The most important reason for the exercise to have an attackers start up higher in the grid is that without this positioning it would not be possible to get a Wall Pass pattern positioned realistically. The pattern in the exercise needs to demand all the same decision making as the game would. The adjustment of starting positions so all the different 2 versus 1patterns created must be understood and done by the players. If they don't get the mixing of starting positions all that will happen is the same pattern(s) over and over again. The coach needs to have this insight so they can instruct the players if they are not adjusting positions to create varied patterns. This understanding of relative positioning is essential to the future recognition and proper use of 2 versus 1patterns within the complex flow of the match.

Diagram 24 D: Starting Up High: Double Pass Pattern with a Diagonal Pass Back

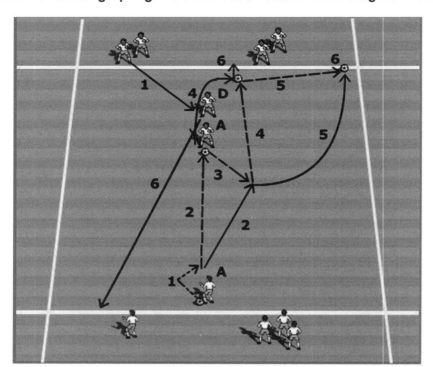

In Diagram 24 D, page 116, the first attacker is pushed up into a high position in the middle of the grid. The first pass by the attack forces the defender to mark the attacker pushed high in the grid. The attacker starting with the ball makes a dribble, numbered 1, and then a pass to their teammate which is numbered with a 2. The attacker then runs forward into a support position that requires a diagonal pass back. That run is numbered 2. The attacker receiving the first pass returns the ball diagonally with the pass numbered 3.

The next movement is for the attacker high in the grid to spin off in the opposite direction from the pass into the space behind the defender. This run is numbered with a 4, while the attacker in possession sends the third pass, numbered 4, straight forward to penetrate. The move is finished off by the supporting attacker making a wide curving run forward, numbered 5 and receiving the ball with the pass numbered 5. The runs numbered 6 are the attacker finishing their run to the end line and the defender switching across. In this example there are twelve players which means the attacking side started with seven and the defending side started with five. These larger numbers will make it possible for the exercise to expand to 3 versus 2 which will teach the players to find and exploit the 2 versus 1 within the larger group.

Remember that there is a second Double Pass Pattern to rehearse that has the visual cue of a straight pass back to the supporting attacker. This movement demands a different solution for the attacker being marked by the defender. The solution is to slide to one side or the other of the defender and open up a passing lane just wide enough to receive the pass but not so wide that the defender could gain time to recover when the pass is made by turning and running to pressure the attacker receiving the ball. The movement by the attacker that is high up on the grid should be with their chest to the defender so they can see the defender.

Diagram 24 E: Starting the Attacker High: Creating a Flick and Spin Wall Pass

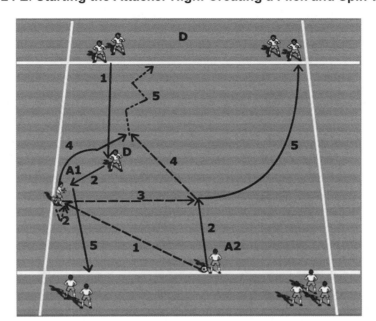

In Diagram 24 E, page 117, attacker A1 has pushed up high into the grid and attracted the defender into the area near them. The pass numbered 1 by attacker A2 pulls the defender into a tight marking position against attacker A1 who must shield the ball to keep possession. The run by the defender into pressure is marked with a 2.

Attacker A1 now shields the ball with a dribble numbered 2. The dribble is a slow movement back towards the grid line with the body of the attacker placed between the defender and the ball. During the time period that the ball is shielded attacker A2 makes a run, numbered 2, into a square position. Attacker A1 uses this support by sending a pass numbered 3 to attacker A2 and then spinning around the defender with a run numbered 4. The spin move is in the opposite direction from the pass so that the vision of the defender is split between the ball and the runner.

Attacker A2 sends a pass numbered 4 to attacker A1 who dribbles across the grid while attacker A2 makes a wide run to the end of the grid. Both the dribble and the run by the attackers are numbered with a 5. The defender moves across the grid once they see that the attack has been successful to the other side of the grid. That run is numbered with a 5. The ending numbers should be seven players on the top of the grid and five on the bottom.

Diagram 24 F: Curved Run Example

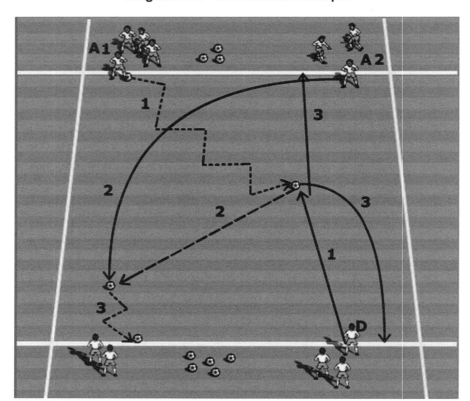

In Diagram 24 F, page 118, the attack starts from the top of the grid. It is a straight forward use of the Curved Run pattern. The attacker, A1, dribbles diagonally with the ball from left to right and attracts the defender to them in the middle of the grid. Both the dribble and the run to stop it by the defender are marked with a 1. The second attacker, A2, then makes a Curved Run out and around the attacker with the ball. The run is numbered with a 2. The attacker, A1, with the ball then sends a pass to the Curved Runner, A2, which is also numbered with a 2. The entire move is finished with a dribble by attacker A2, numbered with a 3, and a wide support run by A1, numbered with a 3 to the opposite side of the grid that the players started on. The defender leaves the grid with a run numbered 3 and ends up on the opposite side of the grid.

Diagram 24 G: X Pattern from Pass Example

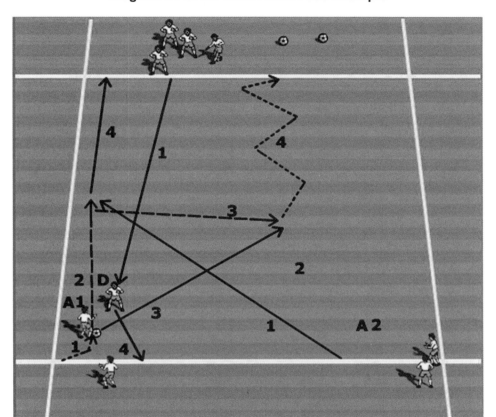

Diagram 24 G, page 119, looks a little ominous but is really just an X Pattern created with two passes. Attacker A1 starts by dribbling into the grid and attracting the defender. The attack is starting from the bottom of the grid and the defense starts from the top of the grid. The dribble by attacker A1 and the run to pressure it by the defender are both numbered 1. Attacker A2 starts a long diagonal run into the space behind the defender with a run numbered 1. Attacker A1 recognizes the run and plays the pass into the space in front of the run. The pass is numbered with a 2. Then attacker A1 makes a run numbered 3 into the space created by the run by attacker A2. Attacker A2 returns the ball with a pass to attacker A1 that is numbered with a 3. The whole pattern is finished with a dribble by A1 to the edge of the grid and a wide support run by A2 both of which are numbered with a 4. The defender exits the grid with a run numbered 4.

The diagrams above were a few examples of how to adjust the starting position to create the 2 versus 1 pattern that you want to use. There are many other choices. The coach merely needs to imagine how to create the other situations that should be rehearsed.

Variation Using 3 versus 2 to Find the 2 versus 1

Diagram 24 H: 3 versus 2 to Allow 2 versus 1 Patterns to be Isolated

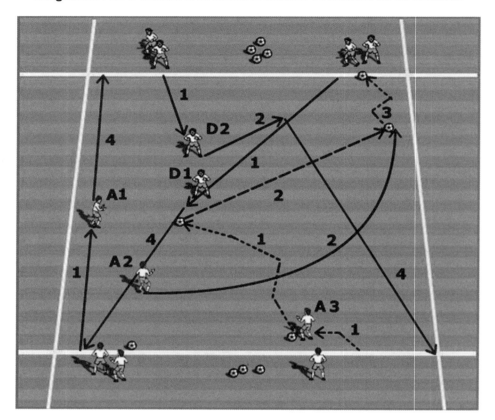

In Diagram 24 H, page 120, all the attackers are designated A1, A2 or A3. The defenders are designated D1 or D2. The attackers in Diagram 24 H, page 120, are starting from the lower edge of the grid. The defenders are starting on the top side of the grid. Defender D1 steps forward to challenge the attacker labeled A 3 who is dribbling the ball forward. The dribble by attacker A3 is numbered with a 1. This defending run is labeled with a 1, while the second defender stays static providing cover on the left. This is particularly intelligent decision by the defender because at this point both of the other attackers, A1 and A2, are on the left side of the grid. This situation causes the attackers to need to spread the defense by moving one of the attackers to the right side of the grid. This is done by attacker A2 with a Curved Run around attacker A3's dribble. The Curved Run by A2 is numbered with a 2. This run creates both a 2 versus 1 possibility on the right half of the grid with attackers A2 and A3 and a 2 versus 1 possibility on the left side of the grid with attackers A1 and A3.

The two attackers, A2 and A3, exploit the situation by combining for a Curved Run. The pass from A3 to A2 is numbered with a 2. The fact that there are now two possible 2 versus 1's temporarily freezes the second defender who makes a run to close down the Curved Run to late and makes the Curved Run pattern successful. The run by defender D2 is numbered with a 2. The movement is finished off with a dribble by A2, numbered 3. All the runs out of the grid to end the sequence are also numbered 4 for both the defenders and other attackers. Remember that the attackers move across the grid to end the sequence in the direction they were attacking and the defenders move across the grid to the opposite side they started the sequence on.

The exciting part of this exercise is that because of how the defenders react to each situation the game more closely resembles the kaleidoscope that the real game becomes for the players.

The fact that the defenders movements will vary and are not rehearsed makes the exercise dynamic. Each situation is different because of all the factors of the game; time, pressure, space, opponents, technical ability, tactical awareness, creativity; all come into play. Coaching and playing this exercise is both challenging and enjoyable.

Quite often it is best to freeze the play and ask questions of the players about the situation that they are in and what the best solutions might be for them to succeed. (This style of asking questions is referred in educational methodology as the **Socratic Method of Teaching).** The coach can use the freeze method, where the players are required to "freeze," stop all movement immediately and completely, the second the coach uses the word. Make sure that the players can look at the positioning exactly as it was when the coach asked for the play to freeze. The biggest issue with this method is how fast the players will freeze. A change in positioning will change what needed to be addressed. If players move or drift a little after the freeze command is given then be sure to get them back in the exact positions required to get an accurate picture. Then the coach can either ask questions to stimulate thought; the Socratic Method, or instruct the players personally to detail the solutions.

Studies suggest that the retention of information learned using the Socratic method of questioning that demands thought and participation by the players is significantly higher than when players are lectured by the coach. Of course the coach must use all three basic means of learning; **seeing, hearing and doing,** but the act of doing in conjunction with players thinking for themselves, seems to solidify information more effectively. One could argue that thinking is just an extension of the doing process.

In Diagram 24 H, page 120, both sides of the grid start with six players each. On the top half of the grid the reader can see four waiting players and two defenders entering the grid. On the bottom half of the grid the reader can see three waiting players and three attackers have entered the grid. This puts six players on each side of the grid at the start of the repetition.

Diagram 24 I, page 122, shows how after the first rotation of the exercise both the players and the ball would have moved to start the new rotation. The attacking side, which is now on the upper side of the grid, would have seven players. The defending side, now on the lower portion of the grid, would start with five. The ball would start this rotation on the upper half of the grid with the seven players, three of whom are preparing to attack. The next rotation would have the numbers back to even on each side of the grid at six and six with the ball starting on the lower end of the grid. This allows the players to rotate the roles of attacker and defender

With a little imagination from the coach this exercise can move to more complex forms. Here are a couple of suggestions:

1) The defending players can add a defender who stays on the line to stop penetration by the attackers. This forces attackers to continue supporting until the move is finished and replicates a covering defender thus complicating the decisions for the attackers. In essence that means that the game is 3 versus 3 with a condition that restricts the third defender.
2) More numbers can be used per rotation which gets the exercise closer to a small sided game.
3) The exercise can require a certain number of passes before penetrating to the end line.
4) The coach can end up having the exercise evolve into a small sided game where goals are scored by stopping the ball on the end line. The game can be directional and a team can score on only one end line or the team can turn and attack the other end of the grid so that possession of the ball is retained for the team with the ball when they score.

The coaches' imagination is the only limitation to how the exercise can be added to or evolved.

Diagram 24 I: Player Alignment: 3 versus 2: After First Player Rotation Example

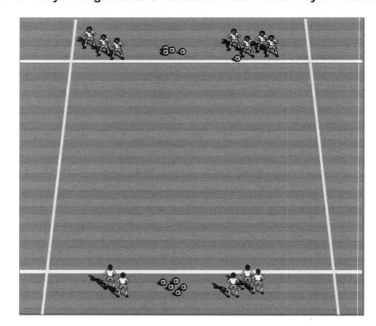

Diagram 24 I, page 122, shows that after starting the exercise with six players on each side of the grid the rotation of players will create seven on one side of the grid and five on the other. The attack will start on the side with seven players and defense will start on the side of the grid with five players. The rotation stays in the same pattern as it did for the 2 versus 1 rotation. (See explanation on pages 113 and 114.)

Exercise 9: Areas of the Field Exercises for the Patterns
(Grid size varies and this exercise can be seen as positional training.)

The variations for this exercise are almost endless. The point of these exercises is to set up the patterns in areas of the field where they may occur more often in an actual match. This book will just give a few examples and let the reader set up other situations as they see the need for the players and team.

Runs used on the flank (See Diagrams 25 A, 25 B, 25 C, 25 D, 25 E, 25 F, 25 F1 and 25 G, pages 125, 127, 128, 129, 130, 131, 132 and 133.)

Keys to Exercise Nine: Diagram 25 A: Curved Run on the Flank (page 125.)

1) The attacking player with the ball must clear the space for the curved runner with a diagonal dribble towards the interior of the field. (See Diagram 25 A, page 125, for a visual of all the following keys)
2) The curved run allows two things to occur:
   a) The ball can be released to the runner at anytime during the run if pressure on the ball gets to be too much. (This release of pressure is why the curved run is one of the safest 2 versus 1 patterns to use when building out of the back.)
   b) The curved run changes from a support run in its' early stages into a penetrating one that can threaten a defense. This penetration often leads to crossing situations; early serves, wide crosses, balls taken to the end line or penetration around the corner of the defense into the penalty box.

3) A hard lunge, body feint or dribbling move by the ball carrier that is made towards the interior of the field will help to open up an easy passing lane to the curved runner. The attacker carrying the ball with the diagonal dribble is getting threatening a penetrating position. Because the defender on the ball needs to respect penetration by the ball carrier towards the interior of the field or towards the goal they must move into the interior of the field with the attacker carrying the ball before they can react to the runner on the flank.

4) The dribble is diagonal for three reasons.

    a) The diagonal dribble allows the curved runner to catch up to the play. A dribble that is straight down the field or uncontested will rarely get caught by a teammates' run from behind.

    b) The diagonal dribble forces the defense to compact centrally in response to the ball movement towards the inside of the field and towards the goal. This dribbling by the player with the ball opens a lane of space out wide on the flank for the curved runner to exploit.

    c) A diagonal dribble only challenges the edge of the 180 degree line that defenders must protect attackers from penetrating through to reach goal. If the ball is dribbled with the top foot away from the defender the dribble is being carried through the edge of the 180 degree defender's line of defense and through the 360 degrees that the attacker has to exploit when controlling or dribbling a ball. This toying along the edge of the 180 degrees that a defender must prevent penetration through makes it difficult for the defender to dispossess the attacker without over committing. Over committing by the defender to winning the ball from the diagonal dribble can lead to the defender being beaten and to potential disaster in the organization of a teams' defense.

5) If the defender of the ball fails to protect the interior of the field from the dribble, the dribbler can penetrate to the interior of the field at will. As the defense either recovers to pressure the ball or rearranges to pressure the ball there is a second option to use the curved runner. It is playing a late pass to the supporting attacker making the curved run. This is done by splitting the defender just beaten and the defender that will step up to challenge the dribbler. This pass is across the grain of the dribble to the runner outside. This split pass back outside to the runner is a thing of beauty that usually leaves two defenders in poor position to protect the team from penetration down the flank by the attacker making the curved run.

6) Combination play can easily occur in this situation. The attacker dribbling to clear space for the curved runner can make a pass to a supporting player in the central area of the field. That central player can then send a second pass back out to the curved runner. This is the cooperation of three players to use the initial 2 versus 1pattern.

7) When this exercise is set up on the flank in the attacking third of the field it replicates a game situation that should allow flank service to central attackers to occur. Using the specific players that will try this pattern in the game will familiarize the players with their roles and the variations that can occur. This is referred to as Functional training.

8) Players that receive the ball on the flank can also look for 2 versus 1patterns with other attacking players or the initial dribbling attacker that penetrates the penalty box.

9) The coach can set up strikers to be in the penalty box to get crosses from the penetration and practice finishing with a central midfielder who after supplying support for passes to the interior can make a late run into the box to supply a third shooting option. The flank should look to cross to any of three options; near post, far post and to the top of the box, sometimes referred to as a trailer.

10) The coach can also set up the situations to penetrate the penalty box with diagonal dribbles from the flank and using their fellow attackers to execute 2 versus 1patterns that will end with shots on goal.

11) The coach is now evolving the 2 versus 1 situation starting with a possible Curved Run into a replication of the game and some of it's' myriad and kaleidoscopic possibilities.

12) If finishing is executed after the Curved Run then the quality of the cross and the timing of

the runs should receive attention as well as the 2 versus 1 pattern.

13) If diagonal runs and other 2 versus 1patterns are being used then the coach will need to replicate the environment that the attacking players will confront from a defense within a game. The coach must allow enough success for the attackers to learn and believe in the patterns. This will mean that there will be fewer numbers of defenders than in a normal match or that there are special conditions that will restrict the defenders from full pressure once attackers have learned how, what, where and when 2 versus1patterns can be used around the box then full pressure should be used.

13) The coach should be sure to point out the role(s) that the attacker who was dribbling and then initially passes the ball to the flank runner can take after releasing the ball. There are essentially four choices:

a) "Sharpen" to support the ball and provide a back pass.

b) The attacker can move into a position where they can shoot the ball on goal if the flank runner penetrates to the end line and can drop the ball back. Sometimes this is called a "trailer" position. In the left/right/split support structure it would be the left support position if the run is on the right flank and the right support position if the run is on the left flank.

c) The attacker can take up a position in the field that will both support the attack in general and be immediately useful to winning the ball back if possession is lost. This is often the same as "sharpening" for a pass behind the attacker with the ball but it could be a more centrally located position that allows a split pass backwards into the interior of the field.

d) The attacker can look to create additional 2 versus 1patterns with the flank attacker. This could be Wall Passes, a second Curved Run, Diagonal Runs to the outside of the field, a Straight Run looking for a Diagonal pass are a few of the possibilities. The list is almost endless and relies mostly on the understanding by the attackers of the physical relationship of the attackers to the defenders and the space available that is in the immediate area. The technical ability of the attackers is also critical to the ability of the players to exploit the space and their understanding level of the tactics available.

14)A good "first touch" is necessary to prepare the ball for the next move the attack wants to make.

15)Be sure to have plenty of extra balls available to keep the exercise flowing.

Diagram 25 A: Curved Run on the Flank with Finishing

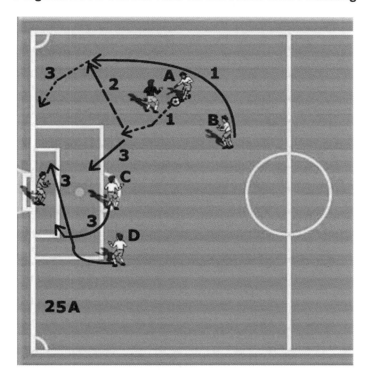

In Diagram 25 A, page 125, the wide flank attacker A dribbles the ball towards the edge of the box. The dribble is numbered with a 1. The attacker from the midfield, attacker B, makes a Curved Run out and around their teammate which is also numbered with a 1. The dribbling attacker then makes a pass to the attacker curving around them. The pass is numbered with a 2. The curving attacker then makes a short dribble numbered with a 3 and prepares to make a cross into the box for any of the attackers, C, D or A to finish. Runs into shooting positions by attacker C, D and A are all numbered with a 3. Attacker D makes a near post run, attacker C makes a far post run and attacker A makes a trailing run that are all numbered 3 as they get ready for the cross from attacker B.

Keys to Exercise Nine: Diagram 25 B (page 127)

The use of two Wall Passes with attackers in central positions allows the flank attacker to move towards the top of the penalty box. The movement does not have to have two wall passes but the flank runner running thirty plus yard with just one wall pass is not realistic to penetrating a compact zonal defense. (See Diagram 25 B, page 127, for all the following keys.)

1) The Wall Pass pattern selected to move the flank attacker into the center of the field is not something that is set in stone. The coach needs to provide different positioning of the supporting attackers so the player making the run from the flank will see different possible solutions to any situation.
2) The run by the flank player takes a diagonal path. This causes the same dilemma for the defenders that the diagonal dribble did in the Curved Run. The run slides across the 180 degree line that the defender is trying to prevent penetration through while the attacker is using the full 360 degrees in which they can carry the ball forward.
3) If the defender of the ball fails to protect the interior of the field from the run and the runner penetrates to the interior it will force the defense to reorganize and in the reorganization be vulnerable to penetration.
4) Combination play can easily occur in this situation. (Combination Play is defined in this book as using more than two players to execute a pattern.)

5) When this exercise is set up on the flank in the attacking third of the field it replicates a game situation that allows flank players to combine with strikers and/or central midfielders to create scoring opportunities using Wall Passing.

6) Shooting opportunities for the striker and flank players' combination can be augmented with drop passes back to oncoming central midfielders that create shooting opportunities. (The central midfielder does not have to shoot. They can slip the ball back into the flank runner or striker and create combination play.)

7) The coach is now evolving the 2 versus 1 situation into a replication of the game and some of it's' possibilities. The more the players can imagine and experience the more fluid and creative the team becomes.

8) If finishing is executed at the end of the exercise, and it should be, then the quality of the pass that allows a first time shot at goal should be emphasized. It is hard to shoot a ball that is placed directly into the players' feet. A ball placed outside of the body allows the player striking the ball to use the movement of opening and closing their hips to provide maximum power. If the ball is placed right under the body of the shooter there are three simple technical solutions.

    a) One is to slice across the ball with the outside of the foot which will create a fair amount of power which will cause a bending of the ball. The advantage of this shot is that it can go out and around the keeper thus avoiding the necessity of maximum power.

    b) The second technical choice is to "snap" the shot from a quick knee movement. This does not maximize power but it does have some quickness to the release of the shot. Timing the strike is critical because hitting it to soon will cause it to rise. Having the foot follow through the ball and metaphorically through to the net also helps create a technique that keeps the ball down. A collogue of mine used the saying; "Foot follow ball;" to describe the motion.

    c) The third technical choice is to toe poke the ball. While frowned on by many coaches, this choice tends to upset the timing of the keeper because the shot comes a little earlier than usual and it tends to have a fair amount of velocity. Personally, I never chide my players for scoring a goal with this option.

9) A good "first touch" is necessary to prepare the ball for the next move the attack wants to make.

10) Be sure to have plenty of extra balls available to keep the exercise flowing.

11) The False Wall pattern in shown in Diagram 25 C (page 128) to emphasize that players can use both the completed form and the threatened form of the 2 versus 1 pattern to be successful.

Diagram 25 B: Diagonal Wall Passing with Finishing 1

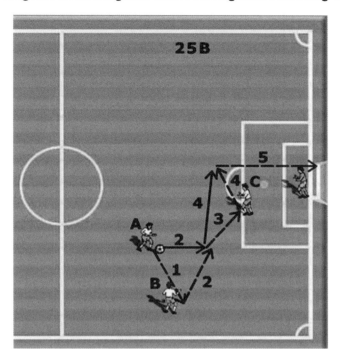

Diagram 25 B, page 127, is a series of two wall passes. The first Wall Pass uses the midfielder in the interior of the field and the second Wall Pass combines with the striker in front of them. This allows attacker A to penetrate into a shooting position at the top of the box. The central midfielder, labeled A, makes the first pass, numbered 1, and makes a run numbered 2. Attacker B returns the ball with a pass numbered 2. A second Wall Pass Pattern is used when the central attacker A sends a pass labeled 3 to the striker, labeled C, at the top of the box. Attacker A makes a diagonal run across the top of the defense with a run numbered 4. The return pass from the striker C to the attacker A is labeled 4 and the shot on goal is labeled 5.

The whole sequence could have started with attacker B using attacker A to start the wall pass and then made the same kind of penetration with their run into the middle of the field. That is the beauty of 2 versus 1 patterns because they can be used in a myriad of ways by a myriad of players it is critical to teach the patterns and then let experience and guidance teach the players where they might find the patterns useful.

The coach should try to create these situations in practice to let the players understand the possibilities. However, the match will force variations based on distance, speed, defenders positioning, teammates' attributes, exact positioning on the field and other variables that will only be a replication of the patterns practiced not an exact duplication. The key issue is that the patterns are appearing in areas of the field where they may be replicated in matches. The coach needs to remember that each situation will always have its' own nuances. Even when all the chips for the patterns are known by the players and coach what they will look like in each instance will be spun into its' own kaleidoscopic forms to create their own beautiful and individual form.

Diagram 25 C: Diagonal Wall Passing Using a False Wall with Finishing 2

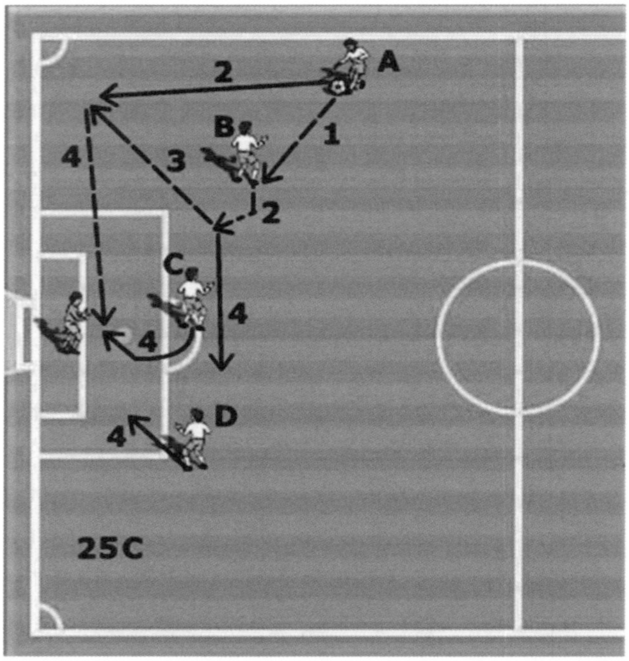

25C

In Diagram 25 C, page 128, the wide attacker A sends a pass to the striker B and makes a run forward that appears to create a Wall Passing opportunity. The pass by attacker A is numbered with a 1 and the run is numbered with a 2. Instead of immediately returning the pass the striker, attacker B, uses the False Wall option to roll away from the runner, dribble to the inside and then lay off a late pass to attacker A on the flank. The dribble by striker B is numbered with a 2 and the late pass to attacker A is numbered with a 3. Attacker D makes a short far post run numbered 4; attacker C makes a near post run numbered 4 and striker B makes a run, numbered 4, to the top of the box to help frame the goal mouth for the cross made by attacker A that is numbered with a 4. In this case the cross is met by attacker C at the near post.

It is easy to see that this level of the exercise is with no pressure. The coach can and must start raising the levels of training pressure as players show better understanding of their options. Limited pressure of a passive or semi-passive defender can be added. Then raise the level again where a defender may interfere but will allow the play to reach the desired result. Then the defender can steal the ball and disrupt the play. Lastly, the defender can steal the ball with a counter-attack objective which will force the attackers to transition to defense to win the ball back just as they would in a game.

As the coach adds supporting player(s) for the defenders or attackers and the exercise becomes more and more game like at each step. Add supporting interior midfielders who can either allow back passes to relieve pressure or to make penetrating runs that make defending the situation more difficult. The coach can add strikers to provide passing and finishing options. Add wide players on the opposite side of the field to switch the point of attack or to cross to for far post finishing and the exercise takes another step towards match conditions. Unfortunately, nothing will exactly replicate the pressure and speed of the match. But from this simple start the coach can end up complicating the training environment until it replicates the game as closely as is possible. Nothing will replicate the speed, pressure, focus and demands of a game except the game itself.

Diagram 25 D: Flank Play with Finishing 3

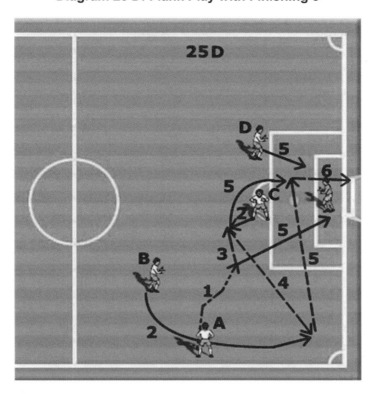

In Diagram 25 D, page 129, the reader can see the 2 versus 1 Curved Run pattern being expanded into a combination play using a striker, player C, to provide support and then a "delayed" pass to the overlapping player, A.

Attacker A dribbles in from the flank which is numbered with a 1 while attacker B curves around attacker A with a run numbered 2. Attacker C makes a short run, numbered 2, to make them self available to attacker A, who then passes to attacker C with a pass numbered 3. Attacker C sends a pass out to attacker B that is numbered 4 which allows the original 2 verses 1 Curved Run pattern to be completed by using three players combining.

Players B and C then make runs, labeled 5, into the box as quickly as possible to finish a shot from a cross from player B numbered 5. Player D also makes a short far post run numbered 5. The cross is finished by player C with a shot labeled 6. The same issues of creating more and more defensive pressure should apply in this situation also.

This use of combination play could be required in the game because:
   a) The immediate pass to player B is blocked by a defender in the passing lane between player B and A.
   b) The space that player A is trying to create is not sufficient for a return pass and by playing the ball first to the interior it forces the defenders to compact to the interior of the field thus opening the flank space more completely for a return pass to player A.
   c) The striker sees that the tactical situation to get other teammates into the penalty area to score requires more time for other attackers to get into effective scoring positions.

There may be other reasons to use the combination play but these are a few of the possible reasons to delay the direct pass back and include a third person in the attack through the flank.

Diagram 25 E: Flank Play with Finishing 4

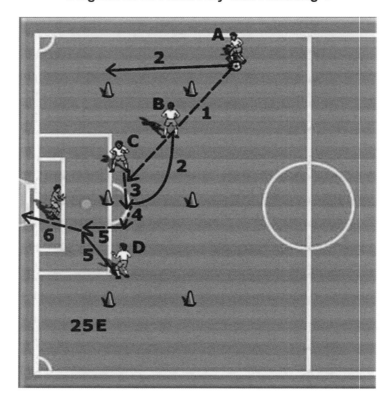

Diagram 25 E, page 130, is coned out so that spacing can be conceptualized. The cones do not necessarily mean that the players must stay in them. In this example attacker A in the top flank position starts the exercise. Attacker A plays a pass to attacker B, the pass is numbered with a 1. Attacker A then makes a run that threatens penetration with a Wall Pass that is numbered with a 2. Attacker B uses a Dummy Pattern to let the ball run to attacker C and then makes a Curved Run around attacker C that is numbered with a 2. Attacker C then pushes off a pass to attacker B that is numbered with a 3. Attacker B makes a short dribble numbered 4 and then sends a Straight Pass to a Diagonal Run to attacker D. Both the run and the pass are numbered with a 5. The shot by attacker D is numbered with a 6. This sequence is just one of thousands of permutations of four decisions possible.

Diagram 25 F: Adding a Defender to Force Accurate and Intelligent Crossing

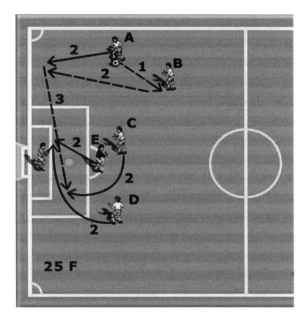

Diagram 25 F, page 131, uses two strikers for finishing work with one defender to cover them. The coach can start to perfect the art of accurate crossing by wide players while practicing 2 versus 1patterns on the flank. In this diagram player A starts the sequence by passing to player B and using a High Wall Pass pattern on the flank. The pass by player A is numbered with a 1 and the run by player A is numbered with a 2. Player A then runs forward to receive the High Wall Pass. Player A then sends in a cross to players C or D who have made runs into scoring positions in the box. The runs by players C and D are numbered with a 2. The use of one defender to mark one out of two attackers starts the process of forcing the flank server to look for who is open and what kind of pass should be sent in to accomplish the task. In this case the defender, E closes attacker C at the near post so the flank player A should pick out the serve to the far post runner. The cross by attacker A into the far post is numbered with a 3.

Diagram 25 F1: Adding Defenders to Get Accurate and Correct Crossing Decisions

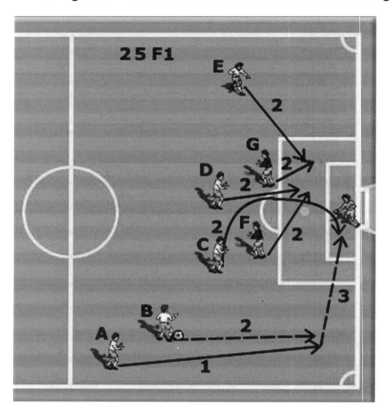

Diagram 25 F1, page 132, has the same concept in mind about picking out the correct runner with the crossing pass. Attacker B is Overlapped by attacker A. The run by attacker A is numbered with a
1 and the pass to attacker A from attacker B is numbered with a 2. (The effect is the same as a Curved Run but the run by the defender A is straight forward to a slow moving or static attacker B. Thus the pattern is referred to as an overlap and not a Curved Run.) There are three attacking players, C, D and E, making runs into the box and only two defenders to mark them, players F and G. Attackers C, D and E all make runs into the box that are numbered with 2's. Defender F marks attacker D and defender G marks attacker E which will leave attacker C making the run to the near post open. Attacker A selects that option and serves a pass numbered 3 to get the ball into scoring position. Once a player has made a penetration behind the defense they must learn to look quickly for their options and then pick out the correct tactical choice. In addition, once the tactical choice is made the player must be able to both select the correct technical choice and technically execute the choice or all is lost. Coaches can never lose sight of the mantra: "technique, technique, technique."

Diagram 25 G: Flank Play Complicated by Multiple Attackers with Finishing

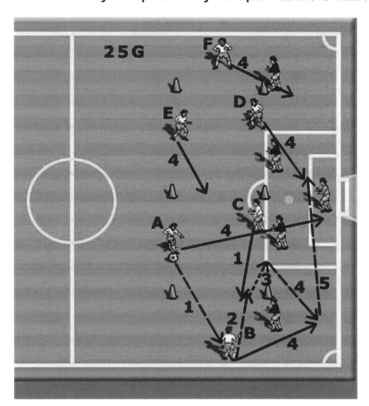

Diagram 25 G, page 133, starts with attacker A passing the ball out to attacker B on the flank. The pass is numbered with a 1. Since there are only four defenders and the goal keeper against six attackers there should be ample opportunities for 2 versus 1 patterns to occur and scoring chances to be taken.

Next attacker C moves to support the pass with a run towards attacker B that is numbered with a1. Attacker B gives a pass to attacker C who uses a False Wall Pass to turn and dribble inside. Since attacker C now will encounter one of the center backs a late pass is made to attacker B who has made a run forward in a Wall Pass pattern that is numbered with a 4. The pass from attacker C to attacker B is also numbered with a 4 because the actions are almost simultaneous.

At this point all the other attackers; A, E, D and F are making runs to frame the goal and get into scoring position for the expected cross from attacker B. All the runs by attackers A, E, D and F are numbered with a 4. The cross is sent in by attacker B and is numbered with a 5 where it is met by attacker D at the far post area.

The area is coned out so that there won't be more than two attackers in a zone at one time. There should also be no more than one defender in a grid. This will allow 2 versus 1 patterns to emerge in any one of the zones.

The defense should be able to build the ball out to the coach or some small goals and if the attack fails to shoot but stays in play the sequence should continue. A new ball is introduced when the ball is scored, shot out of bounds or the defense effectively clears the ball in any manner that the coach asks them to do.

Review of the Keys for the X Pattern

1) The ball must be played a little early into the path of the runner who is making a diagonal run. It is frequently a run that comes out of the middle towards the outside with a diagonal run but there is no reason for the run to go from the outside to the inside. The first pass should arrive on the runners' hip.

2) The X Pattern can also be created by an attacker dribbling the ball diagonally and having the second attacker cross in behind dribbler in the space that the dribbling attacker just vacated.

3) A pass to the runner should be paced to create a shielding motion between the attacker receiving the ball and the defender tracking them.

4) The return pass is made backwards into the space that the runner has just vacated. The space that the runner is vacating is usually centrally located although that is not set in stone. It is most effective if the run or dribble empties the space centrally so that the second runner is attacking that central space with their run and hopefully into a defense that is temporarily disorganized by the first attackers run.

5) The return pass can be made several different ways but the quickest is with the top foot with an outside of the foot flick. This skill requires flexibility in the ankle and hip.

6) Another move that is effective is for the attacker making a diagonal dribble with the ball to stop and leave the ball by stepping on the ball and leaving it for the runner coming in behind. This move requires that the momentum of the defender marking the dribbling attacker be fast enough that they can not stop and back track to defend the ball before the second attacker arrives.

7) The attacker that makes the initial pass will run diagonally into the space just vacated by their teammate. This will make an X on the ground when their diagonal runs cross each other. The run is the same for the second attacker for the diagonal dribble use of the pattern.

8) This pattern can often be used in the midfield, is most often used in the attacking third but is rarely used in the defensive third of the field. Where it is most impressive and explosive is inside the penalty box as shown in the following Diagram 26 A and 26 B, page 135. The use of this pattern often leads to scoring opportunities. In 26 A, page 135, the use of a diagonal dribble is shown with the second attacker running over the space just vacated by the attacker carrying the ball. In Diagram 26 B, page 135 the use of the pass and return pass that creates the pattern is shown.

9) A good "first touch" is necessary to prepare the ball for the next move the attack wants to make.

10) Be sure to have plenty of extra balls available to keep the exercise flowing.

Diagram 26 A: X Patterns from the Dribble and 26 B X Pattern from the Pass

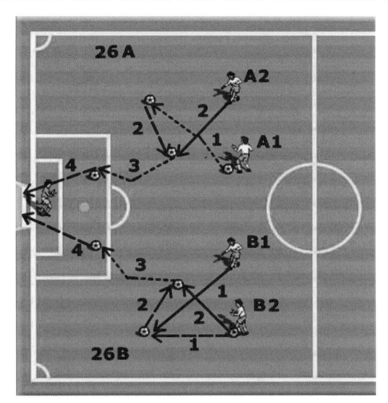

The top half of the Diagram is 26 A, page 135. The reader can see an X Pattern that is initiated by the attacking player labeled A1 by dribbling the ball diagonally. The diagonal dribble is numbered 1. The player labeled A2 crossing over the top of the dribble just made by player A1. The Run by A2 is numbered with a 2. Player A2 then receives a pass, numbered 2, from player A1 back into the space that was just created by the dribble and into the path of the run by A2. A2 then dribbles to goal which is numbered with a 3 and then shoots at goal which is numbered with a 4.

In the bottom half of the Diagram is 26 B, page 135, the reader can see the X Pattern is initiated by player B2 passing to player B1 who has made a diagonal run out in front of player B2. The run by player B1 is numbered with a 1 and the pass by B2 is numbered with a 1. Player B2 then cuts across the diagonal run made by player B1 creating the X on the ground. The run by B2 is numbered with a 2. Player B2 then receives a pass, numbered with a 2, from player B1 in the space that was just created behind the run. The pattern is finished with a dribble by player B2, numbered with a 3 and finished with a shot on goal numbered 4.

Exercise 10: 2 versus 1 with No Pressure, Limited Pressure, Three Quarters Pressure and Full Pressure
(Grid 10-15 x 10-20 yards)
(See Diagram 27, page 137)

Keys to Exercise 10

1) Set up a grid size needed for the players to succeed at an approximate 80 % to 100% rate with room enough for the 2 versus 1 pattern. This will vary from age group to age

group and from skill level to skill level. Only the coach can determine the correct size and this will come from experience and experimentation. A minimum size of 8 to 10 yards is generally the smallest players can handle. (Don't be afraid to stop the exercise and reset the boundaries if the exercise isn't working correctly)

2) If the players have mastered the pattern and can move through it with nearly perfect execution the players may get bored. Have a scoring target for the players to work towards or the effort will fall short of what is needed to get better. The players will lose interest. The coach can award points for success of the desired work, set up a small goal or a large goal or use stopping the ball on an end line to score a point. This point is emphasized to make sure that the coach is aware that players need external goals or motivation to work hard at the required exercise.

3) The reason for this exercise being in the book is to make clear that there are stages to take the players through before they can see and play the tactical situations at game speed. There are three parts to manipulating pressure; time, space and opponent(s). The following are generally accepted steps for increasing pressure on the players through out an exercise's evolution in speed and complexity.

    a) No pressure (Time and space are always present but no opponent is used at this point in teaching the material)

    b) Limited pressure (Defender(s) just move through the exercise to show attackers the visual cues they will run into when the material picks up speed)

    c) Half or three quarters pressure (Defenders may touch or take the ball **if there is a mistake** made by the attackers)

    d) Unlimited pressure (Defender(s) can take away the ball and should have a scoring opportunity themselves of some kind. Examples include but are not limited to, an incentive of starting an attack the other way; passing the ball to the new set of attackers, passing the ball to the coach or target player, attack a small goal of their own, counter-attack to the opposite end line, are a few examples)

4) The coach can up the level of pressure in the situation by adjusting any of the three basic elements to pressure, space, time or opponents. Once an exercise is understood then adding the complexity of more defenders; a 3 versus 2 changing to a 2 versus 2 situation for example, will start to demand both attackers to make decisions about when, where and how to pass the ball without having an extra attacker. The coach providing more opponents or evening up the number of attackers to defenders complicates the visual cues that the attacker receiving the ball must use to make a good decision with the ball. Just having the direct pressure from a defender applied to the attacker as they receive the pass forces passes to be timed accurately and paced properly. In addition a second defender can cause the pattern to become untenable and new choices will have to be made to retain procession or to continue to penetrate the defense. Without these additional complexities the players will learn to be robotic and fail to adjust their game according to what they can take from the oppositions' positioning or how they, as attackers, might need to adjust to be successful. Creating a smaller space will also up the level of pressure as will putting on the pressure of time limits.

5) Ending this series of exercises with a small group game to large goals is beneficial and enjoyable for the players. Awarding points for using the 2 versus 1patterns learned or practiced prior to the small game will encourage the players to use the patterns. Not letting a team shoot at goal until a certain number of patterns have been executed helps to encourage the players to use the patterns. The coach can instruct the players by stopping play long enough to show what was worked on and how it could have been used during the exercise. Methodology Note: Stick to correcting or demonstrating what has been emphasized during this particular practice or in the practice before. If the coach stops to correct and show everything in the book of soccer this will:

    a) drive your players to distraction

    b) lose the focus of the lesson

    c) disrupt the flow of the exercise so much that nothing is

accomplished

Remember, doing is the most powerful form of learning for most people.

6) Be sure to have plenty of extra balls available to keep the exercise flowing.
7) A good "first touch" is necessary to prepare the ball for the next move the attack wants to make.
8) Coaches should be aware that there are three ways to increase or decrease pressure in an exercise. The three elements to be manipulated are: **Time, Space and Opponents.**

Diagram 27: Levels of Pressure

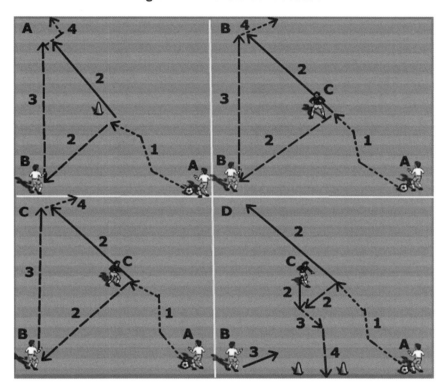

In Diagram 27, page 137, Square A shows there is no pressure on the attackers while they learn the timing of the High Wall Pass. The cone in the middle of the grid takes the place of the defender. Since the cone can not steal the ball only time and space will pressure the attackers. Player A dribbles diagonally, numbered with a 1, at the cone. Then player A sends the ball back up field to player B with a pass numbered 2 and makes a run in behind the cone with a run numbered 2. Player B returns the ball with a pass numbered 3 and player A finishes the attack by reaching the line with a dribble numbered 4.

In Square B the defender is told to go through the motions of defending, limited pressure, but to allow the High Wall Pass to occur. The speed of the defender is about half pace. All the dribbling, passing and running sequences are the same. The defender is there just to let the attackers know what the timing of the pass and run will be as the tempo steps up.

In Square C the defender is told to put on pressure at about three quarters pace and if they can touch the ball they are allowed to do so to let the attackers learn that their timing was flawed. If the defender steals the ball they give the ball back to the attackers. All the dribbling, passing and running sequences are the same as in the other squares.

In Square D the defender is allowed to steal the ball away from the attackers and counter-attack. (See keys to the exercise, point number 3, section d) (See Diagram 27 Square D, page 137) The sequence in Square D starts with attacker A dribbling towards the defender with a dribble numbered 1. But when player A tries to make the pass numbered 2 back up field the defender intercepts it and dribbles forward which is numbered with a 3 and passes the ball through the counter attack goal with a pass numbered 4.

What should now be introduced are small sided games that bring the topic to game speed for the players. This can be done with even numbers or with "Plus" players to lessen the pressure a little. Remember, the concept of a "Plus" player, generally a player(s) that plays for the team with the ball is just a manipulation of pressure using time, space and opponents. In this case a "Plus" player lessens the number of opponents to attackers and lessens the pressure.

Exercise 10 is extremely important information regarding how to progress an exercise from the basic stages through to game speed at a fundamental level of play. It is important to remember that exercise speed is still slower than match speed which can only be replicated by playing real matches. All coaches should have the three components of increasing and decreasing pressure at their finger tips. Manipulating the pressure levels of time, space and opponent(s) is critical to achieving a learning environment that maximizes growth.

A quick aside on methodology might help coaching effectiveness dramatically. Most coaches understand the fundamental levels of a skill or tactic. What gets lost in the translation is the ability of the players to integrate the knowledge into the game itself. The awarding of points inside of a game is a critical half step to using the knowledge learned in the match itself. This is called giving a condition that is rewarded for the behavior desired. Conditioned games are the critical link between structured exercises that teach a concept and learning to use the concept in the game itself.

Finally there is the last level of scrimmaging or playing small sided games where the coach encourages the material to be used and shows positive reactions when the material is used but does not use the awarding of points to reinforce the concepts. This is when the players make the information their own and internalize the concepts into a more normalized use.
Remember that the first part of learning is inside the left brain and is not holistic in nature. It is not until the information is ingrained enough that the player can use the information holistically; a right brain function, that the use of a concept becomes fluid. I often tell the coaches I work with that it will take at least 9 months for knowledge to become fluid and useful to players inside of matches. If one looks at the different abilities of the sides of the brain it is clear that introductory levels of information for soccer will be more likely used in the left hemisphere and spatial awareness and pattern use is a right hemisphere process. To get the whole brain understanding and using the information is a complex process demanding time.

The USSF currently defines this same set of principles of methodology using the terms Unrestricted Space, Restricted Space, One Goal with Counter and Two Goals for tactical teaching. For technique they use the terms Fundamental, Match Related and Match Conditions. It is important to note that there is a progression from a simple form to a complex form of teaching information to players. This is true for how much pressure the coach puts on the player(s) as they progress to the pressure of a match.

Functions associated with hemispheric dominance include:

Right Hemispheric Functions:

- Connected to left side of the body
- Integrates many inputs at once
- Processes information more diffusely and simultaneously

- Deals with space
- Responsible for gestures, facial movements, and body language

Left Hemispheric Functions:

- Responsible for relational and Connected to right side
- of body
- Deals with inputs one at a time
- Processes information in a linear and sequential manner
- Deals with time
- Responsible for verbal
- expression and language
- Responsible for invariable and arithmetic operations

Left Hemisphere

o Mathematical Operations
o Specializes in recognizing places, faces, objects and music
o Does Intuitive and Holistic Thinking
o The Seat of Passion and Dreams
o Crucial side for Artists, Craftsman and Musicians

Right Hemisphere

o Specializes in Recognizing Words and Numbers
o Does Logical and Analytical Thinking
o The Seat of Reason
o Crucial Side for Wordsmiths and Engineers

Left Side Processes

❖ Speech
❖ Analysis
❖ Time
❖ Sequence

Right Side Processes

❖ Creativity
❖ Patterns
❖ Spatial Awareness
❖ Content

Another crucial coaching point to remember in all teaching situations is that an entire shopping list will not be remembered. The brain can not absorb and integrate too much information all at once in a short period of time. If the reader verbally tells someone to go buy two or three items at the store they will be likely to remember and bring them back. If the reader gives the same person an entire list of 15 items or more all at once they will not remember much of it at all. Teaching is one to three blocks at a time. This is why it takes years to develop as a complete player with the entire list memorized, internalized and at their toe tips to command. It is why we value the creative player who sees the game holistically with all of the tools, tactical and technical that the shopping list can have on it. It is critical that the coach understand that it is a long process to get this fundamental understanding of the skill or tactic into proficient use in small games, scrimmages and full matches.

Exercise 11: Switching Grids to release 2 versus 1's (Grid 35-70 x 50-85 yards)
(See Diagram 28, 28 A, 28 B, 28 C, pages 141, 142, 143 and 144.)

Keys to Exercise Eleven

1) Divide the width of the field into four vertical strips headed towards large goals. The width of each strip will vary according to the width of the entire exercise. The time length of the game will depend on what the coach is doing, the skill level and age group the coach is working with at the time. The strips are artificial but will let 2 verses 1 situations develop by restricting defenders to just their strip of territory.
2) Put a defender in each strip.
3) Put an attacker in each strip.
4) Have one or two free central midfielder that is not assigned any particular strip. This makes the game 5 or 6 attackers verses 4 defenders and a goal keeper.
5) Attackers can move from area to area but can not have more than two in any one grid strip at a time.
6) There does not need to be a large goal to attack but it is nice to have a finishing aspect to the exercise. Having a large goal allows keepers to get game like work and attackers to shoot. It can also allow defenders who have won the ball to have a release point backwards to avoid high pressure.
7) The coach can have points scored for the exercise by having the attackers score by reaching the penalty box or stopping the ball on the end line of the strip that they are attacking.
8) Defenders should be able to counter attack by reaching their end line, by scoring on small goals or by getting the ball back to the coach.
9) Defenders can not run offside traps with the intent of pushing all the attackers stating positions up field. If an attacker is making a run that is mistimed then the player can and should be offside. Defenders should try to keep the area they are defending compact.
10) The reason attackers get caught offside is usually because both attackers; the runner and server, make mistakes. The timing of both the run and the pass are critical to penetrating the back of the defense.
   a) First the runner that is moving forward has to time the run correctly.
   b) Secondly, the passer of the ball needs to time the pass to avoid letting their teammate be in an offside position.
11) The extra midfielder will often become a penetrating player but should spend much of their time supporting the play and swinging the ball from area to area.
12) Any attacker can switch channels to create the 2 versus 1. However, there should not be more than 2 attackers in any one grid. A flank attacker can move into the interior and striker can move into the flank area. Penetrating 2 v 1 patterns do not have to be created only from the central midfielders they can be created with diagonal movement by the strikers and/or flank players.
13) Later in the exercise the defenders can be freed up to leave their grids and go where ever they want. The attackers will have to do a better job of moving the ball at speed and recognizing where their advantage is on the field. If the defense is becoming highly successful the coach can let the attackers have more than two players in a grid and the exercise. The only situation now that does not replicate the game is the defenders being outnumbered.
14) Attacking players must visually or verbally communicate to each other. The mentality of the attackers should be a purposeful one. They should be recognizing potential patterns and both moving the ball and runs to create the tactical movements with purpose.
15) A good "first touch" is necessary to prepare the ball for the next move the attack wants to make.
16) Be sure to have plenty of extra balls available to keep the exercise flowing.
17) "Sharpening" by the attackers who are waiting in each strip is essential to create and take care of the numerical advantage of 2 versus 1. This is particularly important in relation to

the players immediately around the ball.

18) Players away from the ball should be preparing to react to what future ball movement will provide in relationship to their position on the field.

19) One example is a wide flank player on the weak or far side of the field away from the ball should be preparing to try and time a run on to a ball crossed into the penalty box from the opposite flank.

    a) The same wide flank player will need to readjust where they position them self when the ball is being held centrally by a midfielder. The questions are can they make a run to penetrate behind the defense with a pass from the midfielder, can they create a 2 versus 1 pattern with the ball carrier or should they move back up the field to support a switch in the attack but not provide immediate penetrating options from this position.

    b) The coach should be "coaching off the ball" and supplying insight for player movement based on ball position, teammates positions, opponents position, relative level of risk, time of flight to attack the ball and a myriad of other factors. ("Coaching off the ball" is making sure that the players without the ball are moving to anticipate what will or can happen. If players are showing no recognition of what is about to happen with their movement the coach should point this out and instruct players "off the ball" how to position themselves to take advantage of impending opportunities or failures.)

Diagram 28: 2 versus 1 Grid Set-Up on Half Field

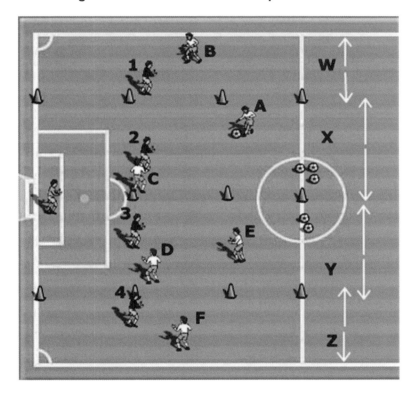

In Diagram 28, page 141, the grid zones for the players are used to restrict them with the exception that the attackers can over load a zone with two people to create 2 versus 1 situations. The zone at the top of the grid is labeled with a W on the far upper right of the diagram. The two middle zones are labeled X and Y. The flank zone on the bottom of the diagram is labeled with a Z. The labeling of the zones is for reference purposes only and essential to the exercise itself.

Zones W, X, Y and Z each have one defender in them with a goal keeper behind. Each defender is numbered with a 1, 2, 3 or 4. At the start of this diagram Zone W has attacker B, Zone X has attackers A and C, Zone Y has attackers E and D while Zone Z has attacker F. Once all this is set up the exercise is relatively simple, create 2 versus 1 patterns in a zone and penetrate to goal. Defenders should have counter attack targets to use when they win the ball.

Diagram 28 A: 2 versus 1 Grid Curved Run Combination Play

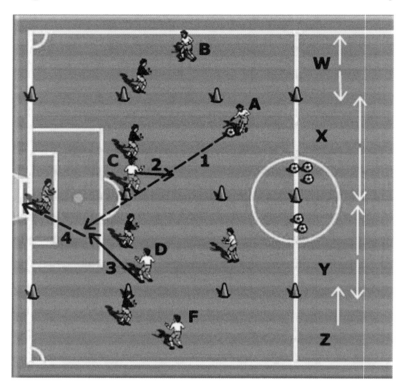

In Diagram 28 A, page 142, the half field is divided into four vertical zones, W, X, Y and Z. The attackers are in white and a labeled A, B, C, D, E, and F. The defenders are in black and are not numbered. The defenders are not numbered so that the ball movement and runs can be numbered and not leave the reader confused.

The pattern used is a diagonal run with a diagonal pass. This pattern is executed by attacker A and attacker D. The pass is numbered with a 1 and the run is numbered with a 3. Attacker C makes a run into the path of the pass numbered one and Dummy's the ball to confuse the defense. The run by attacker C is numbered with a 2. The move culminates with a shot numbered 4 by attacker D.

Diagram 28 B: 2 verses 1 Created by a Striker and Flank Player:

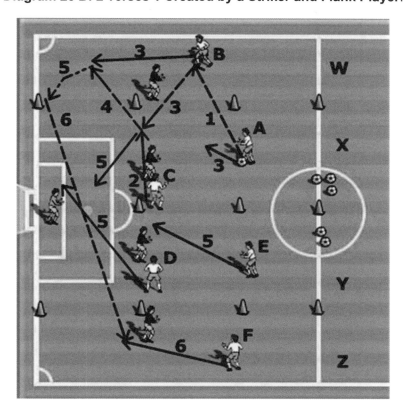

In Diagram 28 B, page 143, the attack has a 3 versus 2 tactical advantage in grids W and X at the top of the grid. Attackers A, B and C outnumber the two defenders that are held in their respective zones; W and X. This advantage occurs in the top half of the grid and it is helpful for the coach to point out that by looking at the two grids together the attack has a 3 versus 2 man advantage in the two grids combined.

The midfielder, A, passes the ball out wide to the flank attacker, B with a pass numbered 1. The striker, C, makes a horizontal run towards the flank which allows them to avoid being in an offside position. The run by attacker C is in grid X and is numbered 2. Attacker B on the flank then combines with attacker C with a Wall Pass. The pass and run by attacker B are both numbered with a 3. The return pass that gets attacker B in behind the defense is numbered with a 4. Attacker B takes a quick dribble, numbered 5, to look for attackers in the box before making a crossing pass numbered 6. Attackers C, D and E all make runs into the penalty area that are numbered with a 5. In this case the ball is over struck and none of the attackers were in a good far post position so attacker F makes a run to collect the ball on the other flank. That run is numbered with a 6.

Diagram 28 C: 2 versus 1 Expands to Combination Play

In Diagram 28 C, page 144, attackers E, F and D start to use a simple 2 versus 1 Curved Run pattern. Attacker F starts by dribbling into the interior of the field with a dribble numbered 1. Attacker E responds with a Curved Run around attacker F from the midfield. The run by attacker E is numbered with a 1. Because the defender is in the passing lane to send the ball from attacker F to attacker E the immediate 2 versus 1 pattern is obstructed. Attacker F solves the issue by passing the ball, numbered with a 2, to attacker D who then sends the ball out to attacker E with a pass numbered 3 to finish the original Curved Run pattern. This is Combination Play used to solve a 2 versus 1 pattern that has been effectively shut down for the direct solution with just the two players.

Exercise 12: 1 verses 1 with a Second Attacker Coming from Different Angles of Support
(Grid 10-15 x 10-20 yards)
(Angles can include behind the attacker, even with the attacker, next to the defender, or up in front of the attacker and defender)

(See Diagrams 29, 29 A, 29 B, 29 C, 29 D, 29 E, 29 F, 29 G, 29 H, 29 I, 29 J 29 H, 29 I, 29 J, 29 K, 29 L, 29 M, pages 145-158.)

Keys to Exercise 12

Reviewing the keys to all 2 versus 1 patterns would be useful. The diagrams are examples of how to organize defenders and attackers to get the desired patterns of play to occur. Without the correct set-up the players can not execute the 2 versus 1 patterns. This practice by the players to see the relative positions of the players to create a pattern is critical to perceiving opportunities in the game and reacting with patterns that are possible to execute given those positions.

Diagram 29: Organization of Wall Pass Pattern

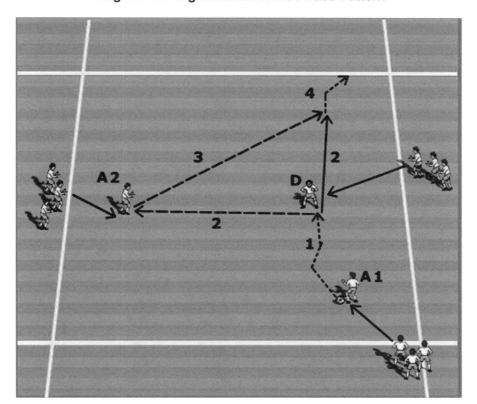

Diagram 29, page 145, is a typical Wall Pass pattern. One attacker, A1 must start on the end of the grid and the other attacker, A2, needs to start on the side of the grid about half way up the grid. The defender can start from the middle of the grid or the end of the grid but where ever they start the attacker, A1, must have the opportunity to commit the defender by dribbling at them and learning to time the release pass to the supporting attacker.

Explanation of Diagram 29, page 145: Attacker A1 dribbles the ball with a move numbered 1 as the defender runs into the center of the grid. As A1 reaches the defender they pass the ball to the supporting attacker, A2, with a pass numbered 2 and then A1 makes a hard run in behind the defender also numbered with a 2. The return pass by attacker A2 is numbered with a 3 and A1 finishes the move to the end of the grid with a dribble numbered 4.

Diagram 29 A: Organization of Parallel Players for a Wall Pass Pattern

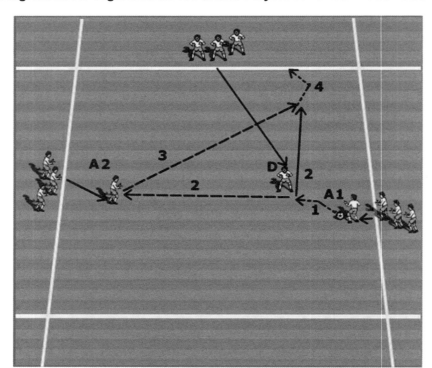

The pattern shown in Diagram 29 A, page 146, .is a way of setting up a Wall Pass from a horizontal approach. The dribble from attacker A1 is horizontal to the grid not vertical. Both attackers can start anywhere along the sides of the grid that leaves enough space for the return pass to be made. It is important for players to see that a wall pass can be created by movement other than one that is vertical down the field. The defender starts at the far end of the grid.

Explanation of Diagram 29 A, page 146: Attacker A1 starts the sequence with a dribble numbered 1. The defender makes a run to put pressure on A1. A1 times the release of the pass to the supporting attacker A2 with a pass numbered 2 and makes a hard run behind the defense also numbered with a 2. The return pass by attacker A2 is numbered with a 3. The whole movement to the end of the grid is finished by attacker A1 with a dribble numbered 4.

Diagram 29 B: Organization of False Wall Pattern

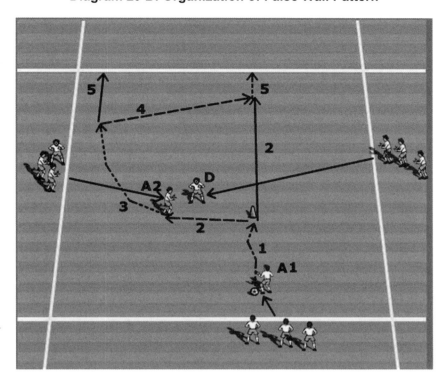

Diagram 29 B, page 147, shows a False Wall Pass. The attacker A2 should start in the middle of the grid and slightly to one side. A defender should mark attacker A2 to start the exercise. There is a cone for attacker A1, who starts at the end of the grid, to use as a marker replicating a defender which gives a reason to make the pass to attacker A2. The defender marking A2 should position them self to obstruct the potential return pass and Wall Pass pattern between attackers A1 and A2. This positioning creates the reason that attacker A2 needs to use the False Wall Pass pattern.

Explanation of Diagram 29 B. page 147: Attacker A1 dribbles, numbered with a 1, into the grid and when they reach the cone sends a pass numbered 2 to attacker A2. A1 then makes a hard run in behind the defense that replicates a Wall Pass pattern. The run is numbered with a 2. Because the defender is positioned to obstruct the return pass in a Wall Pass pattern attacker A2 then rolls away from the intended Wall Pass with a dribble numbered 3. This dribble and the fact that the Wall Pass is not executed gives the pattern its' name, the False Wall. In this diagram A2 dribbles in behind the defense and then gives a late pass to attacker A1 which is numbered with a 4. The movement is finished with a dribble to the end line by attacker A1 and a run to the end line by attacker A2. Both of these actions are numbered with a 5. The initial pass from attacker A1 to A2 should be to the top foot of attacker A2 so that when receiving the pass the ball is automatically shielded.

Diagram 29 C: Organization of Curved Run Pattern

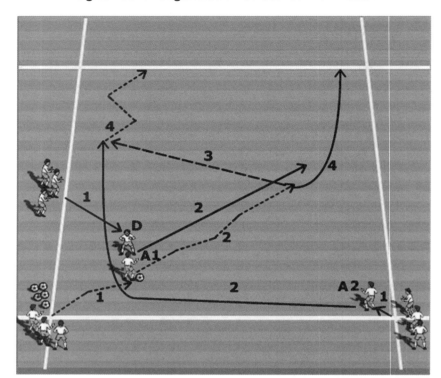

In Diagram 29 C, page 148, the attackers, A1 and A2 should both start at the end of the grid in wide positions from each other. The defender can start on the side of the grid or on the end of the grid. The side of the grid puts pressure on the ball carrier faster than if the defender starts on the end of the grid.

Explanation of Diagram 29 C. page 148: Attacker A1 starts with a diagonal dribble into the grid numbered with a 1. When the defender arrives to put pressure on them the dribble then is numbered with a 2. The reason for that is that there is no reason for attacker A2 to make a Curved Run until there is pressure on their teammate. Attacker A2 then starts a run, numbered 2, behind attacker A1 and then up and around them. Attacker A1 needs to keep the ball shielded while dribbling and then use a move or body feint to create space for a pass to attacker A2 which is numbered with a 3. The move to the end of the grid is a dribble by A2 and a run by A1 which are both numbered with a 4. The defenders' run to pressure and marking run against attacker A1 are numbered 1 and then 2. If the defender does not over commit into the space in front of attacker A1 then A1 can use a Spin move or Turning move away from pressure to create the passing lane to allow A1 to pass to A2.

Diagram 29 D: Flick and Spin Wall Pass Organization

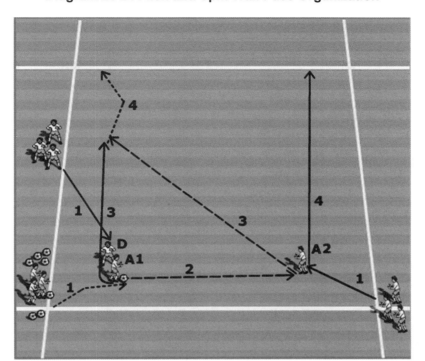

Diagram 29 D, page 149, is a Flick and Spin pattern. The set-up organization is essentially the same as for the Curved Run. The two attackers, A1 and A2 start near the end of the grid on opposite sides of the grid. The defender is best started from the side because the Flick and Spin Move to be used effectively must have a defender marking the ball carrier quite closely.

Explanation of Diagram 29 D, page 149: Attacker A1 dribbles into the grid and attracts the defender into a close marking position. Both the dribble by attacker A1 and the defenders' run are numbered with a 1. Attacker A2 moves into a square support position approximately even with the dribble of attacker A1. A2's run is numbered with a1. Once A1 is marked closely they make a pass, numbered 2, to attacker A2 and then spin away in the opposite direction of the pass with a run numbered 3. A2 returns the pass, numbered 3, in behind the defense. Attacker A1 finishes the move to the end of the grid with a dribble numbered 4. A2 makes a supporting run to the end of the grid that is also numbered with a 4.

Diagram 29 E: Flick and Spin; Down Field Organization

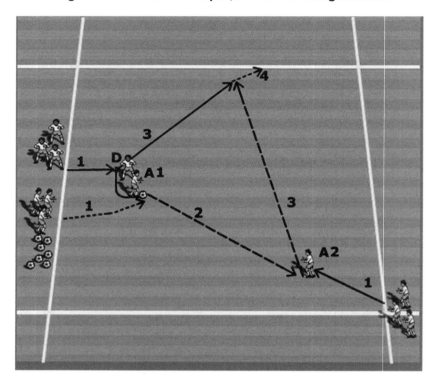

In Diagram 29 E, page 150, the Flick and Spin is shown when the support player is down field from the attacker with the ball. One attacker needs to start from the side of the grid about half way up while the other attacker needs to start on the other side of the grid at lower edge. The defender should start near the first attacker on the side of the grid so that they can mark the attacker fairly quickly.

Explanation of Diagram 29 E, page 150: Attacker A1 dribbles into the grid. The dribble is numbered with a 1. At the same time attacker A2 steps into the grid and the defender makes a run to mark attacker A1. Both attacker A2's run and the defenders' run are marked with a 1. As attacker A1 gets marked tightly they make a pass back down field to attacker A2 that is numbered with a 2. Attacker A1 then spins away in the opposite direction of the pass around the defender and makes a diagonal run, numbered 3, into the space behind the defense. The run needs to be diagonal instead of straight down field to keep the defender from easily stepping into the passing lane which making a straight run up field would do. Attacker A2 then returns the pass, numbered with a 3 back to attacker A1 who finishes the sequence with a dribble, numbered 4, to the opposite end of the grid. Attacker A2 does not need to make a run forward unless the coach wants them to make a Curved Run to the opposite side and upper edge of the grid which would supply support besides a back pass.

Diagram 29 F: Low Wall Pass Organization

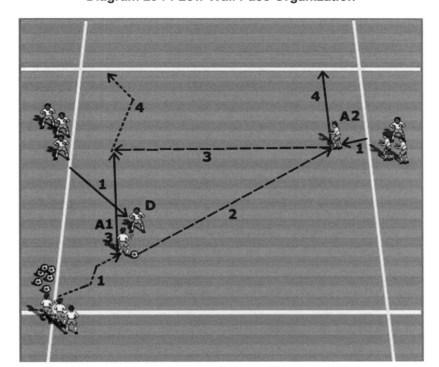

Diagram 29 F, page 151, is organization for a Low Wall Pass. Remember this pass allows the return pass in the Wall Pass pattern to be square and not diagonal. This allows the pass to avoid defenses that have good depth to them. The starting position is that on attacker starts up high in the grid on the edge of the grid opposite the other attacker. The supporting attacker must be on the side of the grid opposite from their teammate. The defender starts on the side of the grid from which the ball will enter the grid. This allows the defender to present the Low Wall Passing opportunity to occur.

Explanation of Diagram 29 F, page 151: Attacker A1 dribbles into the grid. The dribble is numbered with a 1. At the same time the defender makes a run into pressuring attacker A1. That run is numbered with a 1. It is extremely helpful if the defender is making a fast, slightly out of control approach so that their momentum will help attacker A1 make a successful run in behind the defender. If the defender is cautious then the Low Wall pattern is not likely to be successful. Attacker A1 then times their pass, numbered with a 2 to attacker A2 who has made a run, numbered 1 into the grid. The explosive run by attacker A1 and the square return pass by attacker A2 are both numbered with a 3. The move is finished out with a dribble to the end line by attacker A1 that is numbered with a 4. Attacker A2 should push up in wide support and finish with a run numbered 4. If the defender is static the attacker A1 will still need to release the ball slightly earlier than in a normal Wall Pass so that the defender can not close the passing lane to the supporting attacker A2 who is up field. The defender's static position means that attacker A1 must be able to accelerate quickly to exploit the space behind the defender and make up the space between attacker A1 and the defender that must be greater than a normal Wall Pass because of the easier ability of the defender to shut down the passing lane to attacker A2.

Diagram 29 G: Double Pass Organization

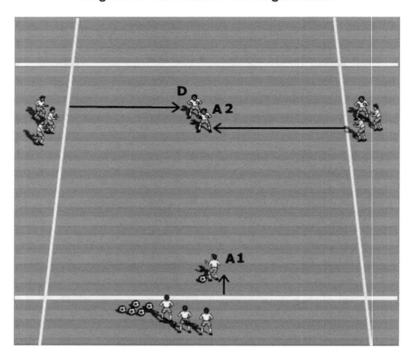

Diagram 29 G, page 152, shows the organization for both Double Pass patterns. The Double Pass Patterns, Straight Return or Diagonal Return pass are both the same in the initial set-up. The patterns them selves are not shown just the organization. One attacker A1 should start the edge of the grid. Attacker A2 should start up fairly high on one side of the grid so they can make a run into the middle of the grid to start the pattern. The defender can start on the opposite side or same side of the grid at the same level at attacker A2. Having the defender and the attacker start on opposite sides of the grid helps keep confusion of who is doing what down to a minimum and the defenders are on the side not on the end of the grid so that as the pattern finishes they won't be in the way.

Diagram 29 H: High Wall Pass Organization

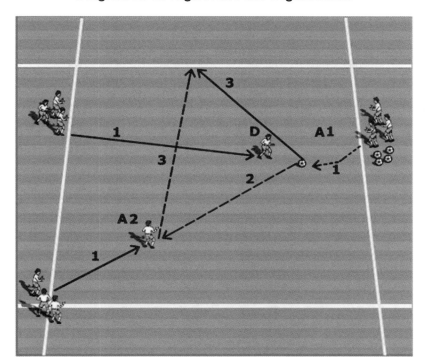

Diagram 29 H, page 153, shows the organization for the High Wall pattern. The starting attacker should start up high on the side of the grid and the other attacker should start down on the bottom edge of the grid. The defender needs to start on the opposite side of the grid from the first attacker.

Explanation of Diagram 29 H, page 153: Attacker A1 dribbles into the grid. The dribble is numbered with a 1. Both attacker A2 and the defender make runs in reaction to the dribble by A1. Both the runs by A2 and the defender are numbered with a 1. Attacker A1 commits the defender and then passes the ball back and diagonally to attacker A2. This pass is numbered with a 2. A1 then makes a hard run in behind the defender and A2 supplies a pass. Both the run and the pass are numbered with a 3. The run must be diagonal to get in a position to receive the ball back and the pass should be nearly straight down field.

Diagram 29 I: Take Over Organization

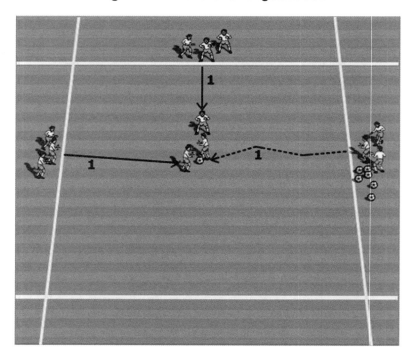

Diagram 29 I, page 154, depicting the Take Over pattern just shows the organization and not the actual movements since there are two possibilities. The first is for the attackers to change possession of the ball and the second is for the dribbling attacker to keep the ball in a False Take-Over maneuver. The attackers should start on opposite sides of the grid from each other. The precise point to start from is not crucial but up the field makes it easier to reach the end line successfully. The defender can start on the end line edge of the grid where the attackers are trying to reach or they can start on the side of the grid.

Diagram 29 J: Straight Run/Diagonal Pass Organization

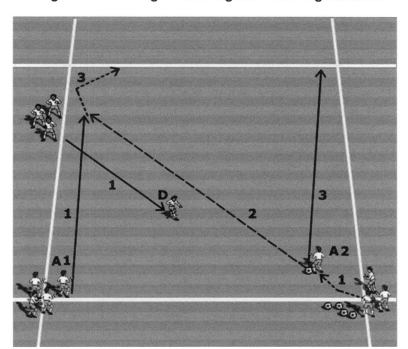

Diagram 29 J, page 155, organizes the attackers on opposite sides of the grid at the bottom edge of the grid. The defender should start from the side of the grid opposite from the ball. The defender should start on the opposite side of the grid from the attacker with the ball. This allows time for the run to develop.

Explanation of Diagram 29 J, page 155: Attacker A2 starts with a dribble numbered 1 to enter the grid. This motion is the signal for the defender to start a run into pressure that is numbered with a 1. Attacker A1 sees the space created by the defenders run towards attacker A2 and makes a Straight Run, numbered 1, up field into the space behind the defender. Attacker A2 sees the run and sends a pass, numbered 2, that must by nature of the relative positioning of the two attackers will be diagonal. The move is finished off with a dribble to the end line by attacker A1. The dribble is numbered with a 3. A2 finishes the sequence with a wide support run, numbered with a 3, to the end line.

Diagram 29 K: Diagonal Run/Straight Pass Organization

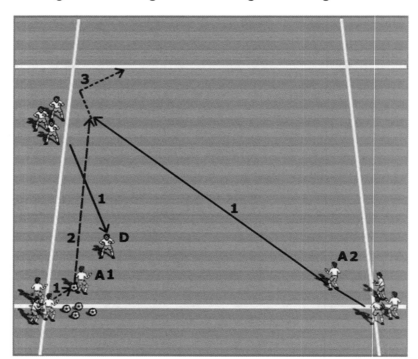

Diagram 29 K, page 156, is essentially the same as Diagram 29 J, page 155. The two attackers start on opposite sides of the grid at the starting edge. The defender should start on the side of the grid but could start on the end line of the grid if so desired.

Explanation of Diagram 29 K, page 156: Attacker A1 makes a short dribble into the grid, numbered with a 1, which triggers a run to pressure the ball by the defender that is also numbered with a 1. Attacker 2 must recognize the situation and start a hard run diagonally into the space directly in front of attacker A1. This run is numbered with a 1. Because this is a long run the coach may need to make an adjustment to get the timing of the run and pass to be correct. The coach can start attacker A2 a little closer to A1 so the run is not as long or start the defender further back. Or the coach may need to instruct attacker A1 that the pass numbered 2 may need to be stuck into the space in front of A2 before they actually get there. This creates the need for learning to pace a pass properly. Because attacker A1 sees the diagonal run of attacker A2 they pass the ball straight up field for A2 to receive and collect to dribble to the end line. The dribble is numbered with a 3. The coach can require attacker A1 to make run forward, usually moving across the grid to the opposite side of where attacker A2 has dribbled. It is a good force of habit to move to support other players who have the ball.

Diagram 29 L: X Pattern from the Dribble Organization

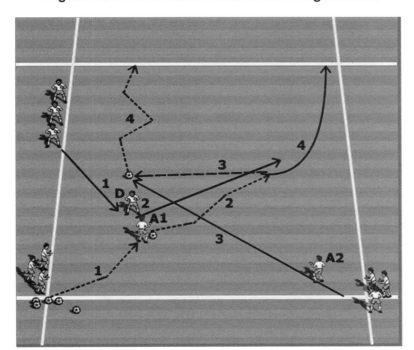

Diagram 29 L, page 157, is the organization for an X Pattern created from a dribble. The attackers need to start at the starting edge of the grid on opposite sides from each other. The defender can start on the side that the ball starts from or on the end line. In this example the defender starts on the side where the ball enters.

Attacker A1 starts with a dribble numbered 1 which triggers a run to pressure by the defender which is also numbered with a 1. Once marked attacker A1 continues to dribble diagonally which draws the defender with them and out of the space that the dribble leaves behind. This dribble with a marking defender is numbered with a 2 and the defenders' run next to the dribble is numbered with a 2. Once the space starts to open attacker A2 makes a run in behind where attacker A1dribbled. This run by A2 is numbered with a 3. Attacker A1 then makes a pass square or slightly backward to attacker A2. The pass by attacker A1 is numbered with a 3. The sequence finishes with attacker A2 dribbling to the end line of the grid which is numbered with a 4 and attacker A1 provides a wide support run numbered 4.

Diagram 29 M: X Pattern from the Pass Organization

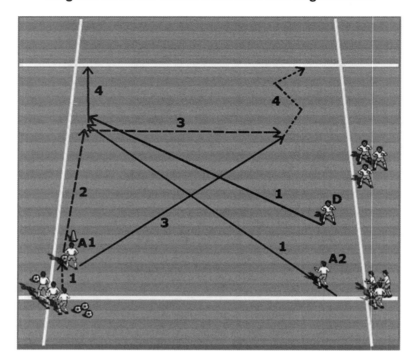

Diagram 29 M, page 158, is essentially the same organization. The attackers need to start at the bottom of the grid on opposite sides from each other. The defender now starts on the opposite side of the grid that the ball starts on. In the diagram there is a cone in front of attacker A1 that replicates a defender. This allows the other attacker to receive pressure from the live defender when they make their run, receive the pass and send the pass back.

Explanation of Diagram 29 M, page 158: The sequence is started by attacker A1, at the bottom left of the grid, dribbling into the grid. The dribble is numbered with a 1. The dribble is towards a cone that symbolizes a defender. Attacker A2 starts a run, numbered 1, to get in behind the cone defender. The live defender starts tracking attacker A2 with a run numbered 1. As attacker A1 reaches an appropriate spot near the cone they make a pass straight up field into the path of attacker A2's run. The pass is numbered with a 2. Then attacker A1 makes a run that crosses over the run by attacker A2. That run is numbered with a 3. Because attacker A2 is tightly marked when they receive the ball they return the ball with a pass, numbered 3, back into the space that they just ran out of and into which attacker A1 is running. Attacker A1 dribbles to the end line and attacker A2 supplies a wide support run to the end line. Both the dribble and the run are marked with a 4.

Having defenders coming at the attackers from different angles, sides, and distances will help the attackers start to adjust their decision making and timing of play. Adding a second defender makes the exercise very difficult and worth doing when players have learned the patterns well enough to start to adjust to all the variables created by multiple defenders. Adding a third attacker against the two defenders lets the attackers figure out where a 2 versus 1 advantage exists and what pattern they should choose to exploit it.

There are lots of ways to set up the preceding exercises. Not every pattern has an example of how to set up the players to start the sequence. The coach can adjust it for anything that is required to be trained or emphasized with the players. Remember, if the coach keeps adding players to the exercise, attackers or defenders, with a "Plus" one advantage or with even numbers they can slowly but surely recreate an environment that closely resembles the game from a very basic exercise. The exercise can be easily expanded to a 5 versus 5 game that is free in nature or that the coach puts conditions on to get the players to use what has been taught earlier in practice. Don't forget that in the end at higher levels of play the numerical advantage will be the defenders' so when the players and team is ready that numerical advantage should be given to the defense.

Exercise 13: Long Service to Striker with Supporting Run to a 2 versus 1
(Grid; Half Field or longer)

The purpose of this exercise is to teach the striker to hold the ball for support to arrive and for the supporting attacker to arrive in such a way as to support the striker by creating good positions to create 2 versus 1 patterns. The long service is in to a striker versus a defender or 1 versus 1 tactical position. The server must then run to create 2 versus 1 from different angles while the attacker with the ball holds it and waits for support to develop the 2 versus 1.

The long service to the attacker makes the attacker hold the ball and wait for the 2 versus 1 to occur. This holding action is important for front runners to learn. This exercise helps develop timing of the 2 versus 1 execution. It also helps with a real weakness in our game at this time which is accurate serves to teammates that are 30 yards or more away. We tend to hit the ball at the area of our teammate and make them work to get it rather than making it an accurate pass that keeps the defender out of the play.

It is of course important that the strikers learn to take opponents on in 1 versus 1 or even 1 versus 2 situations without the hesitation of waiting for a teammate. But the skill to hold the ball and time the 2 versus 1 pattern is one that is essential to good players. Even in counter attack situations when a team is breaking out quickly understanding 2 versus 1 patterns and how to make runs to support the attacker with the ball is critical to good play and good decision making.

Depending on the age and skill level the distance of the long serve will vary greatly. The coach is attempting to allow the serve to have a success rate of around 70 to 80 percent of the time. As previously mentioned this ratio of success is generally needed for players to be challenged without leaving them either bored with to much success or overly stressed and frustrated with failure.

Keys to Technical Issues: Long Service 2 versus 1

1) The server should strike the ball with enough pace on it that it does not allow the defender to run around the receiving attacker and cut the pass out.
2) The pass should draw the receiving attacker either too the side or back and away from the defender.
3) The attacking player should serve balls driven on the ground at first for ease of receiving the ball. Later balls served in the air are needed to increase skill level of receiving and holding the ball.
4) The receiving player should try to turn their body so that their shoulder is into the chest of the defender making the widest possible distance between the ball and the defender. Some people call receiving the ball this way as "sideways on."
5) Using the outside of the top foot to receive the pass helps to create the widest possible position to shield the ball from the defender. If it is not possible for the attacker to receive the ball in this position they should try to get the ball and their body in this position as quickly as possible. Or if the attacker can they should turn on the opponent and face the opponent's goal which puts the defender in a more vulnerable position.
6) If possible the attacker moving backwards to receive the ball should move back towards the server at an angle from the defender so that their peripheral vision allows the attacker to see the defender as the ball is coming in to them. This use of peripheral vision allows three things to occur.

a) If the attacker can see that the defender is over committing the striker can beat the defender without further ado.

b) If the defender is to loose then the attacker can turn with the ball and face up with the defender. This position of facing up to the defender will change the decision making of the supporting attacker and the kind of run that they will make.

c) If the defender marks the attacker well the attacking player can hold the ball in what is essentially a stationary position while waiting for the supporting attacker to arrive. A striker can also buy time for the supporting attacker to arrive by starting to dribble diagonally rather than trying to stay stationary or turn on the defender.

7) The angle of the support run, straight from behind, diagonally from the back, square from the side, will all cause certain 2 versus 1 patterns to be more useful or useable than others.

8) Defenders that mark to tightly can cause the attackers to simply play the ball in behind the defense and go straight to goal without the need of a 2 versus 1 pattern. This is not useful for the exercise as a whole but the positioning of the defender should be something that servers of the ball recognize as inviting a penetrating pass or possession.

9) Defenders that over-commit to winning the ball by pressuring to closely on the back of an attacker as the striker receives it are vulnerable to being turned and beaten directly by the receiving attacker.

10) In matches or exercises the striker must know the ability of their teammate. Do not make runs to get in behind the defense if the player with the ball can not send long enough passes or accurate enough passes. Use the strengths of the player and not cause weakness' to be exposed. This point is constantly true in all sorts of situations. Another simple example is hitting balls to space for a teammate to run onto when that player is not particularly fast and would benefit by the ball being played to feet. Play to a players' strength.

The exercise itself is easy to set up. (See Diagram 30, page 161.)

Keys to Exercise 13

1) A 10-15 yard square can be set up for the receiving attacker to play in with a restraining line for the defender that gives a little extra space and time to receive the ball. The coach can do this exercise without any square restricting the target receiver or holding the defender away to create artificial space. But the creation of a little space to start makes it easier for inexperienced players to succeed.

2) Shielding should be with the attacker positioned shoulder into the defender's chest to maximize the attacker's distance for the defender to the ball.

3) A slow diagonal dribble with either ball or body feints will buy time for the striker who is waiting for support.

4) Serves should come from all angles and sides; square, diagonal and from straight behind.

5) The coach can have the server run or another attacker who did not serve the ball run to support the player with the ball. Which way support is given, by the server or by another player makes no difference.

6) Once the support runner is within playing distance the 2 versus 1 battle can begin using any of the patterns that the players know.

7) The time to release the defender from the small head start given, if any, to the attacker will vary due to the skill levels of the players. The coach can have them release as the ball is being struck, a count of 2 after the ball is struck or after the receiving attacker has touched the ball. The coach has to judge what level of pressure the attacker can handle.

8) A good "first touch" is necessary to prepare the ball for the next move the attack wants to make.

9) While players are waiting their turn to serve the ball to the striker they can work on ball touch, dribbling moves, long serves to other groups are just a few examples. Imagination, player needs and team needs should be the inspiration for what the coach has the players doing.

Diagram 30: Long Service to Create a 2 versus 1 Set-Up

Diagram 30, page 161, allows long services to be sent from all angles to a striker who must hold the ball away from the defender while the server or other designated players make long runs to create a 2 versus 1 situation to exploit to goal. A player who has the ball simply serves the ball into the attacker and then supports the play with a run to create a 2 versus 1 pattern.

Exercise 14: Three Grid Game
(Grid size; 15-25 x 3 segmented grids of 10-20 yards each) (See Diagram 31 A, page 163.)

The exercise area is divided into three segmented grids that are equal in length and width. Each team has two defenders in their defending third, one midfielder in the middle third and one attacker in their attacking third. (Two attackers in the attacking third is a viable variation)

The ball starts with the keeper who uses the defenders and the 2 versus 1 advantage in their defending third to build out of the back. When the ball moves into the middle third one defender may move forward keeping the 2 versus 1 advantage going. When the ball moves into the attacking third a player from the midfield third may also move forward making the situation 2 versus 2 too goal. (In the variation with two attackers it can be 3 versus 2 in the attacking third)

(See Diagrams 31 A, 31 B, 31 C and 31 D, pages 163, 164, 165 and 166.)

Keys to the Three Grid Game

1) The game can either be a static restart after a ball is lost or a fluid game that requires the players to think about how to recover and who should be allowed to move forward or back in any given situation. The better the players and the more experience with the exercise the more it should be fluid.

2) Try to encourage several solutions and how to create them as the game flows along. Otherwise the coach may find that the players will use only one or two patterns over and over again because they get comfortable with them.

3) The grids should be of equal length and width. There should be three grids for the players to attack and defend through.

4) If the coach is using a keeper and not a small goal then have the keeper start the attack with a ball rolled out to the defenders.

5) Defenders should not be shy of using the keeper to maintain ball possession in the defensive third.

6) A good "first touch" is necessary to prepare the ball for the next move the attack wants to make.

7) Be sure to have plenty of extra balls available to keep the exercise flowing.

8) Attackers should prepare that are waiting in each grid. If the players who are in each grid are not preparing mentally for the next tactical possibility the speed of play will slow down and the use in the game itself will become fragmented and disjointed.

9) The players can/should dribble forward through a grid if no defender steps up to pressure them.

10) Players should be encouraged to dribble to commit defenders which helps create 2 versus 1patterns.

11) In the exercise the attacking third will always have a 2 versus 2situation unless the coach uses the variation that either has a second attacker (two total attackers in the grid) already in the grid as their teammate moves forward. Or there is an attacker waiting on the sidelines to enter the exercise when the ball reaches the attacking third. This creates a 3 versus 2 numerical advantage for the attackers and will hopefully allow them to see a 2 versus 1 pattern inside the more complex picture.

12) The game should go from grid to grid to grid and not skip over any one area to start. Later as the players understand the concepts better passing from the defensive third to the attacking third can become acceptable. That would most likely mean that the midfield attacker would be making the run forward because of closer proximity and the defender would step into the midfield third to support the play.

13) If a team loses the ball they must recover into the starting position of 2 defenders, 1 midfielder and 1 attacker immediately. As the game gets more fluid who recovers where can be a learning point for efficient adjustments.

1) At first the 2 versus 1patterns should occur in the area where the ball is located. However, as the players get more proficient with the 2 versus 1patterns they will recognize that an attempted attack will not work and can use a pass to the grid behind them to "reload" and attack again. The coach can allow back passes. Possession can be lost on the back pass. This allowing of back passes has the useful effect of keeping the players in the grid behind mentally working.

Diagram 31 A: Three Grid Game: Set-Up

Diagram 31 A, page 163, shows the organization for the start of the Three Grid exercise. Each group has a goal keeper, two defenders in the grid next to their goal keeper, one midfielder in the middle grid and one attacker in the grid where they can score. The exercise requires four field players for each team and a goal keeper for each team. The black team defenders are lettered B and A. The black midfielder is lettered with a C. And the attacker for the black team is lettered with a D. The white defenders are lettered E and F. The midfielder for the white team is lettered with a G and the attacker for the white team is labeled H. Goal Keepers are stationed on both ends.

Diagram 31 B: Three Grid Game: Moving Out of the Back with a Curved Run

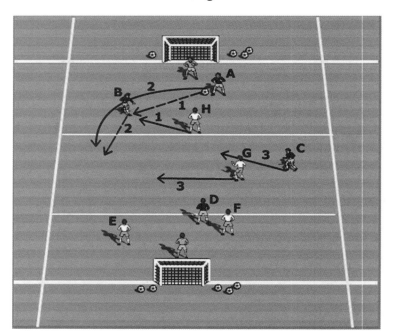

Diagram 31 B, page 164, shows the defenders creating a 2 versus 1 pattern, the Curved run to get out of the back and send a player forward into the midfield where they will outnumber the opposing midfielder two to one. The black team uses player A to pass to their teammate B. The pass is numbered with a 1. The attacker for white, lettered H, makes a run to pressure B that is marked with a 1. Player A makes a Curved Run around player B, which is numbered with a 2, and receives a pass forward into the middle grid that is numbered with a 2. As player A enters the middle grid the white midfielder, lettered G, starts to pressure A and the black midfielder C makes a run to provide a good supporting position. Both these runs are numbered with a 3. Remember that player C's movement to help player A is only one of many choices that are open to them. Player C could have chosen a diagonal run behind the white defender G to create a quick penetration.

Variation Pattern: 3 versus 2: Third Attacker Waits until the Ball Enters Grid

What this variation allows is for the attackers to have a numerical superiority in the final third. This will allow them to find the 2 versus 1 within the exercise that has extra players to complicate the picture. This variation is good for younger or more inexperienced players because having equal numbers in the attacking third may cause the attacking team to be unable to penetrate if the players are not skillful enough. The more experienced the players the more likely they will be able to handle a 2 versus 2 player confrontation successfully. Eventually, if the players are good enough then creating a 2 versus 3 player confrontation that has the numerical superiority given to the defense. This numerical superiority for the defense is most often the case in games. (Diagram 31 C, page 165, shows this variation,)

Diagram 31 C: Three Grid Game with Waiting Attackers to create 3 versus 2

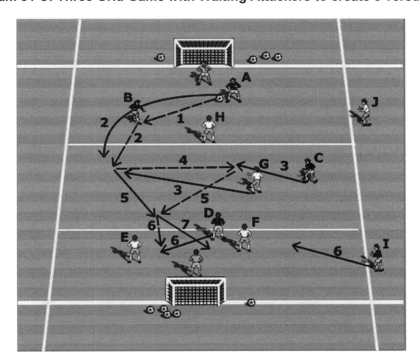

Diagram 31 C, page 165, shows the defenders creating a 2 versus 1 pattern. The Curved run pattern is used to get out of the back and send a player forward into the midfield where they will outnumber the opposing midfielder two to one. The black team uses player A to pass to their teammate B. The pass is numbered with a 1. The attacker for white, lettered H, makes a run to pressure B that is marked with a 1. Player A starts a Curved Run around player B, which is numbered with a 2, and receives a pass forward into the middle grid that is numbered with a 2. As player A enters the middle grid the white midfielder, lettered G, starts to pressure A and the black midfielder C makes a run to start in a good supporting position. Both these runs are numbered with a 3. All of these moves are the same as the previous diagram.

The black defender, A now combines with the midfielder C to create a Wall Pass pattern. Player A passes to player C, which is numbered with a 4 and then makes a run, numbered 5, forward behind defender G. Player A then receives a pass back from player C numbered 5 and gets ready to enter the attacking third.

Player D makes a diagonal run, numbered with a 6, out in front of the ball trying to attract a defender out of the way. Player A passes the ball to player D, which is numbered with a 6, and makes an X Pattern run, numbered 7, in behind player D's run. As the ball enters the attacking third player for the black team lettered I now enters' the attacking grid to create a 3 versus 2 situation. This addition of player I is what creates the variation of the exercise. The coach can have player I stay outside the grid and wait or the coach can have player I already in the grid waiting for the attack to enter their grid.

By slowly conditioning the game concerning where the players can start and allowing passes backwards through the grids the coach can create the situations desired to train. Adding an extra attacker up front can help the number of finishing chances and tactical understanding for the final third. In this exercise most of the conditions revolve around who can be in which grid at what time.

In the attacking grid the condition is that there are two defenders held in place in the grid they are defending. The defenders must stay there until they win the ball and start attacking forward. This means that a 2 versus 2 will evolve when the attackers enter the final grid to create finishing opportunities. (See Diagram 31 C, page 165, for the variation that allows a 3 versus 2.)

The condition of allowing one defender to move forward into the middle third of the field allows for a 2 versus 1 advantage. This in turn allows the creation of patterns that emerge from that numerical advantage. With only one attacker in the final grid the game is 2 versus 2 which means' that the attackers must be much more efficient and effective to create shots on goal. If the coach adds a second attacker into the final section of the grid then that condition will create a 3 versus 2 which hopefully will allow the attackers to isolate and execute a 2 versus 1 pattern. If both defenders respond to the area where the ball is located then the third attacker should be free if they kept any width in their supporting position.

Diagram 31 D: Three Grid Game Freed Up to be a 5 versus 5 Small Sided Game

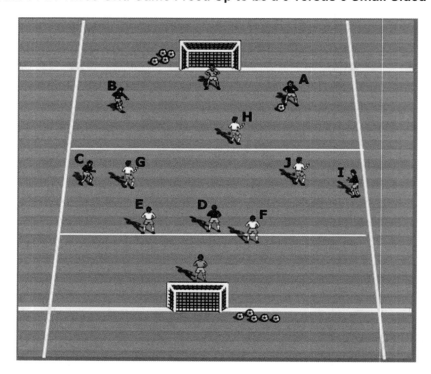

In Diagram 31 D, page 166, the game now involves the same players but is allowed to be free flowing. It is now a 5 versus 5 small sided game with keepers. These numbers are excellent for training lots of issues besides the ones' just discussed in the above exercise. I want to thank Berhane Andeberhan for showing me this exercise.

Definition of Conditions: "Conditions:" the set of rules for the exercise, that cause the desired technical, tactical, psychological or physical demands that are desired. This allows exercises to be game like but controlled by the specific conditions imposed which in turn creates the desired learning points to be performed in an exercise. Players tend to enjoy conditioned exercises that simulate games with the only restrictions being rules structured by the coach that will create the desired training effects. At any level of development and in almost all situations the placing of conditions on an exercise will allow the coach to get the desired training effect for the players.

Using conditions makes small sided games extremely flexible for teaching any issue while essentially providing a game like experience. Since small sided games are already an excellent form of economical training the addition of requiring specific actions to occur makes them one of the most important parts of the coaching arsenal. A few examples of conditions will quickly show that all the coach needs to do is imagine what is required and then impose the condition.

1) The ball must be back passed every four passes.
2) Players must take two touches.
3) Every other pass must be in the air.
4) The ball must switch sides of the field before attacking.
5) All goals must be scored with the head.
6) Players must dribble to attack a defender and then turn away to pass.
7) Players must beat opponents with a dribble before shooting.
8) Players must shoot in one touch.

The list and the possibilities of conditions are endless. Conditioned games are one of the backbones of a coaches' bag of tricks to create a training environment that is both effective and enjoyable.

Exercise 15: 2 versus 2: One Defending Player Retreats to the Line
(Grid size 10-15 x 10-15 yards)

This is a simple exercise where the object is for one team is to step on the ball right on the line of the grid they are attacking. If the skill level is not high then the object is to cross the line of the grid they are attacking. Since both teams have 2 players the team that does not possess the ball must have one player drop back to the line they are defending thereby creating a 2 versus 1 in the area of the grid. (This requirement of one of the defenders retreating to the end line when not in possession of the ball is a form of "Conditioned" play. In this case the condition creates a numerical advantage for the attack in the grid.)

(See Diagrams 32 A, 32 B, 32 C, pages 168, 169 and 170.)

Keys to 2 versus 2: One Defender Retreating

1) Once possession is established by one group the defending team must have a player retreat to the line that they are defending. The defender must stay on the line until their teammate wins the ball, the opposition loses the ball out of the grid or a point is scored by the other team.
2) The defender on the line may move laterally on the line to defend but may not encroach into the grid to defend.
3) The game is directional. This means each group has an end line to attack and an end line to defend.
4) When an attack is successful in stopping the ball on the line then the attackers simply leave it there and immediately transition to defense. One defender stays in the grid while the other assumes the defending position on the end line. The team just scored on takes possession of the ball and starts to attack the other end.
5) Because the defender on the line can move laterally to stop the attacker trying to reach the line the second attacker must continue to work into good spaces to receive the ball. This in turn forces the other defender to read how either to stop the pass to the second attacker or mark the second attacker. This helps defenders to learn to recover. It also starts to teach defenders to recover through passing lanes that are advantageous to the attackers, which makes it more difficult to execute 2 versus 1patterns by clogging up dangerous passing lanes. The lateral movement by the defender on the line forces all the players to keep playing through-out the exercise.
6) Because of the pressure of having a defender on the line the exercise gets much

more game like. Essentially the condition creates depth in defense. However the constraint to stay on the line limits the amount of pressure that the defense can use to stop 2 versus 1patterns. This in turn allows for the attackers to execute the patterns with more success.

7) The defender who retreats should be the one least able to immediately stop the attack in the grid. That would seem to be the defender closest to the line but that is not always the case. The defender closest to the line may be in a better position to pressure the attacker and stop penetration. This would mean that the other defender would need to recover past their teammate to the covering position on the line.

8) The game can be played to a point total or played for an allotted time. Remember that this is a fairly demanding exercise that often exceeds the athletes' anaerobic capacity. Timed games should not be of extreme length. Short passive or active breaks need to be allowed. (A passive break is one that allows the players to stand idle; an active rest means that the players now work on some activity that has a low work rate demand such as juggling the ball) If the coach sees the work rate dropping dramatically it may be because the players have had to switch to an aerobic source of energy rather than an anaerobic energy source.

9) Keep lots of balls near by to keep the players working on 2 versus 1 and not losing time chasing the ball. The extra balls will also keep the work rate up and force a natural increase in fitness.

10) A good "first touch" is necessary to prepare the ball for the next move the attack wants to make.

One of the benefits of this exercise is the transition rate and decisions that the players have to make to go from offense to defense and back again. The exercise is quick and demands clean technical touches, quick tactical execution and a high physical work rate.

Diagram 32 A: 2 versus 2 with One Defender Retreating

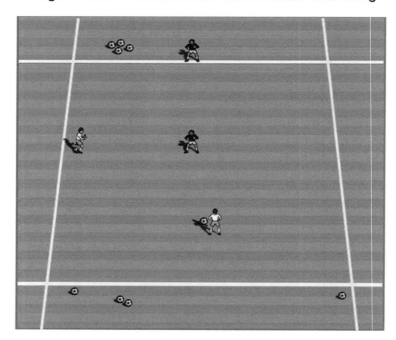

Diagram 32 A, page 168, shows how the players would start the game. The condition here is that one of the defenders must retreat to the line when they lose possession of the ball. In this case the team in black is defending the top of the grid and is currently on defense forcing one of their players' to be on the end line. The white players are currently attacking. This condition creates a 2 versus 1 confrontation inside of the grid.

To score the attacking team needs to step on the top of the ball when it reaches the end line. The defender who has retreated to the line can slide laterally along the line to stop the opposition from stepping on the ball. The ability to slide and defend along the line forces the second attacker to make runs forward and stay involved in the play after the first penetrating pass is made to their teammate. The purpose of most of these runs is to receive a pass that evades the defender on the line with a change in the point of attack. Because of the number of players and size of the grid this switch in the point of attack is small but it is a rudimentary start of switching away from pressure.

The fact that there is a defender on the line waiting to stop an attack will also encourage the other defender to make a continued effort to play defense. It forces the defender to recover in tactically intelligent ways and not just chase after the ball. Becoming aware of where the ball should be passed to next will allow the defender to step into passing lanes as they recover. The defender can also prevent a pass from being sent to the other attacker and close to double the ball making the pressure on the attacker increase as they near the end line.

While this book is primarily about the patterns that can be used for 2 versus 1 there is a time in teaching the points for attacking when defenders must get better. If the defenders do not improve their level of decision making then the attackers will not have to solve tactical problems presented by defenders with brains and experience. Don't neglect to improve the defensive pressure on the attackers by improving the defensive ideas of the players. The improvement of attack demanding an improvement in defense which in turn demands another improvement in attack is a cycle that should go on with all teams.

Diagram 32 B: 2 versus 2 with One Defender Retreating to Line

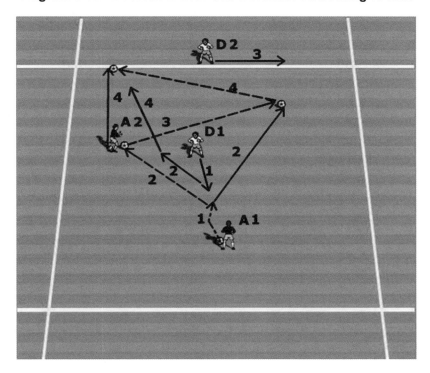

In Diagram 32 B, page 169, the reader can see that the attackers execute a wall pass to get behind the defender in the square. The attacker closest to the bottom of the grid, A1, dribbles forward, numbered with a 1, to commit the defender, D1, who is in the middle of the grid. The defender, D1, steps forward to pressure the attacker, that run is numbered with a 1 also. The attackers, A1 and A2, penetrate behind the defender in the center of the grid with a wall pass.

The pass from A1 to A2 is numbered with a 2; the run by A1 in behind the defense is also numbered 2 and the return pass from A2 to A1 is numbered with a 3. The supporting attacker, A2, sees that the defender, D2, on the line is moving laterally to stop penetration to the line by attacker A1. This defensive run is numbered with a 3. This causes the supporting attacker, A2, to make a run, numbered 4, forward to the end line away from defender D2 on the end line. The defender, D2, on the line tries to prevent the attacker carrying the ball after the wall pass from reaching the line unimpeded. The attackers' teammate, A1, in possession of the ball sees the run and the defender, D2, moving into the space in front of them and elects to pass the ball to their teammate, A2, with a pass numbered 4. The defender, D1, in the middle of the grid does not make a good effort to prevent penetration or to win the ball back. The run by the defender D1 when the first pass was made is numbered with a 2. But then defender D1 hesitated in recovering and their run numbered with a 4, is too late and fails to cut the passing lane that the pass from A1 to A2 numbered 4 is rolling through. Defender D1 has not recovered ball side of attacker A2 to prevent them from reaching the line. So neither the passing lane nor good positioning to stop the attack has occurred by defender D1.

The coach can teach defending as well as attacking. Always remember to keep focused on the primary objective of the practice or exercise but adding a few defensive pointers will only force the attackers to get better at what they are doing. The coach just needs to avoid turning the exercise into one about defending if the purpose is to improve the attacking skill sets. But without good defending there will be little to no growth in attacking skills.

Diagram 32 C: 2 versus 2 Turn Over with One Defender Retreating to the Line #1

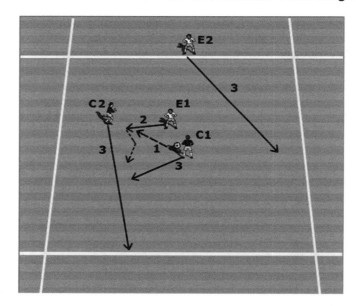

Diagram 32 C, page 170, shows the transition from attacking to defending after a turn over takes place. The attacker, C1, tries to make a pass, numbered 1, to their teammate, C2. The defender, E1, in the center of the grid cuts the pass out with their run numbered 2. The "new" attacker, E1, immediately transitions with a dribble forward numbered 3. Because the defender, E1, cuts out the intended pass it forces the attackers, C1 and C2, to become defenders under the rules of the exercise. One of the new defenders must retreat to the line while the other one stays in the grid to defend. In this example the player who is furthest from the line, C2, decides to retreat to their line. C2's run is labeled 3 and ends on the bottom edge of the grid. C1 makes a run to pressure the ball numbered with a 3 and E2 enters the grid from the line to become an attacker. Their run into the grid is numbered with a 3. It is important to notice that E2 is making an intelligent decision by moving wide of where both the defenders are placed. Coaching this exercise will give lots of opportunities to point out intelligent running and decision making.

Exercise 16: 2 versus 1 through Multiple Grids with a Defender
(Grid size 10-15 x 10-15 yards)

This exercise is also essentially simple. The coaches' set up is a multiple series of stacked grids for the players to attack through. Each grid has only one defender. The exercise will need a line of players at each end of the grid to start playing 2 versus 1.

(See Diagram 33, page 172.)

Keys to 2 versus 1 through Multiple Grids with a Defender

1) The coach needs to have a group of players, 3 or more, at the start of the grids so they can start a 2 versus 1 situation at the start of the first box.
2) Each grid has an attacker who is waiting for a teammate to advance into the grid in which they will be playing. They may start anywhere in the grid.
3) The coach will need a defender starting in each grid. The starting point is the exit line of each grid or the one farthest away from where the opposing attacker enters the grid. When players get very good at this exercise the defender can be allowed to start anywhere in the grid that they choose.
4) Each defender carries a scrimmage vest to designate that they are a defender. Not wearing the vest and simply carrying it will speed up the rate of transition when a defender wins the ball and has to give the vest to another player. (Whenever players will be making a quick transition from offense to defense or defense to offense where they must be designated I have the players hold the vest and not wear them so the work rate stays higher.
5) When a defender wins the ball they throw the scrimmage vest to the attacker they stole it from or made the mistake. They then go join the other attackers at the starting point of the exercise to start another 2 versus 1 attack through the grids. The transition of the vests and roles should be done quickly.
6) Four or five grids in a line should be enough. The coach can decide to make the number of grids less or more in number.
7) The coach can keep score by having an attacker keep track of how many times they get through all the grids successfully. The easier scoring system is to have each player keeps track of how many grids they penetrate through and scores each one as a point. Players are on the honor code to keep score. Since it takes 2 people to penetrate through a grid each time a grid is successfully penetrated through both players get a point.
8) After an attacker has passed through two or more grids another attacker can start through the grids. This keeps the exercise flowing at a higher rate of work.
9) A good "first touch" is necessary to prepare the ball for the next move the attack wants to make.
10) Keep lots of balls near by to keep the players working.
1) "Sharpening" by the attackers who are waiting in each square is essential to create and take care of the numerical advantage of 2 versus 1. Teaching players to prepare for the next movement is an important issue in creating a higher speed of play.

Diagram 33: 2 versus 1 through Multiple Grids

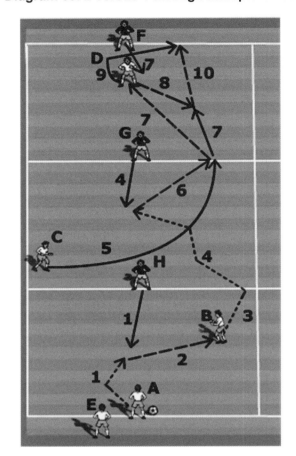

Diagram 33, page 172, has each defender starting at the upper edge of the grid that they are going to defend in when the attackers enter. These players are labeled F, G and H. The attack has started on the bottom edge of the diagram. The attackers are marked alphabetically; A, B, C, D, and E. The first defender, labeled H, steps forward into the grid to play when attacker A starts to dribble into the grid. Both the dribble and the defenders' run are labeled with a 1.

As pressure arrives on attacker A they pass the ball to the supporting attacker B. The pass is numbered with a 2. Attacker B, because they are already in behind defender H simply dribbles into the next square with a dribble numbered 3. Player A would stay in the grid for the next attack and player H would return to the line to prepare to play defense for the next attack in their grid.

In the second grid attacker B now starts a diagonal dribble to draw defender G to them and allow attacker C to make a Curved Run around them. The dribble by B is numbered with a 4, the run by defender G to pressure B is numbered 4 and the Curved Run by attacker C is numbered with a 5. Attacker B now passes the ball to attacker C. The pass is numbered with a 6.

In the third grid attacker C plays a pass immediately to attacker D who is in a position to create a Double Pass pattern. The pass is numbered with a 7 and draws defender F on to the back of attacker D with a run that is numbered with a 7. Attacker D then passes the ball back diagonally with a pass numbered 8 as attacker C steps forward to invite that passing pattern with a run numbered 7. Attacker D then spins around defender F with a run numbered 9. Attacker C finishes the sequence by passing the ball to attacker D behind the defender and on the end line. The pass is numbered with a 10.

The reader can see that as the attackers, labeled A and B, are successful then one of them would move into the next grid and combine with the attacker, C, waiting in that grid to penetrate past the defender, G, stepping off their line to defend. Player D waits to start another 2 versus 1 when the ball moves into the third grid. Remember that if the defender wins the ball they throw their vest to the attacker who lost it and go to the starting point for the attackers and the attacker who lost the ball now plays defense in the grid where they lost the ball.

Occasionally the coach will find an intelligent attacker who will pass the ball forward into the next grid without combining with the attacker in the grid in which they are currently working. This disrupts the use of 2 versus 1patterns to penetrate which circumvents the purpose of the exercise. It does show intelligence and allows for one attacker to run forward into the new grid that has the ball to try and combine there. It is a realistic choice in a game so the coach can decide to allow this pattern or if the coach is more interested in forcing 2 versus 1patterns to appear they must stop this solution of passing the ball from one grid to the next essentially bypassing a grid entirely.

Exercise 17: 2 versus 1: Defenders Can Counter-Attack
(Grid size 10-15 x 10-15 yards)
(See Diagrams 34 A, 34 B pages 174 and 176.)

This exercise is a little harder to get players to understand the organization of at first. The grid size is still 10 to 15 yards wide and/or deep. The coach must have an attacker in each grid and a defender waiting on the exit line of the grid to defend when the ball reaches their grid.

The coach will need two players to start the game at the beginning of the first grid, one to attack and the other to wait to defend if the ball is lost. This is a fast paced game when the players understand it and react to the transition of winning and losing the ball. The object of the exercise is for one team or the other to penetrate through all the grids until they penetrate through the last one. It just needs to be clear who will defend next or attack next so mayhem does not occur. This exercise is much more game like and teaching transition rate as well as 2 versus 1patterns.

Keys to 2 versus 1: Defenders Can Counter-Attack

1) An attacking player should wait in each grid.
2) A defender for the other team should wait on the end line of the grid so they may enter the grid and defend when the attacking team enters.
3) The roles of where the attacking player and defending player start change quickly with each dispossession and repossession of the ball.
4) Play starts with the attacking players entering from the edge of the first grid to combine with the attacker already waiting in the first grid.
5) There should be one extra "defender" waiting at the far end of all the grids to help stop the opposition or help with counter-attacks started in the grid in which they are standing.
6) The defenders will react by trying to stop the attackers from passing through the grid.
7) If a defender wins the ball they attack through the grids in front of them. They combine with their teammates that are in each grid. A defender who has been waiting on the edge of the grid immediately enters that grid when their teammate wins the ball and becomes part of a 2 versus 1 attack through the grid the other way.
8) When the ball is won then a grid will come open without one teams' players in it. The team now in possession needs to move players forward in the grids to anticipate an attacking movement. The team that has just lost the ball needs their players to go to the edge of the grid they are in to await their turn at defending.
9) The team that lost the ball will have two players in the grid where the ball was lost. One of the players from the team that just lost the ball must exit the grid and return to their teams starting point. The other player should defend immediately. Who leaves and who

defends should be based on who has the best chance of winning the ball back right away.

10) When a 2 versus 1 movement is successful one attacker moves forward into the next grid and the other stays behind. This causes another 2 versus 1 to occur with the attacker who has been waiting in the grid and the defender who has been waiting.

11) If a defender wins the ball they attack forward into the grid in front of them. Since there is already a defender on the edge of the grid and only one attacker left from the previous movement this will create a 2 versus 1 going in the opposite direction.

12) Tell the waiting defenders to move one grid line forward if there is no defender stepping back from the grid that the attack just went through when their group wins the ball. This makes it so that if their team loses the ball then the other teams' counter-attack will have opposition.

13) The coach should instruct the attacking group that after they penetrate a grid the remaining attacker needs to back up to the edge of the grid to get ready for the other teams counter-attack should their team lose the ball.

14) Three or four grids are enough so that players can reach one end or the other with successful 2 versus 1attacks. Just having two grids may be all the players can deal with in the beginning.

15) A good "first touch" is necessary to prepare the ball for the next move the attack wants to make.

16) Keep lots of balls near by to keep the players working.

1) "Sharpening" by the attackers who are waiting in each square is essential for speed of play from grid to grid.

Diagram 34 A: 2 versus 1 Counter-Attacking through One Grid (Shown as Two Grids for Clarity)

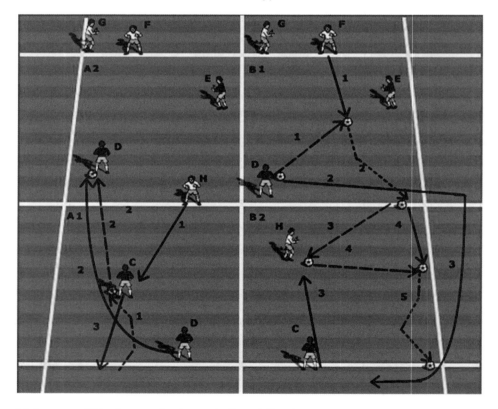

Diagram 34 A, page 174, shows attackers, C, D and E trying to penetrate through the grids and what happens when the ball is stolen. The grids on the left are labeled A1 and A2. The grids on

the right are labeled B1 and B2 to show the counter-attack. Both sides of the diagram show the same group of players and how the exercise plays out. There are not two sets of grids sided by side. The grids labeled B1 and B2 are in fact the same squares as A1 and A2. They are shown separately to clarify how the counter-attack would work. The exercise done in real life would be done with Squares B1 and B2 super-imposed over squares A1 and A2.

In grid A1, attacking players, C and D, execute a Curved Run. Player C enters the grid with a dribble numbered 1 which forces defender H to leave their line to move to pressure C with a run numbered 1. Attacker D makes a Curved Run around attacker C with a run numbered 2 and D receives a pass labeled 2 which allows them to enter the next grid. Since the attack was successful player C then retreats back to their line to prepare to defend if the ball is lost and the other team now attacks. The recovery run by player C is numbered with a 3. Player H would simply wait in the grid to attack the other way if their team wins the ball and starts to counter-attack.

In square A2 player D prepares to pass the ball to player E who is prepared to support the ball for another 2 versus 1 attack. The defender, F, has been waiting on the line to defend the square should the attack in the grid before them be successful. Grid A2 now becomes grid B1. The positioning of the players is the same in both grids. It is shown separately so that the reader can see the counter-attack start from a loss of ball possession.

In the grid labeled B1, player D attempts to pass the ball to player E. The pass is numbered with a 1. Player F intercepts the pass and counter attacks forward with a dribble numbered 2. Player D starts to run to recover which is numbered with a 2 but fails to reach player F before they reach the edge of the grid and ends up leaving the grid and returning to the starting point for future attacks and counter attacks. The run by player D to the starting point is numbered with a 3 and is outside of the grids. Player E simply stays in the grid to await an attack going through the grid. The grey player G would step up to the line and become the defender for grid B1 should the ball possession be lost and the other team attacks into the grid.

In grid B2 Player F then passes to player H. The pass is numbered with a 3. The defender on the line, player C enters the grid to put pressure on player H. Player C's run is numbered with a 3. Player F makes a run, numbered 4 on the opposite side of the grid and receives a pass, numbered 4. The counter-attack is successful with a dribble by player F, numbered 5, to the end line. (See Diagram 34 A, page 174.)

Diagram 34 B: 2 versus 1 Counter-Attack through Multiple Grids (One Grid Shown as Two Grids for Clarity)

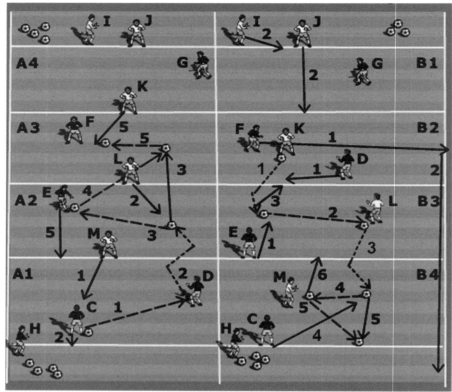

Diagram 34 B, page 176, is also split in half, the left side A1-A4 and right side B1-B4. Both sides of the grid show the same groups of players but it shows what happens when one side is attacking, grids A1-A4 and what happens when the ball is dispossessed and a counter-attack occurs; diagrams B1-B4. It is the same exercise shown above but with multiple grids that make flowing back and forth in a series of attacks and counter attacks possible. In the diagram it only shows one attack and counter attack but possession can be lost back and forth which is why players must recover to their starting points on the line quickly to react to a gain or loss of possession.

The exercise starts in grid A1 with players C and D confronting the defender M. The solution that is used in this example is for player C to hold the ball until pressure from defender M arrives with the run numbered 1. Player C then simply passes the ball to attacker D who dribbles the ball into the next grid. The pass from C to D is numbered 1 and the dribble by D is numbered with a 2. Player C now needs to step back to the line in preparation for defending. This recovery run by player C is numbered with a 2. Player M waits in the middle of the grid to help with a counter attack if it comes.

Players D and E execute a Wall Pass in grid A2 to avoid the defensive pressure of player L. Player L's run to pressure the ball is numbered with a 2. The pass from player D to E is numbered 3 and the return pass from E to D is numbered 4. Player D's run in behind the defense is numbered 3. Player E must now recover to the starting edge of grid A2 to prepare to defend. Player E's run to recover is numbered with a 5. Player L remains in the middle of the grid to help with a counter attack if it comes.

In grid A3 player D attempts to pass the ball to player F and has the pass, numbered 5, intercepted by player K. Player K runs to intercept the pass is numbered with a 5. The reader should now look to the right side of the diagram to the grids labeled B1-B4 where the counter attack now begins.

Player K immediately dribbles forward, numbered 1, from grid B2 into grid B3. The defender, player D, runs to supply pressure in grid B2 but fails to reach player K with their run numbered 1. Player F must leave the grid and run back to the starting point for their team. This run is numbered with a 1. Notice that because the attack forward by player K is successful it means that player J from grid B1 must step forward to the edge of the grid in front of them to get ready to defend against a counter attack. And it means player I is the defender now on the edge of the last grid, grid B1. Both runs by players J and I are numbered with a 2.

Player K, now in grid B3, evades the pressure from the entering defender E who has stepped forward with a run numbered 1. Player K chooses to make a pass numbered 2 to player L who turns and dribbles, numbered 3, into grid B4. Player K now returns to the line with a run numbered 3 to prepare to defend should the ball be lost. Defender C and attacker M react to the new situation.

Defender C moves to pressure the ball, the run is numbered 4, while the attacker M supplies support for a Wall Pass with attacker L. The passes for the Wall Pass are numbered 4 and 5 and the run showing player L getting in behind the defense is numbered with a 5. That run shows player L scoring a point by reaching the end line of the opponent. Player M retreats back to the edge of the grid to prepare to defend and that run is numbered with a 6. (See Diagram 34 B, page 176.)

The player, D, that lost the ball in grid B2 needs to leave the grids and move back to the starting position for their team which is at the bottom of the diagram. Player F in grid B2 and player E in grid B3 would stay in the middle of the grid and await a counter attack if their team won the ball back. One other point is that if player C had won the ball back in grid B4 they would not have had a second player to work with so player H would have had to step in to create the 2 versus 1 while the player who lost the ball exited the grid and returned to the starting point for their team which would be at the top of the diagram. Since the attack was successful player L would return to their teams starting point of the grids. **Remember there is really only one line of grids in this exercise that allow the players to attack and counter attack back and forth.** The lines of grids in the diagram labeled with an A are also the same line of grids labeled with a B. There are two lines of grids in the diagram to show how the game flows back and forth.

This is a confusing exercise at first and takes older players with a good sense of organization to execute it effectively. Players stay in the grid if their team is not in possession and players who are behind the attack, who's team has possession of the ball, recover to the end line of each grid to defend the grid should their team lose possession. The coach will have to spend time guiding the players into the correct starting positions and reorganization of the players within the grids as possession in won and lost.

Exercise 18: 3 versus 2 with Double Grids
(Grid is 10-15 x 10-15 yards)
(See Diagrams 35 A and 35 B, pages 179 and 180.)

This exercise is essentially the same one as 2 versus 1 in a single line. The difference is that there are two lines of grids. Each grid has one defender each. Waiting in the two grids is one attacker who prepares for the penetration of two attackers moving forward when they penetrate a previous square. One of the biggest differences is decision making, two attackers moving forward to combine with one waiting somewhere in the two grids creates a lot more decision to make. Also the 2 versus 1patterns will now start to become combination play more often between three people attacking. This is a difficult exercise.

Keys to 3 versus 2 Double Grids

1) The coach should have at least four to six attacking players waiting to start the exercise at the edge of the first grid.
2) The attackers will have one teammate already waiting in one of the two grids in front of them. The attacking player can straddle the center of the two grids if they want while they are waiting.
3) The defenders will have one player per grid that can not leave their personal grid. (The coach can make a variation where the defenders can leave the grid next to them and combine for two defenders in one adjacent parallel grid. This helps the recognition of numbers and width for the attackers but is harder to play, particularly when they are first learning.)
4) The attackers can only have 2 players in any one grid at a time.
5) The effect of the exercise is to create a 2 versus 1 out of a 3 versus 2. The players need to be able to see which player in which grid will provide the highest level of opportunity to penetrate into the next grid.
6) As the attackers move through the grids successfully they move two players forward. Which attacking player of the three ends up staying behind in the grid just penetrated can change and is not predetermined. This flexibility helps players to make intelligent decisions about their movement.
7) Two to four grids are enough. (More grids and the players may never get through) The players can end with a shot on a large goal if the coach wants some keeper work. Just have a goal set up 20 yards or so beyond the last grid and the player receiving the penetrating pass into a shooting position may do so. Otherwise the players score by stopping the ball on the end line of the last grid.
8) When an attack fails then the attackers start over. Usually two new players start the sequence at the start of the grid area and the players that just failed to penetrate all the way through the grids jog back to the starting point. It does not matter if a player that was in a grid jogs back to the starting position and one of the other attackers decides to stay in the grid. The only requirement is that they should arrange the players around the grids as they would for the start of the exercise.
9) The defending group defends until a predetermined number of repetitions have occurred. Then they should be afforded the chance to become attackers in the exercise.
10) Score is kept by the number of shots taken after getting through all the grids. The coach can also keep score for each grid that is successfully penetrated but it is much more work. Finally, the coach can score the game based not on shots but on the number of goals scored by each team.
11) All the 2 versus 1 patterns can occur in the exercise. It may be necessary for the coach to walk the players through examples of when a specific 2 versus 1 pattern could have been used. The "freeze" method is the best to get the players in the right positions and then slowly walk through the pattern. It is also perfectly acceptable to use the Socratic Method of asking questions of the players in conjunction with the "freeze" method of coaching. Asking about what patterns might work, will hopefully allow them to see the possibilities once the coach has frozen them. If the players come up blank then the coach will need to explain and walk through the choices.
12) Encourage the players to be tactically unpredictable beyond the fact that the defense knows that the players want to penetrate. The decision of who, when, where and how should often use surprise as well as the 2 versus 1 patterns.
12) A good "first touch" is necessary to prepare the ball for the next move the attack wants to make. Creative technical choices are to be encouraged if required. The players I work with understand that the ball is on the ground if possible and in the air if necessary. The players are encouraged to lift the ball if that is what will be effective.
13) Keep lots of balls near by to keep the players working "Sharpening" or pre-positioning by the attackers who are waiting in each square is essential to create and exploit the numerical advantage of 2 versus 1. One of the critical elements in creating a higher level of speed of play is having players who can anticipate what can happen or should happen

before it actually occurs

14) The coach can place a large goal 20 to 25 yards away from the edge of the grid and let the attackers who penetrate successfully take a shot on goal with either a one or two touch restriction. It helps train the keepers who do not get enough work in most practices.

Diagram 35 A: 3 versus 2 through Multiple Grids Set-Up

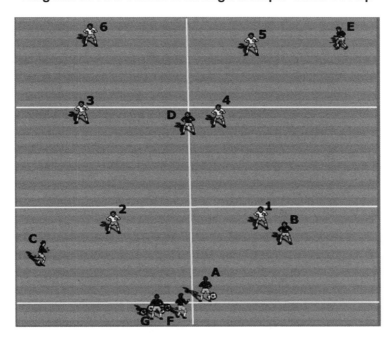

Diagram 35 A, page 179, shows the set-up of how players are organized at the start of the exercise. This exercise looks simple enough but don't be surprised if the players struggle with it for quite some time. Because the defenders have the condition that they must stay in their starting grid there must be a 2 versus 1 advantage in either the left or the right grid through out the exercise. The next set of grids will have two attackers moving forward from the grid before it. Since only one attacker is waiting in the grid two players must step forward to create an advantage of 3 versus 2 for the attackers. Be careful that the attacking group coming forward does not send three attackers into one grid by accident thereby creating a 4 versus 2. In addition the attack can only have two of their three players in any one grid. This prevents the attack from getting a 3 versus 1 numerical advantage in a single grid.

The players that are lettered are the attackers. The exercise begins with attacker A entering the grid and playing with either attacker C or B. The defenders who are numbered can not leave the grid that they are defending. In the first two squares the defenders are numbered 1 and 2. This organization continues through all the grids.

Personally, I like to have a big goal with my keeper at the end of the grids so that the players finish with a shot on goal. The usual condition is that the shot should be in one touch to allow more realistic timing for the goal keeper. However the coach can put on the condition that the attacker must beat the goal keeper with a dribble which will train the keepers to deal with 1 versus 1 finishing situations. This allows the keeper to practice their skills as well as the field players. Make sure you do not make a specialist of a player into goal keeping to soon. The keepers' foot skills need to be trained and tactical understanding will help them even if they stay in goal for life because they will be better at reading the game from having played it. Keepers can do this exercise and other field players' exercises. Keepers need additional training for their particular skill set.

A teaching point that bears sharing is that the waiting attacker should watch what their teammates are doing in the grid before them. This will allow them to anticipate where the ball will enter the grid they are occupying and where their teammates will be. This allows for better supporting positions being made in advance and positioning that will allow 2 versus 1patterns to be executed quickly. Speed of play is increased with intelligent thought.

Diagram 35 B: 3 versus 2 through Multiple Grids

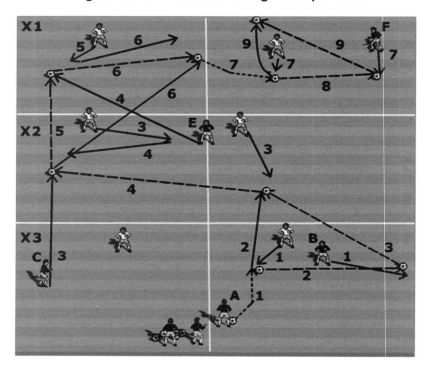

Diagram 35 B, page 180, shows how players might move through the grids. In this example player A chooses to attack the right square in the first grid with attacker B. B widens their position to make the defender less able to mark both attackers with a run numbered 1. Attackers A and B create a Wall Pass pattern. Attackers A and B create the pattern because the defender is moving to pressure player A who has dribbled, numbered with a 1, into the grid. Player B sharpens and improves their support position so that a Wall Pass, numbered with passes 2 and 3 can be made. Player A makes a run, numbered 2, in behind the defender. This allows player A to move forward into the next grid and make decisions on where they should play the ball and with whom.

Attacker C has moved forward into the next grid to supply wide support on the opposite side of the grid with a run numbered 3. Attacker E has chosen to straddle the line to make defending them or the space more difficult. Because of attacker E's position the defender in the left hand grid starts to close down attacker A, who is in possession of the ball. The run by the defender is numbered with a 3.   The defender in the grid next to them has pushed centrally to use time of flight to mark attacker E. The run by the defender is numbered with a 3. Attacker A reacts by making a pass to attacker C to switch the side the attack is coming from as the defender in attacker A's square steps up to pressure them. The pass from player A to player C is numbered with a 4.

Attacker E decides to make a run, numbered 4, forward to create a 2 versus 1 opportunity in the second left grid. The run also penetrates into the third line of grids at the same time. The defender in the left second grid starts a second defensive run, numbered 4, to pressure the ball that was passed by attacker A to attacker C. The penetrating run by attacker E behind the oncoming defender in the left side of the second grid lets attacker C make a penetrating pass to attacker E that is numbered with a 5. Attacker C then makes a run back over the space that attacker E came out of which creates an X pattern. Because the defender in the left side of the third grid reacts to attacker E's run and reception of the ball with a pressuring run numbered with a 5 attacker E passes the ball back across the grain to attacker C with a pass numbered 6. The defender in the left square of the third grid tries to recover from pressuring attacker E into pressuring attacker C with a run numbered 6 but attacker C eliminates the pressure by dribbling into the fright square of grid three with a dribble numbered 7.

Attacker F sees the dribble into their grid and makes a run to support attacker C which is numbered with a 7. The defender steps to pressure with a run numbered with a 7. Attacker C reads the situation and uses a pattern that can be seen either as a normal Wall Pass or if the release of the ball from C to F is late C can use a Flick and Spin move, numbered with a 9, to get behind the defender and reach the end of the grid. The pass by attacker C to attacker F is numbered with an 8 and the return pass from attacker F to attacker C is numbered with a 9. If there is a big goal at the end of the grids attacker C would take a shot at goal.

Exercise 19: 3 versus 2 to 2 versus 1 Counter-Attack
(Grid size is 20-30 x 25-35 yards or 30-50 x 35-60 yards if large goals are used) (See Diagrams 36 A, 36 B and 36 C, pages 182, 183 and 184.)

This exercise is very similar to the 2 versus 1 with one defender on the line. However, the players start with a 3 versus 2 and return back across the grid with a 2 versus 1. The coach should have 6 to 9 players on one side of the grid and 4 to 6 players waiting on the other side of the grid. It is a fast game that requires the element of transition to be part of the focus of the exercise.

Keys to 3 versus 2 to 2 versus 1 Counter-Attack

1) Three attackers start out attacking from one side of the grid to the other.
2) Two defenders come out from the other side of the grid to prevent them from successfully stopping the ball on their end line.
3) The use of two full sized goals, one on each end of the grid, instead of stepping on the ball at the end line is extremely useful. It allows finishing too occur which in turn motivates a higher work rate and lets the keepers work on multiple repetitions of shot stopping.
4) The coach can allow the attackers to finish using shooting that is unrestricted. This will allow the attackers to finish their attacks with 1 versus 1 shooting confrontations against the keeper. It may also be more useful if the players are given a condition of limited touches or shooting before they reach a certain distance to the goal.
5) One of two results can occur from any rotation in the exercise:
   a) One, the attacking team is successful in penetrating the defense and steps on the ball on the grid line or shoots. The attacker scoring the ball must defend against the two defenders who collect the ball and counter-attack or;
   b) Two, the defenders will steal the ball away and counter-attack to the other side. The attacker that lost the ball must try to defend to prevent the counter-attacking defenders from reaching the grid line. This creates a 2 versus 1 counter attack from the 3 versus 2 that was going the other way.
6) The two attackers that do not defend now move to the end of the grid they were attacking when they started the rotation. This will cause them to start at the defending side of the grid and replace the two defenders that left.
7) The two defenders end up on the attacking side of the grid along with the attacker that tried to stop them from counter-attacking, replacing all three people that attacked.
8) A good "first touch" is necessary to prepare the ball.
9) Keep lots of balls near by to keep the players working.
10) "Sharpening" needs to be reinforced in this exercise.

Diagram 36 A: 3 versus 2 with 2 versus 1 Counter-Attack Set-Up

In Diagram 36 A, page 182, the players from opposite sides of the grid are differentiated by color. In the exercise itself it is not necessary to separate the players by color. The pace of the exercise is very high and the players will be constantly switching ends. The players will automatically know who is doing what role each time the exercise goes through a rotation. The initial explanation by the coach may cause a little confusion while the players sort out how to respond to the issue of the defenders that are beaten versus the situation where the defenders have stolen the ball away from the attackers, but a few repetitions should take care of that issue.

Remember that three players, shown in Diagram 36 A , page 182, coming from the bottom of the grid, attack in one direction and two players attack back the other way. If the ball is lost by one of the three attackers or shot at the far end of the grid the player losing the ball or shooting the ball must defend against the two players now attacking the other way.

Diagram 36 B: 3 versus 2 with 2 versus 1 Counter-Attack with Large Goals

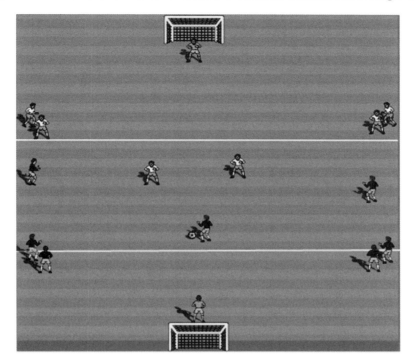

Diagram 36 B, page 183, simply shows the same game of 3 versus 2 with a counter attack of 2 versus 1 attacking to goals set up at each end of the grid. The exercise works very well when using two large sized goals, one on each end, for the players to finish on and for the teams' keepers to get work. The goals should be about 15 to 20 yards outside of the grid. Because the counter-attack is frequently created through the loss of ball possession there will be lots of 1 versus 1confrontations for the keeper to deal with during the exercise. The coach can put on a restriction that the ball must be shot no closer than a specified range and then the keepers will have to deal with timing and reaction. Either way the pace of the exercise is extremely high allowing 2 versus 1patterns to be used and encourages a fast rate of transition.

Diagram 36 C: 3 versus 2 with 2 versus 1 Counter-Attack Example and Rotation

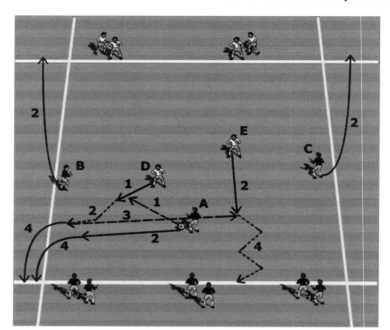

Diagram 36 C, page 184, shows how the loss of a ball creates a counter attack and how the rotation of players keeps three players coming from one side and two from the other without getting overloaded with players on one side of the grid or the other.

Three attackers, players A, B and C have moved into the grid from the lower portion of the grid. Two defenders, players D and E have entered from the top half of the grid. Player A makes an initial pass numbered 1 intended for player B. Defender D cuts out the pass from player A to B with a run numbered 1

Player A, because they lost the ball, must now play defense against the two defenders D and E. Player A makes a pressuring run numbered 2 in reaction to the initial dribble by player D after D won the ball. That dribble is numbered with a 2. Because the pressure is coming player D sends the ball to the opposite side of the grid to their teammate with a pass numbered 3. Player E has stepped forward with a run numbered 2 when they saw that their teammate D had won the ball. Player E receives the pass and dribbles forward to the line to end this sequence. The dribble is numbered with a 4. Players A and D leave the grid when player E succeeds in getting to the end line. Their exit runs are numbered with 4's.

The exercise starts out as a 3 versus 2 and changes to a counter attack 2 versus 1 going the other way. Attacking players B and C jog out of the grid with runs numbered 2 as soon as they see that ball possession has been lost. They move to the opposite side of the grid from the one they started from. This means that they are replacing the two players that came out from the top of the grid. As stated before player A has a run into a defensive position numbered 2 because they lost the ball. However, as soon as the other team succeeds in their attack player A leaves the grid and returns to their starting spot with the two players that just crossed the grid from the top to the bottom.

The exercise always starts from the same side in a 3 versus 2 pattern and ends with a 2 versus 1 counter attack in the opposite direction. If the 3 players reach the top of the grid to shot or score the two players who were defending grab a ball and attack the other way while the player who shot the ball defends against the two players. If the attack that starts with the 3 versus 2 loses the ball to the defenders then the attacker losing the ball must defend the counter attack instead of the attacker who scored becoming the defender. (This exercise was contributed by Van Culver.)

Exercise 20: 2 versus 2 Cross Grid Game
(Grid is 10-20 X 10-20 yards) (See Diagrams 37 A and 37 B page 186.)

This is an exercise that takes four players. Because it is a physically demanding exercise the coach can have another four players waiting passively or actively until the time limit for work has been reached by the four players in the grid. What is different about this exercise is that the two goals for each team are on opposite sides of the grid. One team is attacking North/South and the other team is attacking East/West. In all other aspects this is a normal exercise. What it allows is quick transition when winning the ball away from the opponents. It demands a quick level of play before the disposed opponent can get their defense arranged effectively. This helps train transition rate.

Keys to Exercise 20

1) The players score by stopping the ball on the goal line or by passing the ball through a set of cones that is the goal. After a team scores they turn and attack their opposite goal. Possession of the ball must be taken away from them or they must lose control of the ball outside of the grid for a turn-over to occur that will force them to play defense.
2) Attackers may move anywhere they want in the grid.
3) The coach lets the defenders move freely to defend anywhere in the grid.
4) Instead of using the entire grid line as the goal the coach can set up coned goals on each side of the grid. Remember that this exercise will require four goals, one on each edge of the grid.
5) Help the players understand that quick decision making helps them to be effective. Make sure that quickness by the players is not hastiness or panic. "Be in a hurry but not hurried." (John Wooden)
6) There will be a fair amount of solutions that involve dribbling. This is quite alright both in this exercise and in others that are in this book. Defenders can only shut done the pass or the dribble and the key to success and creativity is learning to read the defenders so the player can know when to dribble and when to pass.
7) A good "first touch" is necessary to prepare the ball for the next move the attack wants to make.
8) Keep lots of balls near by to keep the players working.
9) "Sharpening" needs to be reinforced in this exercise.

Diagram 37 A: 2 versus 2 Cross Grid Game Set-Up

In Diagram 37 A, page 186, the white players possessing the ball to start are attacking from top to bottom on the page. The black players are attacking the goals from left to right on the grid. In this diagram there are goals shown by cones on each side of the grid. The goals can be made smaller if desired. Remember that the game can be played to the edge of the grid line to step on the ball. (See keys to the exercise section 3, page 185) There is can also be a condition requiring a defender to retreat to their end line, once a direction is established. Both conditions will alter the way the exercise works.

Diagram 37 B: 2 versus 2 Cross Grid Game

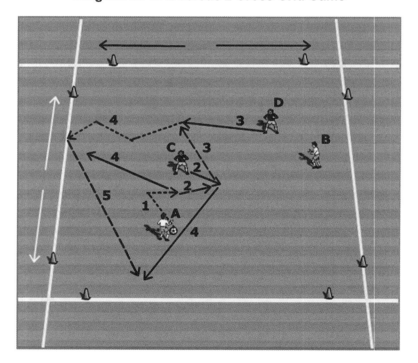

In the first movement, shown in diagram 37 B, page 186, player A dribbles, numbered with a 1 and then attempts to pass the ball to their teammate player B with a pass numbered 2. Player C steps into the path of the pass and steals the ball. Since this is the first possession player C's team can attack in either direction to score on one of their two goals. Player D sees that the opposing player B is in the way of the closest goal and makes a run numbered 3 to attack the opposite goal. Player C sends a pass numbered 3 to player D who then dribbles into the goal with dribble numbered 4. Player A, who lost the ball, makes a run to recovery the ball which is numbered with a 4 but is too late to stop the score. Players D and C then start to attack the opposite goal. Player C makes a run, numbered 4, to the lower edge of the grid which splits the vision of player A from them and the ball carrier D. Player D makes a pass numbered 5 to player C and the attack is now started towards the other goal. The opposing players defend, trying to steal the ball back and thwart the opposing groups attempt to score. When they win the ball back they attack the goals set up for them on opposite sides of the grid.

The coach will need to encourage the use of 2 versus 1patterns during the exercise. This exercise tends to be very high paced and players get caught up in rushing from side to side without thinking or using their teammate. If players do this through-out the exercise then very little learning about 2 versus 1 will occur. Awarding points for 2 versus 1 patterns as well as getting to one side of the grid to the other is probably the best way of encouraging the players to work with each other.

Exercise 21: 2 versus 1 for Possession
(Grid is 10-15 X 10-15 yards)
(See Diagrams 38 A, 38 B and 38 C, pages 189, 190 and 191.)

In any manual about 2 versus 1 there should at least be a cursory examination of two players trying to keep the ball away from one defender. There are at least three variations that I use for teaching my players.

   A) 2 versus 1 where the play is continuous. The defender becomes part of the attacking team and the attacker that lost the ball becomes the defender until they can win the ball or force an error where the ball leaves the grid. This change in possession forces the attacker who lost the ball to become the defender. There should be a time limit on this exercise because doing it well requires a fair amount of anaerobic work by the players. (See Diagram 38 A, page 189.)
   B) 2 versus 1 from teams from 2 versus 2. When players are defending one of the defending teams' players stands just outside of the grid and waits for their partner to win the ball and then joins in the attack. The defending team can switch defenders if the active player in the middle becomes too winded. This game can last a little longer before the players wear out but it should also have a time limit so that the players do not go into slow motion from lack of energy.
   C) 2 versus 1 for possession that has a predetermined number of passes that when that number is reached will allow the players to attack a goal for a shot. This allows some keeper training if using a big goal. The coach can also set up a small goal to pass the ball through or just let the players step on the ball on the line are also acceptable goals to attack.

Keys to Exercise 21

   1) Getting players to understand how to help their teammate is sometimes difficult, particularly at the younger ages. I use a concrete picture to solve the problem. Tell the players that the ball is the sun and the defender casts a shadow from hitting the sun. Then ask the supporting attacker if they are currently in the shadow of the defender. If they are then they are in the wrong spot.
   2) If the player that a teammate is passing the ball to is closer to the defender then the

player passing the ball then the player is probably making a poor choice in passing the ball. Passes should not put more pressure on the player receiving the ball than is on the player who currently has the ball.

3) Shielding the ball is a common solution to buy time to get help from a teammate that is currently unavailable.

4) The supporting player may need to run around in a form of a curved run or to create a take over situation to release pressure on their attacking teammate. Players should understand and be willing to move anywhere they need to so they can receive the ball and release pressure on their teammate.

5) After the players understand that they need to get out of the shadow, a one word reference, to the supporting runner called "sharpening" can be taught or reinforced. Other coaches use the word "showing" or getting a better "angle". The concept is the same. "Sharpening" requires a supporting player to create a passing lane from their teammate to them by running into an available spot. This relates to the concept of getting out of the shadow of the defender.

6) The coach and team will be well served by encouraging players to be patient and attempt to keep the ball so that confidence replaces panic when players are under pressure.

7) Players should try to move so that they have an "open" body shape that allows them to see the field of play. If the players' runs are constantly causing them to turn their back and lose vision of their teammate and the defender then the players in possession of the ball are more vulnerable to losing the ball. Movements like backing out towards the edge of the grid or side shuffling their feet laterally helps keep vision of the ball, their teammate and the opponent through-out the exercise.

8) Methods of scoring for this exercise can vary.

    a) A pre-determined number of passes gets a point. Each attacking player gets a point and at the end of the exercise each individual adds up their points. The player that has the most points, which means they were better as possessing the ball than the other two players, wins. (Used for Diagram 38 A, page 189.)

    b) Each player on a team that scores on a goal are awarded a point. Each individual keeps their total number of points separately but both attackers receive a point when they are part of a sequence that scores a goal. (Used for Diagram 38 C, page 191.)

9) A good "first touch" is necessary to prepare the ball for the next move the attack wants to make.

10) Keep lots of balls near by to keep the players working.

Diagram 38 A: 2 versus 1 for Possession Set-Up

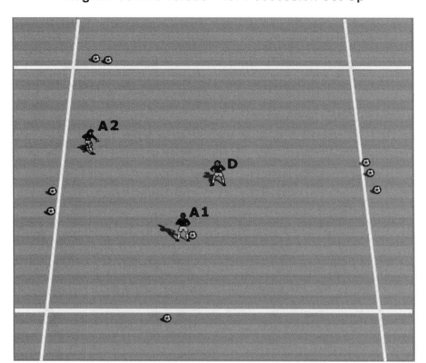

Diagram 38 A, page 189, has three players inside of the grid. The two players in possession of the ball at this moment are labeled A1 and A2. The other player is playing defense and is labeled with a D. In the exercise player D would be just carrying a scrimmage vest to let people know that they are defending. When they win the ball they become an attacker and the player that lost the ball has the scrimmage vest thrown to them to make clear who is defending. This exercise is fairly anaerobic and can not go for to long a time period without some short rest periods. If the exercise just goes on indefinitely then the players will drop their work rate. Score can be kept by each individual if their team of two gets to a certain number of passes. The individual keeps their own score and a point is added to their score regardless of which of the other players are working with them at that moment.

A side note about a general coaching skill and coaching any exercise is that the coach will have multiple grids working at the same time. When setting up the grids try to do it in a way that will allow the instructor to be able to walk around the edge of the entire area so that they can watch all the players at once. This will help avoid getting to focused on just one group and keep the coach more involved with the entire team.

This also allows the coach the ability to monitor the behavior and focus of the players without having to constantly turning to see the players. This helps keep the players stay on task and allows the coach to quickly see if some of the players do not understand the exercise and make corrections so that the coach can help the players correct any flaws. If the players are acting inappropriately the coach can deal with the issue quickly and easily. This can be particularly important if the players are acting in a way that may cause harm to them self or others.
On the positive side it also allows the coach to see and applaud the players who are being dedicated, working on task, show comprehension of the exercise and/or are improving. Acknowledging improvement can be for every player and not just the best. A little positive feedback can go a long way to getting higher work rates. Make sure that average or even below average players are "caught" doing something right and applaud it. Players work harder when they all know that they are being evaluated and valued.

Diagram 38 B: 2 versus 1 for Possession with Resting Partner

In Diagram 38 B, page 190, there are two teams of two. The team that is defending has a resting player on the side of the grid. They enter the grid when either of two situations occurs.

a) One, their teammate wins the ball and they can now play 2 versus 1 for possession against one defender from the other team. The other teams' player steps out and rests when possession is lost.
b) Two, the teammate of the resting player runs out of steam to defend and they need to swap roles for a short period.

Diagram 38 C: 2 versus 1 for Possession with a Large Goal for Shooting

Diagram 38 C, page 191, is the same exercise but when a team reaches a set number of passes they may shoot at a goal.

Exercise 22: Plus 1, 2 or 3
(Grid size will vary.)
(See Diagrams 39 and 39 A, pages 193 and 194.)

This exercise could easily be under listed under the Conditioned Game section. However, the concept of "Plus" players is too critical not to point out separately. Essentially this exercise puts a player(s) into the exercise that play attack for both teams. (It can also put a player that plays' defense for both teams in the exercise but this use is of the concept is less frequently used.) The coach can use more than one player to create a plus situation. This is extremely helpful at the younger ages or at the initial stages of teaching an exercise.

The coach can use any exercise when using this concept. Players can create 2 versus 1patterns that allows only one defender against two attackers and allows one of the players to play with which ever player has the ball is a "Plus" one exercise. In other words one of the players will be designated a permanent attacker. The exercise title would be 1 verses 1 Plus 1. What it does is create a 2 versus 1 pattern to occur.

The key to understanding the "Plus" one player(s) is that the extra player(s) are neutral and will play for both teams. The exercise that the coach is using can be keep-away in nature or directional to goals. The goals can be line goals, coned area goals or net goals. Scoring methods are not relevant to the concept. All that is needed for the "Plus" one concept is that both teams get to use the extra player(s) when they are in possession of the ball. The essence of this concept and the exercises that occur is to create attacking advantages in numbers. (It can also be used for defensive advantages in numbers but is not used this way as often.)

When ever an exercise has a 2 versus 2 structure and a "Plus" 1 it creates a 2 versus 1 numerical advantage for the attack. The 2 versus 2 "Plus" 1 creates a 3 versus 2 numerical advantage for the team in possession of the ball. For this manuals' purpose this creates a 2 versus 1 situation which occurs within the 3 versus 2. Because there is a "Plus" attacker in this situation the ability to find and exploit the 2 versus 1 is critically important.

Grid size has no effect on the concept. The coach will need to assess the number of players involved, the technical ability of the players and the tactical understanding of the players to create the right amount of space and time for the players to be successful. The ability of the players and the time needed to make decisions will influence how many "Plus" players a coach uses in any given exercise. The weaker the players the more "Plus" players will need to be added to the exercise to create success.

Keys to Exercise 22

1) The "Plus" player concept does not have a specific number of players to play the neutral role in an exercise. "Plus" numbers can be from a single player up to a large group of players. "Plus" players play offense for both teams. They can also play defense for both teams. The concept is not used very often for defensive purposes because the creation of play is harder for developing players to grasp and execute than the destruction of play.
2) The biggest key is to get the players with the ball to recognize or create the numerical superiority that the "Plus" player(s) allows to occur by being inserted into the exercise.
3) The "Plus" player concept allows numerical advantages to occur, which makes creating 2 versus 1 patterns easier and allows those patterns to occur much more frequently.
4) This understanding can lead to players knowing when to speed up an attack in a game because a numerically superior situation exists. If the decision is not made quickly the advantage will often disappear in the game.
5) The understanding also teaches players to learn to see the advantage of switching the point of attack as quickly as possible to create situations of numerical superiority from one side of the field to the other.
6) Selecting the right number of "Plus" players and the right grid size is part of the art of coaching. All the factors of time, space and opponents should allow the teams in the exercise to have a success rate that encourages them to keep trying and at the same time is not so easy that they are bored by the exercise. That success rate should be in the B- to A- range if the coach wants the players to be motivated and challenged.
7) A good "first touch" is necessary to prepare the ball for the next move the attack wants to make.
8) Keep lots of balls near by to keep the players working.
9) "Sharpening" will need to be reinforced in this exercise.
10) Keeping an "open body shape" will be important for the players to use.

Diagram 39: Plus Player Set-Up: 3 Verses 3 Plus 2 Example

Diagram 39, page 193, is an example of a "Plus" 2 situation. The players in labeled C are the 2 extra players who will play for which ever team has possession of the ball. The other teams in the grid have three players each. One team is designated with an A and the other team is labeled with a B. The "Plus" concept is very helpful in creating exercises for all sorts of learning environments including the creation of 2 versus 1situations. Learning to support the ball through keep away games, creating larger numbers of shooting opportunities, learning to switch the point of attack and many other concepts are enhanced by using "Plus" players to make the desired outcome more easily attainable.

As already stated there are two "Plus" or neutral players that play for each team in Diagram 39, page 193, which creates a 5 versus 3 player advantage for both teams at all times that they possess the ball. The players are playing keep away since there are no goals or direction to attack indicated in the diagram. However, the numerical advantage will create 2 versus 1opportunities to occur.

In this manual it would make sense that scoring would be kept in this exercise by the number of 2 versus 1 patterns used successfully. The coach should also award points for 2 versus 1patterns that are threatened to be used so that the defense is beaten by illusion of the 2 versus 1 pattern and makes the mistake of jumping a passing lane allowing an attacker to dribble successfully because of the threatened 2 versus 1 pattern.

Since the exercise in Diagram 39, page 193, shows a keep away sequence scoring can also be kept by a number of passes being reached to score a point. This method of scoring will slow down the number of 2 versus 1patterns used or even looked for by the players. The coach can of course choose to combine both methods of scoring; the 2 versus 1patterns as well as a certain number of passes score points. Jim Lennox once said: "That if a coach can see what it is that they want to teach, isolate that topic in an exercise and then reinsert it into the game a coach will never need a drill book again." In the above diagram and explanation of how to use it the reader has been given several possible ways of conditioning the rules and approaching the exercise. The choices for the coach will always be free and predicated on what the coach needs to have the players learn. The coach just needs to know clearly in their mind what the players need to be instructed about, isolate it with conditioned rules like a "Plus" situation and then reinsert it into the game to see if the players have learned what they needed to correct.

Diagram 39 A: Plus Players to Goals

Diagram 39 A, page 194, does not show any patterning by the players but the patterns are limitless. In this exercise the coach can continue to award points for a set number of passes being achieved but the game is now directional in nature because there are goals inserted into the exercise. In this diagram the team labeled with an A combines with the "Plus" players labeled C to attack the goal from bottom to top. If the players labeled with a B win the ball they combine with the "Plus" players labeled C and attack across the grid from top to bottom. The players can create 2 versus 1patterns more easily because of the directionality of the exercise. The 2 versus 1patterns can also score points for the team executing them and the teams can now score on the goals placed at each end of the grid. Awarding points for 2 versus 1patterns is very important in the beginning stages of learning the patterns because players do what they know and are comfortable with, thus awarding points for the patterns will encourage them to use them. "Plus" exercises are great for the coach to start teaching concepts, lessen the pressure on the players so more success is created and are superior in teaching younger players so that success rates are high enough to encourage them to keep working on the topic being taught.

Exercise 23: 4 versus 4 versus 4
(Grid size 25-40 X 25-40 yards)
(See Diagram 40, page 196.)

In essence this exercise is 8 versus 4. Two groups of 4 cooperate as one team working against the other 4 players. One group of four will all have the ball and the other four players are support players. The last group of four will work as defenders.

During their timed competition the 8 players try to create as many patterns of 2 versus 1 that they can or a specific pattern that the coach requires them to create. What it allows is that when a group is attacking they will get two attackers for every one defender. This creates multiple 2 versus 1situations. The coach rotates the groups from offensive role to supporting role to defensive role. The grid size is up to the ability of the players to handle the space, time and opponents and have some success. The reader could look at this exercise as a Plus 4 exercise but it has a different feel about it. The exercise itself is a bit chaotic but forces players to create 2 versus 1patterns even without a specific direction to attack. (See Diagram 40, page 196.)

Keys to Exercise 23

1) Each offensive group should have four balls in the exercise, one per player, which allows for a 2 versus 1 situation to occur constantly.
2) The exercise has three groups of 4 players. The coach can use more or less numbers if numbers dictate this or the coach wants to enlarge or shrink the group size.
3) During a timed period one group of 4 players takes the offensive role. Another group of 4 takes the supporting roles. And the last group of 4 takes the defending roles.
4) If a ball is stolen by a defender they will pass it out of the grid as near to the side line as they can. Smashing the ball long is counter productive to the exercise.
5) In each timed sequence by a group of offensive players use the supporting players to create and execute 2 versus 1patterns. Score is kept by adding up each successful pattern that the offense executes. They must call out the pattern when it occurs and what pattern it was to get it scored.
6) If a 2 versus 1 pattern ends with the supporting player in possession of the ball they quickly pass it back to the offensive player so that they can keep trying to create and execute 2 versus 1patterns. One example of this problem is that a Curved Run would leave the supporting player in possession of the ball so to let the "offensive" group continue to produce 2 versus 1patterns the ball must be passed back to a member of the offensive group.
7) The players must learn to commit defenders to create 2 versus 1patterns. This is accomplished most frequently by attackers dribbling at the defender.
8) Some 2 versus 1patterns do not require dribbling at the defender but rather that the attacker commits the defender to them in a shielding or holding pattern. The committing of a defender by getting marked and then having a supporting player come to relieve the pressure often includes a 2 versus 1 pattern.
9) Supporting players must work hard to help the offense. Lack of quick, intelligent support will cause the exercise to break down and become useless.
10) Defenders must be constantly trying to pressure an offensive player. Lack of work will cause the exercise to break down and become useless.
11) The coach can specify what 2 versus 1 pattern they want used to score points.
12) The coach can let the players use any pattern they wish to create to score points.
13) The exercise should be timed but can be to a set number of 2 versus 1patterns created. The advantage of a timed period is that it can become a contest between groups as they rotate their roles. The coach can see who can create a set number of patterns in the fastest time frame. This method of scoring will tend to cause the players to work harder at committing the defenders and the off the ball players to support faster. It can also have the deleterious effect of causing players who are not ready for this level pressure to panic or force the play rather than have it occur in a natural way or pace. The coach must be able to assess the developmental level of their players.
14) A good "first touch" is necessary to prepare the ball for the next move the attack wants to make.
15) Keep lots of balls near by to keep the players working.
16) "Sharpening" needs to be reinforced in this exercise.

Diagram 40: 4 versus 4 versus 4: Set-Up

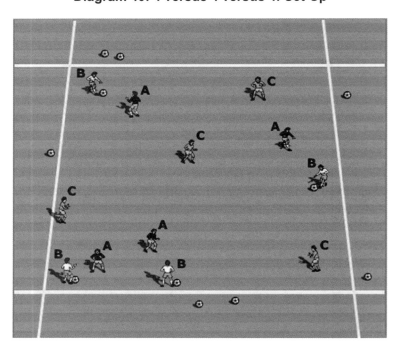

Diagram 40, page 196, illustrates how the 4 v 4 v 4 exercise works. All the players labeled A right now are defending. All the players labeled B have the ball and are trying to combine with the players marked with a player marked with C to create a 2 versus 1 pattern. The C group is the supporting player group in this sequence. The coach must remind the defenders that they have to be aggressive about trying to win the ball. Also the players with the ball should look to try and commit the defenders by dribbling at them. If a ball is lost the player winning it simply passes it gently out of the grid and the player who lost it retrieves it to start creating 2 versus 1 patterns again. If a 2 versus 1 pattern leaves a supporting player in possession of the ball, as a Curved Run would, then the supporting player quickly gives the ball back to the player who is attacking and trying to create points for their team by executing 2 versus 1 patterns. Without a specific direction to attack it is sometimes hard for the players to see the patterns but with patience and time they can see and use them in this exercise.

Exercise 24: Asteroids
(Grid size is 35 x 30 yard up to ¾ of a field)
(See Diagram 41, 41 A, 41 B and 41 C; pages 198, 199, 200 and 201.)

1) The exercises' has many mini-games but the exercise will last 1 to 10 minutes depending on the fitness level of the players and the age group. The exact length of each sequence is not determinable.
2) The players in the middle keep playing until the ball is scored or the ball is shot over the end line.
3) Each rotation of Asteroids can be scored independently or as a part of a series of games that add up to a winning amount of points.
4) A team scores a point when one of its' players shoots and scores on a goal.
5) The game starts when one team, the "attacking" team enters the grid with the ball. They stay the attacking team until they score, they shoot over the end line or the other team wins the ball and becomes the attacking team.
6) All players sprint back to the end line that they started from when a sequence ends in a goal or a shot passes over the end line.

7) Each time an attacker enters the grid then a defender can enter to oppose the attacker. No defender may enter the grid unless the attack adds a player.

8) The attacking team controls how many players are playing inside the grid. The attacking team has no rule that makes them enter. The attacking team chooses to enter to gain an advantage for their team.

9) When possession of the ball is lost in the middle of the grid in a sequence, from the attacking team to the defending team, then the initiative to enter a new player turns to the team with the ball. The former defending team can now enter players because they have possession of the ball. If the new attacking team adds a player then the former attacking team, now defending, may enter a player to help defend. This swinging regarding who gets to have the initiative to enter the players and who must react to the entering of the grid moves back and forth several times within a single sequence. Which team has the ball predicates who can choose to enter and who must respond to attackers being added to the playing grid.

10) The number of players for the entire exercise is adjustable but I like to use five or six players per side. If they all enter into the grid over time then the exercise sequence changes into a 5 versus 5 or 6 versus 6 small sided game.

11) The game restarts with the team that didn't start the attack the last sequence. This way both groups get to try and control their destiny.

12) The coach can use small goals or full sized goals with keepers in them. If a keeper catches the ball they throw it out to their team which switches the initiative for who is attacking and getting to add players.

13) Have four to six extra balls by the grid so the game does not have to stop every time there is a ball from the immediate grid area

14) One of the great advantages of this exercise is that a coach can show players' how and when making runs is advantageous to the group. Most of the runs come from behind but as soon as a ball is back passed then runs made by forward players become available.

15) The coach can have a player from each team start in the center of the grid if they want to create the tactical situation of passing forward to a "striker" who has a defender on them.

16) The coach can also instruct defenders how to position them self to be most effective in reacting to the attackers runs.

17) Most of the 2 versus 1 patterns can and do occur in this exercises. The coach should not be hesitant to stop and show how a pattern could be used. Double pass patterns are the hardest to recreate for this exercise but they can be induced by requiring one attacker to start in the center of the grid with one defender marking them. (See the variation explanation and Diagrams 41 B, 41 C, pages 200 and 201.)

18) An attacker can dribble by the defender in a one on one confrontation and never have any other attacker join the sequence. The coach will find that this does not happen very often and may even need to be encouraged.

19) As the exercise adds more and more players in a sequence the coach should start to instruct players about small group shape, support, penetrating runs and the timing of the decisions.

20) Players should try and find 2 versus 1patterns that will help them penetrate to goal and score.

21) A good "first touch" is necessary to prepare the ball for the next move the attack wants to make.

22) Players should maintain an "open" body shape.

23) Players need to "sharpen" into available passing lanes.

24) Players should look to create left/right/split support when numbers dictate it.

Variation:

a) An attacker is positioned in the center of the grid with a defender marking them. This allows the attack to start working as if they had a striker. (See Diagrams 41 B and 41 C, pages 200 and 201.)

b) The exercise becomes a little more realistic with this starting position. In essence it means that the game starts with a pass and not someone dribbling into the grid. This could mean that the striker and the player who passed the ball in could already provide two attackers by entering the grid. However, the teammate that sends in a pass in can (See Diagram 41 B, page 200.) chose not to run at all. In Diagram 41 B, page 200, the attacker who passed the ball into their teammate in the center of the grid makes a Curved Run. The defenders must stay at a 1 versus 1 situation until the Curved Run is made, then the defenders can enter a player and the exercise becomes a 2 versus 2.

Diagram 41: Asteroids Set-Ups

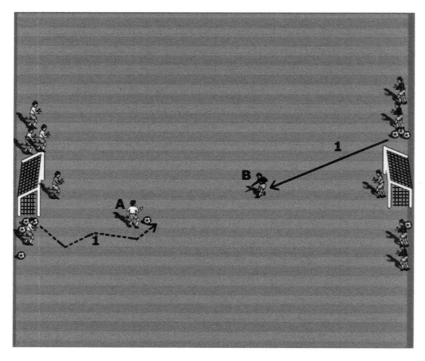

In Diagram 41, page 198, the players on the left of the grid are starting the attack. At this point in the exercise only one defender may enter the grid in response to one attacker entering.

The timing of the support run and where it comes from is a source of excellent teaching points for the players. The timing of a run may allow a defender to move into good supporting position to stop an attack that is using a dribble because defensive cover can now be applied. Any time a team has the ball they may add a player into the attack.

Diagram 41 A: Asteroids Exercise Example

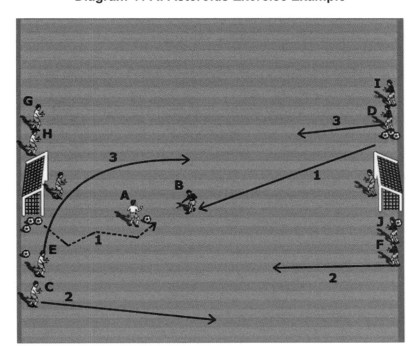

Diagram 41 A, page 199, shows two attackers, player C on the far left bottom of the grid and player E making runs to support the dribble of attacker A. Player B has come to pressure attacker A. The players on the far right of the grid are responding to the runs entering the grid by the attackers C and E. Player D is responding to player E and the defending player F is responding to the run by C. Each action by an attacker is numbered and the responded defensive action has the same number attached to it. When attacker A entered defender B entered and both a numbered with a 1. When attacker C entered defender F entered and both a numbered with a 2. When attacker E entered defender D entered and both a numbered with a 3.

This exercise requires the players to stay focused. It also illustrates what runs can help their team and teaches defenders to react intelligently to runs made by attackers. It might be important to point out that the attacker with the ball can choose to simply dribble 1 versus 1 and shoot without help or using their teammates by passing to them.

Players tend to get very absorbed by this exercise. Younger players will constantly ask if they can play it during practice. It is a fun, fast moving exercise that starts a thinking process to the sport. Players should be encouraged to have a reason for what they do. The Socratic Method of asking questions can help the thought process. There is the unique ability for the exercise to be simply a 1 versus 1 confrontation all the way to a small sided game. Since there are no set time limits a sequence can last 20 seconds or 10 minutes depending on the results of the decisions by the players. Add the variation of having a striker and marking defender start in the middle of the grid and the exercise can start with a realistic bang. (See Diagrams 41 B, 41 C, pages 200 and 201.)

There is another reason for the waiting players to pay close attention to the game. If the ball is stolen then the team with the ball is the attacking team and that team now gets to add players when they want. The exercise can go back and forth several times as to who gets to add players or not depending on the possession of the ball.

Diagram 41 B: Asteroids with Player in the Center of the Grid Started with a Pass

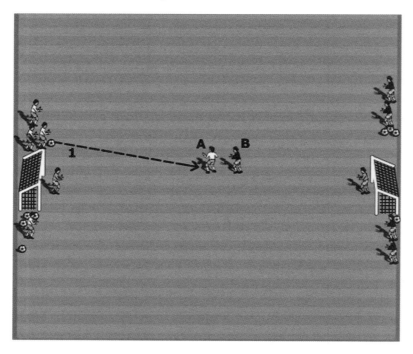

Diagram 41 B, page 200, shows the organization of having a striker and a defender start in the middle of the grid. This allows some learning for front runners that would not occur in the first version of Asteroids. Checking angles, timing of runs, how tight the defender is, can the attacker turn on the defender, should the attacker run the defender out of the way, should the attacker try to make a run in behind and when, how can the striker split the vision of the marking defender and their teammate so that it is harder to track them are just a few of the new ideas that starting with a striker can introduce.

Diagram 41 C: Asteroids Started with a Player in the Center Started with a Dribble

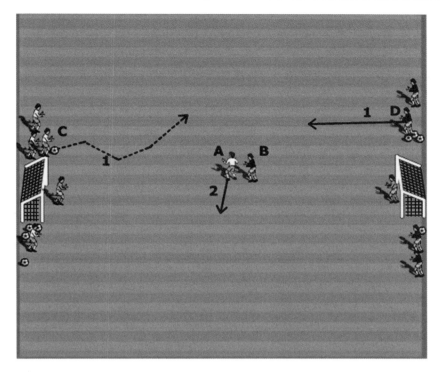

In both Diagram 41 B and Diagram 41 C, pages 200 and 201, the Asteroids Exercise starts with an attacker and defender in the grid. In 41 B the play is started with a pass into the grid and in 41 C play is started with a dribble into the grid. As the ball enters the grid with a dribble the striker makes a run numbered 2 that starts to split the vision of the defender marking them from the player with the ball. (See Diagrams 41 B and 41 C, pages 200 and 201.)

Exercise 25: Conditioned Games
(Grid size varies.)
(See Diagram 42, page 202.)

There is no set grid size for a Conditioned Game. The size of the grid not only relies on how well the players can handle the pressure of time, space and opponents but on what the coach is trying to teach.

First, a short review is required about the concept and use of "Conditioned Games." The definition of a "Condition" is any rule(s) that requires the players to perform a desired activity that the coach wants to be trained. If the "Condition" is met then either the team is awarded a point or an opportunity to score is allowed as a reward. If the "Condition" is not met then no point is awarded, shooting is not allowed or goals scored are not counted. The coach can also set up "Conditions" that if not met mean that the other team gets to have the ball.

Once a coach understands this concept completely they can train any part of the larger soccer game that they want to emphasize. The concept of "Conditioned Games" extends from 1 versus 1training all the way to the full 11 versus 11 team training. All coaching issues involving technical, tactical, physical or psychological aspects of soccer can be inserted into an exercise and trained by demanding specific "Conditions" requiring the behavior desired. Any numbers of players can be used. The concept of a "Plus" number of players is itself a condition, for one group or for both groups of players and can help in aiding the desired training effect to occur.

A "Condition Game" is an exercise that has a rule that the coach puts into an exercise to get a desired action from the players. Here are a few possibilities, but the list is nearly endless.

a. All players must play in two touches or less.
b. A wall pass must occur before a shot on goal can be taken.
c. The ball must switch points of attack from one side of the field to the other before a team can attack goal.
d. The striker must receive the ball and combine with a midfielder before an attack on goal is made.
e. All attacks must end with a serve from the flanks.
f. All passes must be made with the outside of the foot.
g. Every other pass must be in the air and the ball must be laid off in one touch to a teammate when it is received from the air.
h. Every fourth pass needs to be backwards.
i. A point is scored for every curved run made by your team.
j. One touch is used for speed of play, two if they must and dribble only when advantageous.
k. The team with the ball has a "Plus" 2 advantage, two neutral players that play for the team in possession of the ball, and you score by stringing six passes in a row.
l. The defending team can not win the ball back unless they are in their defending third of the field.
m. The defending team must attempt to win the ball back immediately all over the field.
n. In an area that is two penalty boxes face to face a group of players must execute a 2 versus 1 pattern before they can shoot.

The list is endless. Jim Lennox was teaching a class at the NSCAA that I attended and remarked: "Once you understand this concept you can take any part of the game you want to train, make up your own exercise, train the particular point you want and then reinsert it in the game." I personally have lived with this truism ever since that day. When creating "Condition" the coach will have spectacular successes and occasional failures. Do not be afraid to try and if something isn't working to either adjust it or abandon it. This is a delicate balance that often comes only with experience and experimentation. Since we have been dealing with 2 versus 1 let's set up a grid and suggest some conditions that would be useful in this context. (See Diagram 42, page 202.)

Diagram 42: 5 versus 5 Add a Condition

Diagram 42, page 202, simply shows a 5 versus 5 exercise being played. Set the players up in a small sided game and give them a condition(s) that force the training environment desired.

Some suggested Conditions specifically for 2 versus 1: (The list is only as long as the reader's imagination.)

a) The players must execute a Wall Pass or False Wall before shooting
b) The players must execute a Take-Over or false take over before shooting
c) The players must execute an X pattern before shooting
d) The players must execute a Curved Run before shooting
e) The players must execute a Double Pass before shooting
f) The players must execute a Lower Wall pass or False Wall before shooting
g) The players must execute a Flick and Spin Wall pass before shooting
h) The players must execute any 2 versus 1 pattern before shooting

This concept of Conditioned Games is one of the most important tools in the coaching trade. The coach can keep the players working hard on tactical and technical concepts while fitting them into the structure of the game. They usually enjoy the playing, the coach gets the desired training and it becomes a win-win situation for both the players and the coach.

Exercise 25: Grid the Area
(Grid varies)
(See Diagrams 43 A and 43 B, pages 204 and 205.)

This is a simple concept that can take many, many forms. The form can range from a non-directional area to setting grids in specific areas of the field or attacking specific targets that can range from crossing a line to shooting at goal. What must occur is the creation of a numbers up situation inside of a grid. All this requires is that one more attacker can move into a grid than defenders can enter into the same grid. This game is much like a Plus One game or a Conditioned Game. Exercise 11 in this book would be an example of this concept.

Keys to Exercise 25

1) Speed of movement by the attacking players is extremely helpful most of the time. Speed in a game is a combination of three smaller components: a) physical speed b) tactical decision making and c) technical control.
2) Look for times where the players must be concerned with working their timing together to be successful. If the support player is not in a good position for the pattern then the players are really just playing 1 versus 1 instead of 2 versus 1. Don't let the attackers forget that the choice for them to pass or dribble is made in part by the defenders reaction to their movements. It is also the ability of the attacker to manipulate the opponent with dribbling, shielding, threatened passing etc.
3) Committing defenders and not trying to avoid them is often critical to creating and succeeding in performing 2 versus 1 patterns.
4) Don't let the players get technically afraid to try things like lifting balls in tight spaces to achieve their ends. As a country we are always hearing that we need technically gifted players and then coaches go about stifling players as they try technically creative solutions. If the coach needs a guide line for directing their players on when to use technical flair then I believe strongly in the following concept for players to understand technical decision making: "On the ground if you can and in the air if you must."
5) The defenders should have a counter-attack goal of some kind, reaching the half line or small goals set up in each grid area. Even just passing the ball back to the coach will give the defenders more motivation to work harder.

6) The coach can add defensive players (see Diagram 43 B, page 205.) to make the exercise more complex for the attackers.
7) The coach can continue to add defensive players making the exercise more complex and harder to create pure 2 versus 1situations. This can be done until the coach can add another large goal and goal keeper and turn the exercise into a normal scrimmage. If the players are having problems creating a 2 versus 1 situation inside the game then the coach can temporarily add "Plus" or extra players who play for the team that currently is in possession of the ball.
8) A good "first touch" is necessary to prepare the ball for the next move the attack wants to make.
9) Players will need to "sharpen."
10) Attacking players should keep the concept of left/right/split support alive.
11) Attacking players should keep their body shape "open" when ever it is possible.

Diagram 43 A: Grid the Area with Plus 2

In Diagram 43 A, page 204, the ball and the attacking players may move freely from grid to grid so long as there are no more than two attackers in any one grid at a time. This is essentially a Plus 1 situation inside of that grid. In this diagram there are 7 attackers and 5 defenders so the restriction or condition for this exercise is that two grids can have a 2 versus 1 number advantage. In the diagram as it is drawn out the advantages are in grid B and in grid C. (See Diagram 43 A, page 204.)

If the coach changes condition that would allow attacking players' to move any where they want then the advantage could become 3 versus 1 in a single grid. This is an example of how a "Condition" can change the structure of an exercise and dramatically change the effects of the exercise. Make sure that what you as the coach wants is what the condition achieves and what the players are doing.

Diagram 43 B: Grid the Area with a Defensive Midfielder Added; This Causes a Plus 1

In Diagram 43 B, page 205, there is an extra defender currently in grid C. This player is referred to as a defensive midfielder in the diagram heading because they screen the back defensive five. The presence of this player can add a new dynamic (the coach can add or subtract other defenders as desired) to the exercise.

By manipulating the conditions that allow the extra defenders movements the coach can create many new situations. Holding the defensive midfielder to only grids B, C, and D the white players should adapt to this by creating 2 versus 1's in the flank grids labeled A and E. The attack should have a man advantage on the flank because of the conditions imposed.

If the coach allows the defensive midfielder to move into any grid the coach is essentially creating a 3 versus 2 in the two grids around the defensive midfielder. This should help the attacking players to recognize the tactical situation and start to change the point of attack to gain or regain a numerical superiority around the ball. The attacking players must be able to switch the point of attack faster than the defensive midfielder can recover or the numerical advantage will disappear.

The coach can also help the defensive to restructure by allowing the reassigning of roles. By allowing defenders to move from one grid to the next in adjustment to the switching of the ball then the exercise becomes more complex. This would mean that the defensive midfielder, if caught in a flank grid, could stay there as other defenders pushed over from grid to grid. This would allow the extra defender to reappear near the point of attack much more quickly because instead of one player having to run 35 yards to recover a series of players can all adjust 15 yards or less to get pressure back on the ball. This adjustment by the defense from grid to grid is excellent zonal training if a little bit stilted by waiting until the defender from the grid behind a player forces them into the next until the defense has two players in the grid where the attack is located.

The coach can allow this defensive adjustment to be performed all at once as a group and not contingent on each defender having left their grid before the next one can move on to the next grid. The added advantage to this condition is that the attacking players must pick up the speed of their movement to avoid the defenders adjustments to gain any advantage from switching the point of attack.

As the game is added to in complexity by adding players, particularly on defense, the exercise becomes more and more game like. Don't forget to allow defenders a counter-attack option so that they are rewarded for stealing the ball away from the offense. The coach can continuously keep adding players and complexity to the exercise until the coach adds a second goal and goal keeper and the exercise essentially evolves into a scrimmage. Remember that players learn from the simple to the complex.

Chapter 4

Observations

Some Final Thoughts Concerning 2 versus 1: Insight into Where and How to Use the Patterns

The main purpose of 2 versus 1 is to accomplish penetration of the defense. This gives rise to its' prominent use to penetrate in the attacking third of the field. All the patterns can and will be used successfully in the attempt to score goals. Personally, one of the most exciting moves is the use of the X Pattern inside of the opponents' penalty box. It has often been used as a passing pattern but I saw it used by the German National team when one player, who was dribbling at high speed on a diagonal from left to right, stepped on the ball leaving it for the runner coming in from an opposite diagonal run. The dribblers' run pulled the defense out of the way and the other diagonal runner scored a brilliant shot in a electrifying use of the 2 versus 1 X Pattern.

It is interesting to watch how players reflect the mentality of the coach. One can see when coaches trust and expect their players to use their technical and tactical abilities to solve problems. The teams playing both short and long passes in combination out of the back are teams where the coach trusts the judgment and the skills of the players. Good support of the ball and the use of two players combining passes out of the defensive third shows' a trust in the players.

Despite the fact that 2 versus 1 is most often clearly seen and remembered in the attacking third the patterns are effective tools all over the field. In the modern game we see many teams willing to pass their way out of the back under pressure. The old soccer truism: "When in doubt bang it out;" still lives on in many minds and in many teams. But it is a dying truism for the best teams and the top players. It is true that even the most skillful and intelligent of team's clear balls out of the back to relieve pressure, gain time to organize, or to preserve scores in the waning moments of a game. Still, it is not the primary solution for high caliber teams. Excellent players and teams build good shape and support around the ball so they can keep possession of the ball and build towards the opponents' end. Longer penetrating passes are used for specific tactical purposes and are not the main weapon or pattern for higher level teams. Having said all that, there are some interesting patterns to the use of 2 versus 1 that while not lengthy are worth noting.

Curved runs are done most often on the flank and out of the back. Why? There are two main reasons. First, and foremost, is that the curved run is one that allows the release of the ball to the player making the Curved Run at any time that the player in possession of the ball needs to pass it. Any time that it is needed the ball can be given to the runner without undue risk of losing possession. The minimization of turning the ball over makes the Curved Run outside on the flank an excellent choice in the defensive third of the field. There isn't any moment where passing is not an option. (See Diagram 42, page 202.) In wall passing and runs behind defenders there are moments where the passing lane can be closed by a clever defender by closing through the passing lane and a 1 versus 1 confrontation can be created. The defender by closing through the possible closing lane effectively eliminates the second player from the immediate play.

Diagram 44: Advantage of the Curved Run for Building Out in the Defensive Third

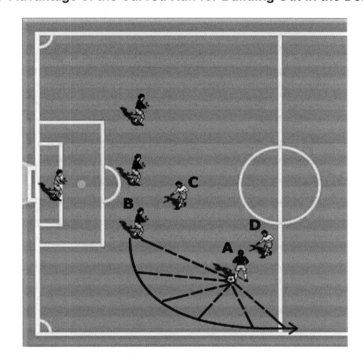

Diagram 44, page 209, shows how the Curved Run by the player, B, out and around the flank midfielder, A, is supported at all times. When ever pressure becomes too great for player A to handle then player A can pass the ball to player B anytime during the Curved Run. The almost spider web like lines show how the ball can be played back at any time. The defender, D, if they try to jump the passing lane, will allow the attacker, A, to dribble the ball up the field. If the defender, C, marks the player B in a man to man fashion, side by side, then the Curved Run will be closed down but it is the only way to close the run down. This man to man marking will leave other players behind attacker A open to receive a pass thus negating the run by defender C.

The play is being brought wide by the Curved Run and the passing option. This position on the field is easier to transition into defense from if possession of the ball is lost. The first reason that it is easier to defend from is that it is farther from the goal mouth than movements up the center of the field. The second reason is that the team shape to support the run will automatically place players in the path of an opponent that might have dispossessed the attacking team. Unless the opponent brings numbers forward to press the ball in the defending third it is almost impossible for the pressuring defenders to get the numbers around the ball to take away both men and the space. Without closing both the man making the run and the space that is being used then the option to use the run will stay wide open.

This is the great dilemma of all defenses and defenders, how does one take away man and space at the same time. It is even more difficult for defenders in the modern game when individual attackers with their technical dribbling abilities are extremely hard to stop in 1 versus 1situations. If a team plays hard man to man marking then there is space for players to run into and exploit. If a team plays zone then they must concede certain areas of the field and give some space to opponents to receive the ball. The field is just too large for 11 people to close down all the available space. Defenders must choose areas of the field where they can constrict the space and use each other to cover both the space and attackers running through it. Lines of restraint and collective efforts are the hallmark of modern defenses.

This dilemma of needing more than one defender to stop individual attackers is why the game has evolved to over rotating zonal defensive structures to the ball side to get numerical superiority, play a zonal man to man in the immediate area of the ball and zone the space on the weak side of the field. In addition teams often rotate an extra man into the area of the ball to supply cover and extra pressure on the ball. This inability to stop individual attackers with individual defenders consistently because of individual attacking abilities; that man to man marking causes huge gaps to occur in defensive structure as attacking runs pull defenders out of the way; coupled with a defensive concept referred to as "Time of Flight" is what makes modern defenses so intricate and interesting to watch. It is however a topic for another book.

Curved or Overlapping runs are good ways to get out of the back and to send defenders into the attack. (Some runs out of the back are just straight runs made by players who are in wider positions on the field. They can be categorized as "Curved" Runs while others refer to them as Overlapping Runs for simplicity of grouping.) The space in the wide area of the field can be held open by players holding the ball inside or dribbling diagonally into the center of the field. The need to stop the point of attack, the player with the ball, and to have a second layer of defense behind the pressuring defender opens up the flanks for runners going forward into the attack and to make runs to support the ball for possession. Over-rotated defenses attempt to make the flank space constricted on the ball side.

Wall passing in the defensive third can be a good way to get out but there is a moment of risk in a Wall Pass that allows an astute defender(s) the chance to turn the 2 versus 1 situation into a 1 versus 1. The attacking and midfield thirds are where defenders can benefit most by gambling attempts to regain possession or strip teams of the ball as they are building out. This is why a defender will gamble on jumping a passing lane and what makes Wall Passing a more dangerous option. The moment of vulnerability happens during the return phase of the Wall Pass.

Just after the initial pass of the ball by the player starting the pattern being sent to the supporting attacker the initial passer must make a diagonal run behind the defending player. If the defender is astute enough to recognize their recovery angle and the correct moment they can jump into the return passing lane and close the ball which will force a 1 versus 1 confrontation. In the defensive third this ability to close the return passing lane may be a risk that a team may not want to take. The situation worsens for the players building out of the back with the Wall Pass if there is also a defender marking the player that is playing the support position and is intending to play the pass back to the runner. (See Diagram 44 A, page 211.)

Good players can judge this issue and make good decisions within the context of the game but the coach needs to be aware of this potential risk and educate the players to it. There are no hard and fast rules that can not be bent, broken or at least bruised in the game. Great players and great teams bend, break and bruise the "rules" at great moments with great results. But Wall Passes allow themselves to be isolated and are riskier than other ways of building out of the back. Additionally, if the Wall Pass is made from the inside then there is often a hole for opponents to counter attack through should possession of the ball be lost. This is caused because an interior player is making a run up the middle of the field. The temporary loss of defensive structure would be immediately apparent and easily exploitable if ball possession is lost.

Diagram 44 A: Disadvantage of Wall Passing out of the Defensive Third

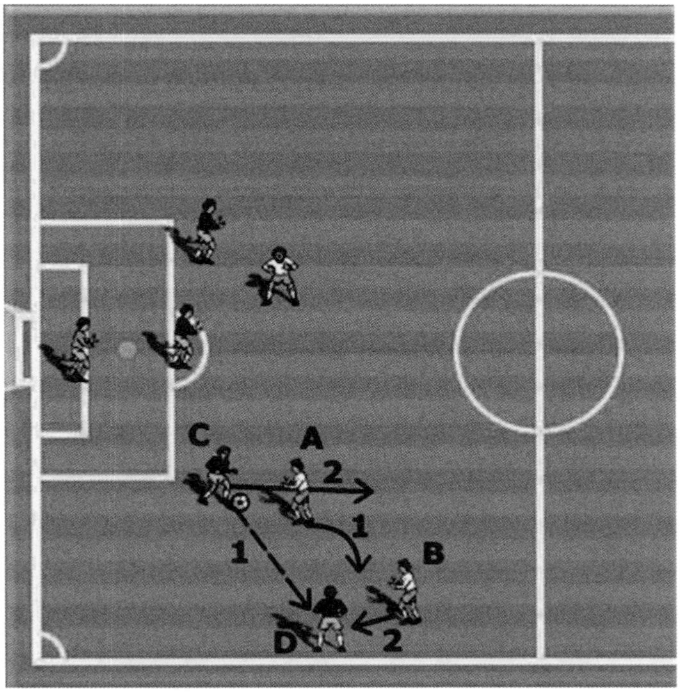

In Diagram 44 A, page 211, the reader can see how the attacker, C, can be closed down if the white player labeled A steps into the return passing lane correctly after the pass by attacker A and not allowing an easy return pass from attacker D. The defenders can create a difficult situation for player D. Defender B can press and defender A in optimum conditions could double the ball leaving attacker B with only the options of either dribbling or hopefully making a back pass to the keeper to relieve the pressure.

Diagram 44 B: Disadvantage of Wall Passing out of the Defensive Third Diagonal Run

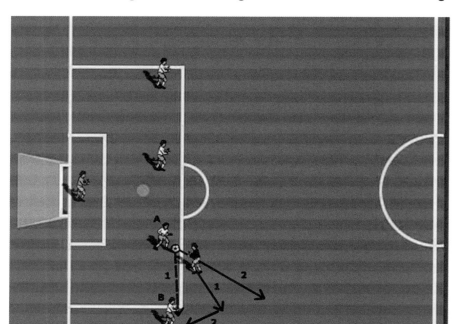

Diagram 44 B, page 212, shows the risk of using a Wall Pass by a center defender that uses a diagonal run out towards the flank. Player A sends a pass numbered with a 1 out player B and then makes a run diagonally behind the defender in black. The run is numbered with a 2. The defender responds immediately with a recovery run into the passing lane numbered with a 1 and then closes to pressure player B who now has the ball with a defensive run numbered 2. With intelligent defending the defender can isolate player B by clogging the passing lane and then closing the ball. This makes the Wall Pass pattern a little more dangerous than the Curved Run in the defensive third.

Some 2 versus 1situations for penetration are most effective and safely used in the middle third and attacking third of the field. In the defensive third a coach tends to find excellent support shape around the ball with good angles of support allowing easy inter-passing to provide a safer way to build out of the back. Where players will find 2 versus 1 play in the defensive third is wide on the flanks as a team tries building out of the back. Mostly this takes the shape of Curved or wide Overlapping runs. All patterns can and may be used to build out of the back. But patterns of 2 versus 1 play for possession, by quick inter-passing between players, is most usually applied to relieve pressure and start building out of the back. Switching or swinging the ball through the back is a standard method of building out of the back that creates less danger of having the ball dispossessed. High quality players playing center back will occasionally use wall passing patterns out of the back with central midfielders. But almost never will a person see a center back wall passing from the inside and then running to the outside using a Wall Pass to combine out of the back.

In the middle third and attacking third teams can benefit greatly by players exploding past defenses and forcing the next layer of defenders to react and reform their defensive shape to the new threat. Every form of 2 versus 1 can be used in midfield play. Every form can also be used in the attacking third. Some of the greatest passing sequences I have ever had the joy to watch were simply a series of 2 versus 1patterns being used. Patterns that were either executed or the false version of the pattern was used, sometimes with other players becoming involved creating combination play. This unpredictable use of the 2 versus 1 patterns and technical choices that create the kaleidoscope of soccer twisting quickly and effectively into a graceful dance of interaction resulting in a goal or shot on goal.

All of us can remember having our breath taken away by these moments of genius when each player in a group saw the correct tactical decision and had the technical command to react with the "right" choice. All of the tactical knowledge and technical skills by players ending in a series of choices, unique in existence, that as a whole were exquisite and every fan waits' to see. A great deal of the exquisite play is 2 versus 1 patterns flowing from player to player, teammate to teammate. 2 versus 1 is one of the major cornerstone chips in the kaleidoscope of attacking soccer. All players should have a complete command of these chips in the kaleidoscope.

It is hoped that the information contained in this book will be of great use. Teams and players that can use this information at will are extremely hard to defend and a joy to watch. If the players have the cornerstone chip of technical command the number of solutions to defensive problems are undeterminable. It is the authors' hope that as a coach and that the players on the team can use this information and bring beauty to the dance that is the great game of soccer.

Closing Thought

While this information about 2 versus 1 is immensely valuable it is useless without understanding the Methodology of Coaching/Teaching. Coaching is in truth teaching. Some of us understand teaching intuitively but even those gifted with intuition hone their teaching skills over the years.

There have been a few asides about methodology in this book. The Socratic Method of teaching was examined and it was pointed out that students that think out the answer them self have shown a higher level of retention than students that are simply given an answer when confronted with a need to grow their knowledge. In addition it was pointed out that a majority of people learn most effectively by doing. It is hoped that this information is of use. The communication of information; which must occur in teaching, so that it is understood and accepted is almost certainly the most important element in coaching.

A coach can have the world in their head but if they can not put it into their hands to exchange it with players it means very little. It has been my experience that a coach with marginal information but who can convey that knowledge, gets the players to use it and motivates the players will end up more successful in the long run than a genius with all sorts of knowledge with out the skills to teach.

It is also important to remember that players are not all alike in their learning methods. When a player or subset of players do not seem to understand what it is being asked of them then the coach should examine the methodology being used and see if it reaches the broad spectrum of learning styles. Some students learn by hearing, some by doing and some by seeing. But even within these categories an astute coach will use several verbal descriptions if a player does not comprehend a particular lesson. It may be necessary to stop talking and walk through the exercise with that player so that they learn by doing at a slow pace. It may be necessary to have the player watch the exercise so that they comprehend it. It may be that the player just needs to do until between the successes and the failures they learn what is being taught. Not all players are the same and the more a coach can vary their methods of teaching and communicating the better the chance that they will reach the majority of the players. In addition, players emotional and confidence levels should be examined and be accounted when teaching information.

To each of you who have taken the time to read the material; all the best in the pursuit of knowledge and even better in passing it on to the players. Thank you for taking the time to read this book and it is hoped that the information will progress the players and the great sport of soccer.

Index

Index of Diagrams:

Index of Exercises:

Index of Key Words:

Index of Teaching Points: